Praise for works by Colin Wilson:

"A wonderfully smooth writer, Wilson challenges and engages in this (*The Misfits*) radical reassessment of sexuality."

—KIRKUS

"A long, ambitious, immensely stimulating analysis (*A Criminal History of Mankind*) of crime down the ages."

—DAILY EXPRESS

"*The Mammoth Book of True Crime* is a depiction of the troubled and tormented mind in society and the end result when such minds snap. Wilson is always readable, informed, and never dull."

—THE COAST BOOK REVIEW

"*Beyond the Occult* serves up hours of entertaining reading and hundreds of captivating glimpses into all aspects of the paranormal, ranging from ESP and precognition to poltergeists and reincarnation."

—BOOKLIST

Other books by Colin Wilson available from Carroll & Graf

- Beyond the Occult
- A Criminal History of Mankind
- The Misfits
- The Mammoth Book of True Crime
- The Mammoth Book of True Crime 2

BEYOND THE OUTSIDER

COLIN WILSON

Carroll & Graf Publishers, Inc.
New York

Published by arrangement with the author.

First Carroll & Graf edition 1991

Carroll & Graf Publishers, Inc.
260 Fifth Avenue
New York, NY 10001

ISBN: 0-88184-704-6

Cover painting:
LINDNER, Richard.
The Meeting. 1953.
Oil on canvas, 60″ × 6′ (152.4 × 182.9 cm).
Collection, The Museum of Modern Art, New York. Given anonymously.

Manufactured in the United States of America

To Bob Ardrey
with affection and admiration

ACKNOWLEDGEMENTS

This book owes so much to so many people that it is impossible to thank them adequately, or even list them. First I should thank Robert Ardrey, Maurice Cranston and Sir Julian Huxley for reading it in manuscript and making many suggestions that I was happy to adopt; in fact, Mr Cranston's comments led me to re-write the book from the beginning, while Sir Julian Huxley's led to several rewritings of the biology chapter. But it should not be assumed that the views expressed here are wholly, or even mainly, acceptable to Mr Cranston and Sir Julian Huxley. I also wish to thank Mr Ian Willison of the British Museum for his help and advice, and Bill Hopkins for many stimulating discussions. Finally, I should thank my hostile critics for endless stimulation.

C. W.

As a machine, man is hopelessly inefficient. Unfortunately, no science of human engineering has yet been invented – GUSTAV NEUMANN: *Necessary Doubt*

Only giants can save the world from complete relapse and so we – we who care for civilisation – have to become giants. We have to bind a harder, stronger civilisation like steel about the world – H. G. WELLS: *The Croquet Player*

CONTENTS

PREFACE

Beyond the Outsider is the sixth and last volume of a 'cycle' in my work, a series that began in 1956 with *The Outsider*, and continued with *Religion and the Rebel, The Age of Defeat, The Strength to Dream* and *Origins of the Sexual Impulse*. These books are closely linked – so closely that it is impossible for any one of them to be fully understood without the others. Each approaches the same problem from a different angle, and attempts to develop the viewpoint outlined in the previous book.

As these books appeared between 1956 and 1963, I was surprised that no reviewer appeared to notice that all were a part of the same thesis. Only *Religion and the Rebel* seemed to be regarded as having any connection with *The Outsider*. *The Age of Defeat* was reviewed as a book about 'the vanishing hero', *The Strength to Dream* as a book about the imagination, *Origins of the Sexual Impulse* as an attack on Freud, and so on. And it was generally alleged against them all that no consistent viewpoint was presented, that they were, so to speak, anthologies of ideas rather than an attempt to develop a thesis. Only one reviewer of *The Strength to Dream* observed that I seemed to be trying to produce a 'new philosophical synthesis' based on existentialism and romanticism.

To some extent, the reason for this was obvious enough: before the publication of the present volume, it would have taken a fairly careful reading of the previous five volumes to recognise the direction in which they were tending. But there was another reason, having little to do with the books themselves, and which is my excuse for writing this preface.

When I wrote *The Outsider* in 1955, I wanted to make the point that existentialism seems to have drifted away from its true basis, the personal. Moreover, some of the most eminent of existentialist philosophers have dressed up certain of their personal prejudices and shortcomings in an impressive and abstract language, thus making the various issues all the more difficult to sort out. I felt that my presentment of the central problem, with its re-emphasis on the personal, was a modest but worthwhile contribution to existential thinking.

My point was taken – at least, I suppose it was, for the book achieved a success beyond anything I had expected. But critics were not slow to point out that its statement of the problems was a great deal more satisfying than its attempt at solutions. I myself became aware, in the discussions that followed, that a broader standpoint was needed, and *Religion and the Rebel* was an attempt to establish such a standpoint.

At this point, I was in for a surprise. When *The Outsider* was received with so much interest, I had assumed that I was mistaken in supposing that existentialism was a subject of narrow appeal. However, it soon became apparent to me that I had been caught in a curious social vortex which had nothing to do with my book or its ideas. In fact, I owed my sudden notoriety to the accident of being a contemporary of a number of writers who were labelled 'Angry Young Men'. (I never quite discovered what I was supposed to have in common with Mr Kingsley Amis or Mr John Osborne.) By late 1957, everyone was heartily sick of the angry young men. *Religion and the Rebel* received the backwash of their publicity – and my own. The fury the book seemed to arouse was startling. Even the least 'intellectual' newspapers fell on it with scorn and dismissed it as a kind of confidence trick. 'Mr Wilson's game of intellectual hooky is certainly up' declared a popular magazine designed for weekend reading. But a well-known critic who called *Religion and the Rebel* 'a very bad book indeed' (admittedly in the course of defending me) later admitted to me that she had not read it, and one of the reviewers who had praised *The Outsider* later defended himself by claiming that he had only read the publisher's blurb, and thought it deserved a good review.

There was no point in getting upset. I continued with my third book, *The Age of Defeat*. In the last pages of that book, I realised that what I was trying to do was to create a 'new existentialism' to replace the bankrupt article of Sartre and Heidegger. The sudden fall from popularity was disconcerting, but I accepted with the reflection '*Time* hath given, and *Time* hath taken away'. The conclusions I had reached in *The Age of Defeat* seemed to me exciting, and in many ways completely new; the cultural problem was 'the fallacy of insignificance', and it was a philosophical form of this fallacy that had somehow landed existentialism in a *cul de sac*.

The Age of Defeat appeared in 1959. To my irritation, the intellectual atmosphere had not changed noticeably in the three years since *The Outsider* was published. The criticism still had the same note of violence, as if my publishing a book were somehow a calculated affront. A critic who had hailed *The Outsider*, explained to his Sunday newspaper audience that the book was a kind of literary sight-seeing tour. I began to feel as bewildered as Einstein might have felt if the *Daily Mirror* had dismissed relativity as an attempt to replace the crossword puzzle with a more pretentious type of conundrum. What I was trying to do might be rather dull, might be of very limited interest indeed. To me it seemed important and exciting, but I would have been the first to agree that its interest was probably limited to a few dozen readers. But the tone of the reviews began to make the whole thing seem like a Ionesco comedy of non-communication.

Nevertheless, the problems were beginning to fascinate me, and there was nothing for it but to go on writing. The dangers of worrying too much were obvious. I had seen several young writers badly hit by critical malice – the backwash of the Angry Young Man publicity – and a few of them had simply ceased to write. Work seemed a good way to avoid self-pity. I produced three novels dealing with different aspects of my existentialism, and another 'philosophical' book, *The Strength to Dream,* dealing mainly with the problem of nihilism in modern writers. I even underlined my rejection of Sartre's abstractionism by making an encyclopedia of murder a vehicle for expounding my theory of the 'intentionality of values'.

When these books had been published, I had to acknowledge that I was still back where I started, six years before. Ignoring the ideas in my books now seemed to have become a critical tradition. Reviews still tended to be personal. Sometimes a critic admired my persistence in writing the kind of books I wanted to write 'in spite of the vertiginous ups and downs of my literary career'; others declared angrily that it was time I stopped regurgitating the books I had read or that publishers stopped accepting my work. By now, I felt like jumping up and down and shouting: '*But what about the ideas*?'

I recognised that this indifference was partly because England and America have no tradition of interest in ideas. But more basically, it was the result of the curious reputation I had acquired in 1956, which made it impossible for critics even to take the preliminary step of assuming that I might have something worth saying.

In the autumn of 1961 I went to the United States to make a tour of universities. The attempts to compress my ideas into ninety-minute lectures provided the stimulus for a projected final volume of the 'outsider cycle', to be called *An Outline of a New Existentialism*. This volume was started early in 1962, but I soon began to encounter difficulties. To begin with, it was difficult to know how much knowledge of the previous volumes could be assumed in my readers. Second, the section dealing with the phenomenological analysis of sex threatened to occupy half the volume. I solved this latter problem by detaching the section and publishing it as a separate volume. Even so, the book was too long. Since it would obviously be the most important of the series, it was necessary that the argument should be presented as cleanly as possible. Several revisions and rewritings have compressed it to its present size.

At first I was dubious about speaking of 'the outsider cycle', since a cycle returns to its starting point. But when I was writing the final chapter of this book, I found myself summarising the problem – and my solution of it – in terms of Sartre's *Nausea* and Wells's *Mind at the End of Its Tether*, the books analysed in the first chapter of *The Outsider*. In a sense, therefore, it can be called a cycle.

The impetus behind these books has been a kind of frustration. I felt like a mathematician who has been handed a problem that has baffled the ingenuity of several earlier generations of mathematicians; the last page has the word 'insoluble' scrawled over it. It seemed to me that constructive philosophical thinking is impossible in the face of this 'insoluble'. Philosophical thought needs a sound basis if it is to develop and expand in the way that scientific thought was able to develop after Newton. The 'outsider cycle' is an attempt to provide such a basis; the attempt involved a careful analysis of the cultural trends of the past three hundred years, a 're-checking' of the previous calculations. The present book offers my conclusions in as orderly a manner as my naturally untidy mind will allow. What is presented is not a 'system' in the Hegelian sense – although it is self-complete – but the preconditions for a system.

I should conclude with an apology. This is about my use of the phrase 'St Neot margin', which I define in Chapter one. This notion of a tax on consciousness, an indifference threshold, has seemed to me for many years now the central problem of existence philosophy. Unfortunately, no other existential philosopher seems to have made use of the concept; and try as I will, I cannot think of a phrase that defines this tendency that might be called 'the law of entropy in prehension'. 'St Neot margin', apart from being merely a personal label, is unsatisfactory in that it seems to apply to a thing rather than to a tendency: to the door-spring, as it were, rather than to the door's tendency to close. So at the risk of seeming egoistic, I have retained the phrase 'St Neot margin' – enclosing it in inverted commas to indicate that I am not too happy about it.

Introduction

This book, which was published twenty-five years ago, is the last volume of my 'Outsider cycle,' but was intended to stand on its own. It is not as deliberately 'popular' as *The Outsider*, with its emphasis on despairing romantics and suicidal men of genius, but it still strikes me as the best and most compact expression of my ideas.

The preface tries to explain something of its background, but for those readers who were not alive in the 1950's, it may help to sketch in a broader picture. At the end of the Second World War, the continent of Europe was in a state of intellectual ferment, due mainly to an exciting new philosophy called existentialism. The difference between existentialism and the older, more academic types of philosophy was that the existentialists were asking questions about human freedom: they were all obsessed by H.G. Wells's question: 'What ought we to be doing with our lives?' Sartre and Camus—its leading figures—had both been in the French Resistance. And it was Sartre who made the interesting comment that he had never felt so free as during this period, when he might have been arrested and shot at any moment. The war had obviously given them a sense of what freedom was really about. Camus had been the editor of the underground newspaper *Combat*, and one of its last editorials was written as the Germans were being driven out of Paris. It was called 'The Night of Truth,' and began: 'While the bullets of freedom are still whistling throughout the city, the cannons of the liberation are entering the gates of Paris amidst shouts and flowers . . . . It is the night of truth.' Never—he is saying in effect—shall we forget the meaning of freedom; never shall we again allow ourselves to drift back into the old boredom and stupidity . . .

But Simone de Beauvoir's best-selling novel *The Mandarins* provides an ironic commentary on this optimistic affirmation. It describes Paris immediately after the end of the war, and its two central characters are thinly disguised portraits of Sartre and Camus. The whole novel is soaked in an atmosphere of boredom: the characters sit around in nightclubs, drink and smoke too much, and indulge in a kind of aimless promiscuity. What had happened to the 'night of truth?' The answer, of course, is that human beings forget terribly quickly. Fichte said: 'To *be* free is nothing; to *become* free is heavenly.' It is absurd, but it is true. 'Even war cannot frighten us enough,' said the Greek poet Dimitios Kapetanakis, quoting Auden.

Now Great Britain and America had never seen much of the war at firsthand, although London had its air raids, and they were bad enough. So, in both these countries, the intellectual atmosphere at the end of the war was a great deal staler than in France. In America, Mailer's *Naked and the Dead* became an instant best-seller, not merely because it was a good novel, but because it brought home to thousands of Americans what the war had been like, and gave them the same elusive whiff of freedom that Sartre and Camus had conveyed so well. The same was true of James Jones's *From Here to Eternity*. But these novels were soon swamped by commonplace best-sellers about booze and adultery. While in England, exhausted by five years of war and always disinclined to ponder intellectual issues, the cultural atmosphere was even staler. Its prevalent philosophy was a fashion called logical positivism, which declared that it is useless and pointless to talk about truth, and we had better lower our sights to more mundane issues, such as the nature of sense perception . . . And in literature there was nothing whatever to relieve the sense of emptiness. The writers of the thirties—Auden, Isherwood, Henry Green—were middle-aged, and there was apparently no new generation to take their place.

Now I had always been obsessed by the problem of human freedom. No doubt this was because I had been born into a working-class background, and had left school at sixteen to take a series of dead-end jobs in factories and offices. Discouraged and bored by what Heidegger calls 'the triviality of everydayness,' I had retreated into a mental world, and devoured the writings of the mystics, the novels of Dostoyevsky, and the poetry of T.S. Eliot. Later, in London, I discovered the ideas of Gurdjieff—whose fundamental assertion is that human beings are fast asleep—and the works of existentialists like Sartre and Camus, as well as their great predecessor Kierkegaard. One of the few American writers who interested me was Thomas Merton, who was also oppressed by a sense of meaninglessness and futility until he became a Catholic, then a Trappist monk. I even devoted some careful consideration to the idea of becoming a monk, but gave it up when I began to take instruction in Catholicism and found its fairy tales impossible to swallow. I began writing a novel—called *Ritual in the Dark*—about a young man who is obsessed by this same problem of freedom, and the apparent inability of human beings to even begin to understand what it means. ('To *be* free is nothing . . .') I was writing this novel in the reading room of the British Museum in the autumn of 1954 when the superintendent—a novelist named Angus Wilson—engaged me in conversation and subsequently offered to read it. He took it home with him for Christmas, and I, having nothing better to do, sketched out a non-fiction book called *The Outsider*, which was basically about men who are obsessed by the problem of how to escape the sheer triviality of everyday life and experience what I called 'the vibration of seriousness.'

To my astonishment, this was accepted by the first publisher I sent it to, and it appeared in May 1956 to an acclaim that startled me. Moreover, a play called *Look Back in Anger* had just caused something of a sensation at the Royal Court Theatre, and its author, John Osborne, also found himself an overnight celebrity. Reviews of his play appeared on the same day as reviews of *The Outsider*, and the British critics were suddenly convinced that the long-awaited 'younger generation' had at last arrived.

I was astonished, not merely by the success of the book—which I knew to be good—but by the fact that British critics had hailed it as important. The British are notorious for their lack of interest in ideas; Carlyle once said that if Jesus came to modern London, people would invite him to dinner, listen to what he had to say, then laugh at him behind his back. Nineteenth-century 'Outsiders' like Carlyle and Ruskin had worn themselves out trying to persuade the British to take important things seriously. But apparently things had changed for the better since 1880 . . .

It took only a short time for me to realise that it had all been an absurd misunderstanding. The 'intellectuals' assumed that this new generation of writers—which now included Kingsley Amis, John Braine, and Iris Murdoch—were social critics with a left-wing bias, and in most cases, they were perfectly correct. These writers were labelled 'Angry Young Men,' and myself and John Osborne were regarded as the founding fathers of the movement. In fact, the real preoccupations of *The Outsider* escaped them. I once gave a lecture entitled 'The Power House' in front of an invited audience at the BBC, the central theme of which was my conviction that human beings possess hidden powers which are called forth only by crisis. One gentleman at the end of the programme raised a laugh by saying that what he had inside him was not a power house but a doss house. I had a despairing feeling that he was speaking for the majority of Englishmen.

In due course, my second book *Religion and the Rebel* appeared, and was slaughtered by the same critics who had hailed *The Outsider*. I was not surprised, for I had realised even as I was writing it that I had no real audience in England.

It hardly mattered. In fact, it followed naturally from my basic thesis: that only a tiny minority of people are obsessed by the problem of freedom. What also followed was that these 'Outsiders' have to get used to working alone, and not to fall into the trap of self-pity when their ideas are ignored. At least I was lucky in one respect. I was happily married—at least, happily settled down with the girl who is still my wife—and *The Outsider* had brought me enough money to retreat to a remote cottage by the sea where I could get on with writing *Religion and the Rebel* and rewriting *Ritual in the Dark* (which finally appeared in 1960). I had hoped that, when my 'Outsider cycle' was finally completed with *Beyond the Outsider*, my contribution might be reassessed. It was, but not in England or America; the only country that took my work seriously was Japan. (There are still more of my books in print in Japan than in England.) But soon after writing *Beyond the Outsider*, I spent two years as a Writer in Residence in America, first at Hollins College in Virginia, then at the University of Washington in Seattle, and was surprised by the warmth and understanding shown towards my ideas. And in 1988, when I returned to America for the first time in fifteen years, I was amazed to discover—at lectures and book-signings—how many people had large collections of my books. As I approach sixty (I was born in 1931), it begins to look as if the last thirty-five years haven't been wasted after all. But it seems typical that *Beyond the Outsider* has had to be republished in America; in England, it is still a rare collector's item costing around thirty times its original price. And as I look around at the England of the 1990's, I still feel that it is the cultural wasteland that it has been since the end of the Second World War.

Chapter 1

THE SOUND BARRIER

> One sticks one's finger into the soil to tell by the smell what land one's in; I stick my finger into existence – it smells of nothing. Where am I? Who am I? How did I come to be here? What is this thing called the world? What does the word mean? Who is it that has lured me into the thing, and now leaves me there? ... How did I come into the world? Why was I not consulted, why was I not made acquainted with its manners and customs, but was thrust into the ranks as though I'd been bought from a kidnapper, a dealer in souls? How did I obtain an interest in it? And is it not a voluntary concern? And if I am compelled to take part in it, where is the director? I would like to see him.

This passage from Kierkegaard's novel *Repetition* could be taken as the starting point of existential philosophy. It expresses the fundamental question. And the situation in which such a question could be asked was expressed by Sartre*:

> 'God is dead ... Hegel tried to replace him with a system and the system foundered ... Comte by a religion of humanity, and the positivism foundered ... God is dead, but man has not, for all that, become atheistic. The silence of the transcendent, and the permanent need for religion in modern man – that is still the major thing ... '* And elsewhere, Sartre writes: 'There does exist a universal human condition ... Historical situations vary; a man may be born a slave ... or a feudal lord or a proletarian. What does not vary is the necessity for him to exist in the world,

* *Situations*, 1, p. 153.

to be at work there, to be there in the midst of other people, and to be mortal there.'*

For mediaeval man, these reflections would have been meaningless. He looked at the world as a savage might look at a power plant; it was bewildering, noisy, overwhelming; still, *somebody* understood what it was all about. It had purpose.

But this simile fails to convey an important aspect of the mediaeval world-view. If a workman in a factory accidentally knocked over a bucket, even the savage would infer that this action was not as purposive as the movement of the conveyor belts. But in the mediaeval world picture, there were no accidents. A sparrow falling from a tree was part of the design of providence.

The basic problem of human existence is so simple that no philosopher has succeeded in stating it. People do not spend their time 'weighing up existence' in order to get through the average working day. And yet everything we do betrays a basic attitude to life, revealing that, in a certain sense, everything *has* been weighed up and judged. A man's handwriting, even the way he ties his shoelace, reveals his character, and character itself is nothing less than a series of acts that 'pass judgement' on human life.

An example may clarify this. In Conrad's *Heart of Darkness*, Mr Kurtz dies muttering 'The horror! The horror!' And Conrad's narrator comments: 'He had summed up – he had judged.' All this makes it sound as if Kurtz had had some final glimpse of all the evil in the universe opposed to the good, and had decided that evil has the last word. And yet when Marlow describes his own glimpse of the 'heart of darkness', it is clear that it is not a summary at all:

> It is the most unexciting contest you can imagine. It takes place in an unpalpable greyness, with nothing underfoot, with nothing around, without spectators, without clamour,

* *Existentialism*, p. 45.

> without glory ... in a sickly atmosphere of tepid scepticism, without much belief in your own right, and still less in that of your adversary ... I was within a hair's breadth of the last opportunity for pronouncement, and I found ... that I would have nothing to say.

This is closer to it – to the basic atmosphere of human life, and human death. It is not merely that there is no 'opportunity for pronouncement'. Pronouncement is irrelevant to it, and this is part of the 'horror'.

It is not a conflict between Carlyle's 'eternal yes and eternal no', which is stated so clearly by Van Gogh or Ivan Karamazov. It is an even more fundamental conflict. It is the question of whether it is even worth making an act of will.

There is an immense basic problem here, and if it could only be stated clearly, it would be somewhat nearer solution.

To begin with, this attitude of 'unheroic nihilism' might be called an indictment of human existence, or perhaps of the meaning of human existence. What exactly does this indictment amount to?

Basically, it is a feeling that human beings can never escape illusions, that they live and die enmeshed in them. The feeling is expressed with considerable power in Eliot's *Hollow Men*, which has an epigraph from *Heart of Darkness*. Its best known lines certainly express the sense of life as anticlimax: 'This is the way the world ends. Not with a bang but a whimper.' But perhaps its most important statement is contained in the lines:

> Remember us – if at all – not as lost
> Violent souls, but only
> As the hollow men
> The stuffed men.

That is to say, human beings are incapable of good or evil; evil is only uncontrolled emotion, and deserves contempt or pity rather than condemnation. Men walk around in an ego-dream, certain of their own identities, unaware that they are scarecrows, *pagliacci*. One line speaks of 'crossed staves in a field', and apparently refers to A. E. Waite's book on the tarot, where the five of wands is represented by a card showing youths fighting with staves in a field, and has the comment 'mimic warfare'.* The 'battle of life' is an illusion.

In the fifties, this attitude was again expressed by Samuel Beckett. His characters seem incapable of motion; they lie on beds, or sit in wheelchairs or dustbins, thinking about their past lives and wondering what it was all about. Over them all seems to hang the question: 'Why should I do anything?' Beckett characters are solipsists. They do not believe in external reality; and yet they can find no purpose or meaning inside themselves.

One of the clearest statements of the attitude of 'unheroic nihilism' occurs in a short story by Hemingway called *A Natural History of the Dead*, which opens by describing an episode from the travels of Mungo Park: how the explorer was fainting in the desert when he noticed a small flower growing in the sand. He reflected that if God can water and protect a mere flower, how could he possibly abandon a creature made in his own image? This thought gave him courage, and he soon found water. Hemingway then proceeds to 'disprove' Mungo Park's belief in divine providence rather in the manner of Voltaire in *Candide*: by citing examples of pointless and futile deaths, and by emphasising the indifference of death. 'I do not know, but most men die like animals, not men.' And the humanists and idealists die like everybody else.

In that case, what had man better do with his life? Hemingway's answer is not encouraging: live like a cave man; think as little as possible; make the best of food, sex and the primitive sports. Above all, avoid thinking.

The chronic alcoholism of Hemingway's later years, leading finally to suicide, seem to emphasise that he held this view in complete sincerity; the later Hemingway had become a Beckett character.

What is being asserted, in fact, is that our 'values' are really only physical reflexes. One is reminded of the story of Carpenter's

* In *The Waste Land*, line 51, Eliot makes the clairvoyant refer to 'the man with three staves', which apparently refers to the three of wands from the same book on the tarot. In this case, it refers to the great merchant, the man of enterprise.

monkeys, cited by Robert Ardrey.* The zoologist C. R. Carpenter decided to settle 350 rhesus monkeys on Santiago Island. In their natural surroundings, the monkeys usually divide into social groups, and defend a certain area of 'territory' against all members of other groups. On board ship, it was naturally impossible for the monkeys to choose 'territory'. The result was startling. Husbands ceased to protect their mates, and mothers lost interest in their young. The monkeys were starved, to accustom them to a new diet, and mothers would often fight their babies for a scrap of food. The infant mortality rate soared. Once established on the island, the monkeys again separated into social groups, and each group selected its territory. Immediately the husbands again protected their mates and the mothers became capable of self-sacrifice for their young.

All this is only to say that monkey values seem to be *completely dependent on their social habit*. Conrad was making a similar point in *Heart of Darkness*, where the idealist Kurtz, left totally alone in Central Africa, sinks to the level of an animal. Similarly, William Golding's novel *Lord of the Flies* shows how a group of schoolboys cast up on a desert island lose all their 'moral reflexes' and descend into anarchy. (Golding seems to think that this is evidence of original sin; in that case, monkeys are also subject to original sin.)

According to this view, then, 'values' are actually social habits, the result of an agreement between the individual and society. Society offers certain advantages: security, a sense of belonging, perhaps a sense of conquest – if one happens to be one of the lucky few who become 'leaders'. In exchange, it asks that one places certain social values above self-interest. In making this sacrifice, the individual's life is given meaning; he comes to believe in external values. Admittedly, he has a right to opt out – particularly if he feels that society is not keeping its half of the bargain and making him feel as if he 'belongs'. He can revert to total self-interest, and become a criminal. But this revolt is only a half measure, for while rejecting society, the criminal continues to accept that he is a part of it. If he were courageous enough to

* In *African Genesis*, chapter 3, section 5.

carry his individualism to its limits, to turn his back completely on other human beings, he would soon revert to the purely animal level; the rejection would hurl him into a void of meaninglessness. In the words of Henry James senior, society 'redeems' men from their animal selves. But if values are merely a social invention – a part of a system of mutual admiration, as it were – then Eliot and Beckett and Hemingway are right: we are biological accidents, hollow men. The universe is indifferent to us. We had better make the most of one another, huddle together to gain a little warmth, and recognise that death is the end.

And yet, somehow the mind cannot accept that values are completely relative, even allowing that most of our 'value reactions' are emotional rather than intellectual. If they are, then the Marquis de Sade was right, and there is no good reason why we should condemn him for indulging in daydreams of firing pregnant women out of cannons. Individual pleasure is as valid a standard as social duty – more so, in fact, because the advocates of duty imagine it to be an objective value, and are therefore deceiving themselves. De Sade's relativism is all very well, but the nose detects something wrong with it, just as it detects something wrong with Beckett's attitude. We feel like pointing out to Beckett's Molloy that from the evolutionary point of view – survival of the fittest – he can expect to be exterminated. He would probably agree, and ask 'Does it matter?' In that case, it seems that the only answer is to apply the test that G. K. Chesterton suggested in *Manalive* – point a revolver at him, and propose to blow out his brains on the spot. If he remains indifferent, then his nihilism is sincere.

The problem is this: that the basic human relation to existence *seems* to be static. The image that can be found in so many modern novels – of the hero staring at a cobweb in the corner of the ceiling, and feeling no desire to do anything – is a symbol of a certain aspect of modern consciousness. We examine life; it is poker-faced, apparently meaningless. Modern man lives amid an immense, complex civilisation that he did little to create; it is not surprising if he feels passive, if he feels that he is acted upon rather than an actor. His inclination to act is poisoned at the root by a feeling that anything he does takes place in a vacuum. He is like an orator addressing a sleeping audience; there is no response. The problem of modern man is summarised in the first line of Rilke's *Duino Elegies*: 'Who, if I cried, would hear me among the angelic orders?' Everything that mediaeval man did took place against a meaningful universe, with God and the angels looking on. One feels about St Augustine that if some catastrophe destroyed every other human being on the earth, and left him totally alone, he would somehow go on living and praying. If the same situation could happen to a modern man, he would feel that all the clocks had stopped, and that nothing he did mattered any more.

THE INCONSISTENCY OF NIHILISM

In essence, this is the situation as presented by some of the most influential writers of our time; by Sartre, Camus, Hemingway, Beckett, Marcel, Eliot, Graham Greene. The last three believe that the situation is redeemed by the existence of religious values, but their estimate of the human world is much the same as Beckett's.

The first question worth asking is how far these writers are consistent in their presentation. Beckett is not, to begin with. For, in a short mime called *Act Without Words* (printed together with *Endgame*), he tries to show the reasons behind the indifference of his characters, and seems to suggest that they amount to wounded over-sensitivity. His man is tempted to act by whistles from above, accompanied by the lowering of various objects on a rope. But whenever he tries to reach these objects – by piling boxes on top of one another, etc – they are raised beyond his reach. Finally, in disgust, he lies flat on his face – the position occupied continually by the hero of his latest novel *How It Is*, – and refuses to be tempted to act. So it seems that Beckett's fundamental complaint is that the universe is *not* indifferent, but is actively malicious. God may be dead, but the devil isn't. Clearly, Beckett is unaware of the illogicality of this position. The same might be said of Camus, who in *L'Etranger* shows the universe as actively hostile, viciously 'absurd'. This attitude strikes us as a version of the pathetic fallacy – a man swearing at the bed on which he has stubbed his toe.

Similarly, we are reminded that Graham Greene admitted, in *Journey Without Maps,* that the danger of the African journey revealed in him something he has not been aware he possessed, a love of life.* But he seems unaware that this is an admission that his usual jaundiced view of the universe may be something to do with his perceptions rather than with the universe. Again, in an essay called *The Revolver in the Corner Cupboard,* he tells how, as a boy, he used to dispel total boredom by playing Russian roulette with his brother's revolver – spinning the chambers with a single bullet in, and firing at his head. This seems to support Chesterton's idea – that nihilism is a form of spiritual dyspepsia based on laziness and self-delusion.

All this indicates that the charge of total meaninglessness brought against human existence by Sartre, Beckett, etc, is not entirely fair. It seems that the indictment should at least be softened a little, and some of the blame put on human nature. When a Beckett character complains that nothing is worth doing, or Greene declares that life is a long drawn out defeat, we might at least ask how far this is our own fault.

THE INDIFFERENCE THRESHOLD

All this brings us back to the old woman in the vinegar bottle, who symbolises the defeated aspect of human nature. Raskolnikov decides that he would prefer to stand on a narrow ledge for all eternity, rather than die at once. If an alien intelligence from another solar system could observe human beings in the face of death, he would conclude that men love life above all other things, and that anything that increases the pleasure of life is good. He would therefore be somewhat baffled to see a play by Beckett, or to study the figures for the suicide rate in any large city. If they love life with such intensity, how can they treat it with such indifference, when they have no cause for complaint?

The answer can be expressed in two words – the indifference

* Part 3, chapter 1.

threshold. One of the most curious characteristics of human beings – particularly westerners – is that *pain and inconvenience stimulate their vitality far more than pleasure*. In a very precise sense of the word, human beings are spoilt. A spoilt child is one who has come to expect certain privileges and accepts them as rights. He is not grateful for these privileges; in fact, they bore him. The only time he feels strongly about them is when they are curtailed; then he sulks. All human beings take their happiness for granted, and only question life when they are in pain, as Pirandello pointed out.

I shall refer to this margin of human consciousness that can be stimulated by pain, but not by pleasure, as the 'indifference threshold'.* William James uses the word 'threshold' (of consciousness) 'to indicate the amount of noise, pressure or other outer stimulus which it takes to arouse the attention at all'. A person with a high noise threshold will be able to sleep through a racket that would rouse another person. A low pain threshold or misery threshold is the sign of an oversensitive nature – and, if there is no compensating self-discipline, of a neurotic. The old woman in the vinegar bottle had a high indifference threshold – using threshold, this time, to refer to the consciousness itself rather than to the stimulus. It might be said that the indifference threshold is the extent to which the vitality is asleep. The Greek poet Capetanakis has a brilliant passage on this subject in his essay on Rimbaud:

> One of the most disappointing truths we are taught by this war is that 'not even war can frighten us enough', as Auden remarked a little while ago. 'Well', I thought when the war started, trying to hope for the best, 'it will be horrible, but if it will be as horrible as to frighten and wake up the mind, it might become the salvation of many. Many are going to die, *but those who are going to survive will have a real life, with the mind awake*.' ... But I was mistaken ... The war is very frightening, but it is not frightening enough. The fear cannot go deep enough to shake the mind. The grief cannot go deep enough to make

* For convenience, I shall also refer to it as 'The St Neot margin'.

the mind bleed. It seems that as long as the mind sleeps, no horrible situation can be grasped in all its horror. One might get physically frightened, but this fear is only the fear of the flesh, of the animal, not the fear of man facing his fate.

Capetanakis goes on to suggest that Rimbaud's strange life of extremes and self-torment was an attempt to 'keep the mind awake', analogous to a saint's self-flagellation. Rimbaud 'realised, to his horror, that human beings are condemned to live perpetually in a happiness they can never escape. This discovery horrified him, because he also knew that happiness is an obstacle to real existence; it gives us a feeling of security and comfort, which allows our minds, so lazy are they, to retire and sleep undisturbed.'*

This is the problem: the 'St Neot margin', the old woman in a vinegar bottle, the curious inadequacy of human consciousness. All human beings are like children who get bored with a holiday after the first week. Or they might be compared to grandfather clocks driven by watch-springs; their appetite for life is too feeble. But this is only a partial answer. Why is the human 'mainspring' so weak? Why is our capacity for freedom so limited?

Writers like Eliot and Greene would no doubt answer: that is original sin. But before accepting this, let us try some of the commonsense explanations. A child's capacity for freedom is smaller than an adult's, and for obvious reasons. A child's internal resources are smaller; this is why adults, on the whole, are less subject to boredom than children.

In the same way, the uncultured adult tends to be bored more easily than the man of intelligence. One has only to read a book like Dana's *Two Years Before the Mast* or Mailer's *The Naked and the Dead* to see what can happen to men with nothing to occupy their minds. The endless dreary card-playing of Mailer's soldiers would seem a death-in-life to a man like Capetanakis. Man's evolution depends on motive and purpose. Without purpose, even a cultured man can sink to the level of an animal – like Conrad's Kurtz.

* Demetrios Capetanakis, *Essays and Poems,* John Lehmann 1947. Capetanakis, who died at the age of thirty-two in 1944, is too little known in this country (where he spent the last years of his life.) His writings and literary personality are in many ways reminiscent of T. E. Hulme – although the resemblance did not extend to their personal lives; Capetanakis was modest and self-effacing.

It might be objected that it is the barbarity of Kurtz's environment that robs him of motive and mocks his idealism. This is only partly true. Young and alert minds are always overcoming a brutalising environment, and apparently experiencing no ill-effect – consider Richard Wright's account of his childhood in *Black Boy,* or Andersen-Nëxo's in *Pelle the Conqueror*. On the contrary, the evidence seems to indicate that pessimism is often related to lack of early struggles. Kierkegaard, Andreyev, Proust, Beckett, Greene and Eliot were all born in fairly comfortable circumstances; Proust frankly admits that most of his later troubles were the outcome of being spoiled by his mother. But the intelligent man who starts 'at the bottom' of society cannot afford the luxury of cynicism or pessimism; he harnesses his mind to the problem of improving his position as he might harness a dray horse to a cart that is stuck in the mud. If he succeeds – as Lawrence, Wells, Shaw, Nëxo and Gorki succeeded – then he has also taught himself a practical view of the intellect and its relation to civilisation, so that he feels that the next step is to harness it to the problems of his age. Beckett's 'Nothing to be done' never enters his head, because if he believed it, he would still be drudging at some badly paid job.

The keyword here is purpose; without purpose, the mind is left to support its own weight. Shaw's St Joan comments: 'Minding your own business is like minding your own body – it's the shortest way to make yourself sick.' The heroes of Proust and Beckett are a case in point; they have nothing to do but mind their own business and their own bodies.

The question: What purpose? is not of primary importance; but it is usually connected in some way with society. Even D. H. Lawrence, who disapproved of Christ as much as of Caesar, believed that the artist is a spiritual leader of society, whose task is 'to reveal the life mystery and by his revelation create a new possibility, a *strange element* in life'* (my italics). These words 'a strange element in life' go to the heart of the problem. For Beckett characters, life is boring and limited: one of them says that 'the earth is extinguished, though I never saw it lit'. This is

* From *The Plumed Serpent*; cited by Henry Miller in *Shadowy Monomania* (*Sunday After the War,* p. 266).

only to say that, unlike Lawrence, he has never seen life as a realm of supra-personal possibility. Laziness, habit and weakness limit us. The answer is self-discipline, self-control. Shaw points out that self-control, 'a highly developed vital sense, dominating and regulating the mere appetites', is the fundamental quality needed for survival and evolution. Since Beckett characters feel they have no reason for self-discipline, it follows that they are doomed to remain spiritually static. The adult's capacity for freedom is superior to that of the child because he is more capable of self-discipline.

Purpose means *escape from the personal.* This is superbly expressed by H. G. Wells in a passage of *The Undying Fire,* where Job Huss talks of education:

> Man ... is born as the beasts are born, a greedy egotism, a clutching desire, a thing of lusts and fears. He can regard nothing except in relation to himself. Even his love is a bargain, and his utmost effort is vanity because he has to die. And it is we teachers alone who can lift him out of that self-preoccupation. We teachers ... We can release him into a wider circle of ideas beyond himself in which he can at length forget himself and his meagre personal ends altogether. We can open his eyes to the past and the future and to the undying life of Man. So through us and only through us he escapes from death and futility.

At first sight, this may seem only a re-hash of the naïve optimism of the nineteenth century, with its belief in endless progress through education. But the implications are deeper, as Wells makes clear in the opening pages of his *Experiment in Autobiography*. These raise so many questions and suggest so many lines of thought that they are worth considering in some detail.* Wells begins by expressing his annoyance with various trivialities that are preventing him from settling down to work. He then goes on:

> There is nothing I think very exceptional in my situation as a mental worker. Entanglement is our common lot. I believe this

* I have quoted part of these pages in chapter 4 of *The Strength to Dream*, in connection with the problem of imagination.

craving for release from – bothers, from daily demands and urgencies, from responsibilities, is shared by an increasing number of people who, with specialised and distinctive work to do, find themselves eaten up by first hand affairs. This is the outcome of a specialisation and a sublimation of interests that has become frequent only in the last century or so. Spaciousness and leisure, have so far been exceptional. Most individual creatures have, since life began, been 'up against it' all the time, have been driven continually by fear and cravings, have had to respond to the unresting antagonisms of their surroundings, and they have found a sufficient and sustaining interest in the drama of immediate events ... Essentially, their living was continuous adjustment to happenings.

That is to say that man in recent centuries has been presented with more freedom than his forebears knew, and has come to realise that life is more than keeping his head above water. Like Nietzsche, he becomes aware that the question: 'Freedom *for* what?' is more important than the question 'Freedom from what?'

So that now, Wells goes on, 'people can ask ... what would have been an extraordinary question five hundred years ago. They can say: 'Yes, you earn a living, you support a family, you love and hate, but – *what do you do*?'

... We originative intellectual workers are reconditioning human life ...

We are like early amphibians, so to speak, struggling out of the waters that have hitherto covered our kind, into the air, seeking to breathe in a new fashion and emancipate ourselves from long accepted and long unquestioned necessities. At last it becomes for us a case of air or nothing. But the new land has not definitely emerged from the waters, and we swim distressfully in an element we wish to abandon.

I do not now in the least desire to live longer unless I can go on with what I consider my proper business ... I want the whole stream of this daily life to flow on for me – for a long time yet – *if what I call my work can still be, can be more than ever the emergent meaning of the stream.* But only on that condition. (My italics.)

Wells's image of the early amphibians goes to the root of the problem. We are neither one thing nor the other. Education has emancipated the mind, taught it impatience with the mere pressure of events, given man a taste for freedom. But an unmixed diet of freedom is too much for the mind. We prefer breathing the open air; but we still have flippers instead of legs, and it costs a tremendous effort to move far on the land. It is a temptation to dive back into the water.

THE SPIRIT OF ROMANTICISM

When we consider the problems, as expressed by philosophers and poets over the last century and a half, it is clear that Wells has grasped their essence. Let us look at this matter in some detail.

For most animals, 'life' means adjustment to the problems of their surroundings. Survival power means power to adjust. The descendants of the mammoth and sabre toothed tiger are still with us because they had learned the trick of adjusting their bodily temperature to a change of environment. The dinosaurs – like the reptiles of today – had a constant body temperature; consequently they disappeared.

Early man had yet another faculty to help survival: language. Many animals – monkeys, for example – have cries that express a definite meaning: 'Enemy approaching', 'Baby fallen out of tree', etc. Human language no doubt began in this primitive way, and developed under the pressure of the need to survive. And yet no theory involving enemies – animate or otherwise – can explain the development of these natural cries into a symbol language. Anyone who has worked with navvies or farm labourers knows how little language is needed for co-ordinated work. Instead of enemies and dangers, it is now necessary to posit another equally important pressure: boredom. Perhaps some sudden improvement in natural conditions allowed our primate ancestors to relax after thousands of generations of hard struggle that demanded cunning and vigilance. This relaxation would have the effect that prison has on the criminal; for an enormous percentage, it would cause degeneration, and lower the survival capacity. But a very tiny number would be the equivalent of the modern man of genius; the energy would flow inwards, animate the brain. So it may be that we owe all our civilisation to some chance improvement in environment – like the warm periods between the great ice caps of the Pleistocene – that created the most valuable of all commodities, leisure, and its concomitant, boredom.

The earliest development of the brain was not in the direction of language, but simply of imagination – the power to envisage something beyond the immediate environment. W. Grey Walter points out that all animals but man lack the ability to envisage any change in environment.* 'Unable to rehearse the possible consequences of different responses to a stimulus, without any faculty of planning, the apes and other animals cannot learn to control their feelings.' The chimpanzees, nearest creature to man, 'cannot retain an image long enough to reflect on it'.

The human brain, more or less identical with the brains we know today, has existed for about half a million years, possibly longer. And yet learning, science, has come into existence only in the past three thousand years. It is true that the earliest development of religion was also the development of science. When a man was frightened by the thunder, and concluded that it was an angry god, he had advanced a hypothesis to unify his experience of storms. This is the definition of science – the creation of unifying hypotheses. And all evolution is an unconscious urge of the whole being to unify its experience.

Changes in a species occur by what biologists call mutations. These mutations may explain how some early ape man decided to walk on his hind legs or to make language grunts, but they cannot explain why certain civilisations showed particular aptitudes. The Chaldeans seem to have been the first to have noted the arrangement of the stars; the Egyptians invented geometry; the Hittites learned to smelt iron. The Ancient Greeks took a step that was greater than any of these, and invented science and philosophy. We know of no previous development of civilisation that will explain why the Greeks developed this love of 'knowledge for its own sake', as distinguished from knowledge for practical

* *The Living Brain,* chapter 1.

purposes. Possibly the Greeks had more leisure than the Chaldeans or the Hittites, and invented science as modern journalism invented the crossword puzzle. Whatever the reason, the leap forward was unexpected and incredible. The sudden development of the human mind was like an aeroplane taking off. And yet the aeroplane is a bad simile; for in a way, the human mind remained earthbound; it had merely learned to take a fantastic series of kangaroo hops. Speculative thought was a new instrument; but to begin with, its use was curiously limited. Human beings find it difficult to break old habits, and the habit of merely adjusting to life was some millions of years old. So Greek science reached a certain point, and then stopped dead. It was as if the 'evolutionary force' was exhausted, and decided to take a rest for two thousand years. From Aristotle onward, the major thinkers tended to be 'system builders'; it was not enough for them to explain one aspect of the universe or the human mind; everything had to be fitted in – the sun, moon and stars, God and the devil, trees, animals and human beings. Inevitably, this entailed much loose thinking and wild guessing. Saint Thomas Aquinas (1226-1274) can be taken as typical of post-Platonic system-builders. His two *Summas* are an immense attempt to summarise all knowledge and 'complete the human mind'. The sheer physical effort of writing so many millions of words killed him in his fortieth year.

The *Summas* are like a tower of Babel, dominating the landscape of the fifteen hundred years since Aristotle. They also illustrate perfectly the limitations of the system-building mentality. Aquinas was a formidable logician and a profound psychologist, with a sure instinct about the direction of human evolution. But wherever there was a gap in his structure, he patched it over with the likeliest Christian dogma that would fit. Consequently, one is always aware that his logic or his knowledge reaches a limit, which he attempts to disguise. His leaps are long and bold; but they only remind one that the human mind has not yet discovered the secret of flight.

The breakthrough came three hundred years later, exactly two thousand years after Aristotle. It was largely the work of six men: Copernicus, Tycho Brahe, Kepler, Galileo, Huygens and Newton. Newton stands above them all, as possibly the greatest single figure in the history of human thought. His greatness is so remarkable that he seems inhuman. If we compare Aristotle's *Physics* with Newton's *Principia*, the exact nature of the revolution becomes clear. Aristotle is like Aquinas; his thought proceeds in kangaroo hops. With Newton, one has a feeling of a new *method* of thought, as different from the old one as aeroplane travel is unlike travel by automobile. By his invention of the calculus and its application to a physical science based on experiment, Newton had opened up infinite vistas of possibility. The human mind was suddenly the potential king of all knowledge. In a sense, it was the most incredible evolutionary leap since the first man burst out of the Pleistocene eight hundred thousand years ago.

It took some time for the full import of Newton's revolution to dawn on the western world. Newton himself never realised; he thought that his most important work was his interpretation of the Book of Daniel, based on the chronology of Archbishop Ussher (who believed that the world was created in 4004 B.C.). In his plodding, unemotional way, Newton was a religious man. But what he had done, without realising it, was to dispense with the necessity of God. The *Principia* destroyed the authority of the scriptures at one blow. With the discovery of the scientific method, the human mind became airborne; what was to prevent man from learning anything, *becoming* anything? From the earliest times, it had been universally taken for granted that God never intended man to know too much; what else is the meaning of the legends of Prometheus or of Adam and Eve? Man was a creature. His relation to God was like that of a dog to its owner. Suddenly, the dog had discovered how to use the arts of its owner; not only that: the owner had totally disappeared, and there was every reason to believe him dead.

Newton was the true father of the French revolution, not Rousseau. The storming of the Bastille was a symbolic act; it was the official coronation of Newtonian man as Lord of the Universe. The Marquis de Sade wrote a curious pamphlet called *Frenchman, one more effort if you want to be Republican*, in which he told his countrymen that they should follow their execution of the king with the execution of God. And he took in one stride the step that has taken other European thinkers a century and a half of nervous edging forward: the idea that values are relative, and that therefore all men should adopt Rabelais's motto: 'Do what you will'. In a sense, De Sade's pamphlet might be regarded as the true assault on the Bastille. It was the first great gesture of romanticism: the formulation of the question: 'Why is man not a God?'

THE FAILURE OF ROMANTICISM

This was a question that would never have occurred to the men of earlier centuries. They took their limitations and their sufferings for granted. Now romantic man asked questions. He was outraged that he should be a prisoner of the body, a captive of the earth. The great symbol of romantic man is Byron's Manfred, standing on a mountain top and shaking his fist at God.

And yet romanticism failed. The nineteenth century began with Schiller's Karl Moor declaring that man should have absolute freedom. (A German military man once said: 'If God could have foreseen *The Robbers*, he wouldn't have created the world.') It ended in the world-weary, twilight romanticism of the 1890s, in the poetry of George, Verlaine and Dowson.

> The fire is out, and spent the warmth thereof.
> This is the end of every song man sings.

It was not that the late romantics had ceased to believe that man is a potential god. But they felt the odds were too heavily stacked against him. The human spirit, they implied, was like a flame burning at the bottom of a river. Like an oxy-acetylene flame, its sheer heat could keep the water at bay. But a time would come when the flame would lose its strength, and the water would close in ...

How had it come about that romanticism collapsed from its defiant Man-worship into the self-pity of the *fin de siècle*? Some of the reasons are obvious. Schiller could talk about man's absolute freedom, but he himself was poor and sick. A great number of romantic poets were sick men; so many as to raise the old Greek dualism in another form; this time it said: 'If you care for things of the spirit, the world will squash you. If you reject the world, then you are rejecting life.'

But another aspect of the problem was expressed in *Faust.* Faust has suddenly become aware that all the knowledge in the world will not free man from his limitations; that, in a fundamental sense, we can know nothing. And when Mephistopheles places his magic powers at Faust's disposal, Faust only uses them to slip into Gretchen's bed. The man who began by demanding: Why am I not a god? ends by accepting the forgetfulness of a peasant girl's body.

Faust's failure is the failure of romanticism. At first, romantic man believed that he had been granted a new kind of freedom; before long, he was more aware of its limitations; like Faust, he envied the happiness of less complex creatures.

THE FAILURE OF LANGUAGE

But the fundamental reason for the collapse of romanticism was to do with its language.

At its best, language might be compared to a sensitive membrane that separates man's inner being from the world. The membrane should pulsate to every shade of meaning that the man wishes to express. Unfortunately, language is subject to a kind of inflation. Words are used until they lose their original force. Finally, the language membrane becomes as thick and as tough as a football. The romantics used words like 'rapture' and 'ecstasy' until they were almost meaningless. It is impossible to read the prose of even an early romantic like Goethe without feeling that it is stiff and cumbersome. Finally, romantic language collapsed under the weight of its verbal imprecision. Like the dinosaurs, it died from sheer clumsiness and size.

But in another sense, language might be compared to a microscope. It takes things that are dimly felt, and gives them precision. Now pre-Newtonian man had accepted that life has a meaning, because he accepted God. Romantic man could no longer believe that life had this kind of meaning, so he scrutinised it for some other meaning, some sign that man is an important part of the order of creation. It was like taking a piece of some unknown substance that might be wood, and peering at it through a microscope to see whether it has a grain. Romantic man scrutinised life under his language-microscope, and concluded that the wood had no grain; life was meaningless. Goethe at least believed in an 'unseen world' of which this one is merely a reflection. But as the century went on, and science progressed, the romantics became gloomily certain that, for all his immortal spirit, man is an accident in an indifferent universe. For all his aspirations, he suffers from boredom, lack of purpose, weakness, sickness, a sense of futility. The poet Kleist was a kind of living Faust, who was so overcome by the philosophy of Kant and the feeling that human beings can never know certainty, that he committed suicide.

THE NEW ROMANTICISM – EXISTENTIALISM

And yet although romanticism ended in exhaustion and defeat, a third 'assault on the Bastille' was being prepared. Existentialism was founded by a typical romantic, Kierkegaard, who felt that the world and the spirit are forever at war. But in the twentieth century, it was taken up by a number of thinkers who had no such romantic predisposition to defeat. Men like Heidegger, Jaspers and Marcel recognised that the failure of romanticism was due to the failure of language. Their 'existentialism' was only a new romanticism, given the added precision of a philosophical vocabulary. It should not be assumed that new language is merely a matter of inventing new words, or even new ideas, like Heidegger's 'authentic and inauthentic existence'. First of all, a whole new framework of ideas has to be created; new language then develops naturally from new ways of seeing the old ideas. Karl Jaspers was concerned to relate the new 'philosophy of existence' to the history of philosophy since the Greeks. Heidegger proceeded to develop a new psychology of man based upon the idea that all our modern ills spring from 'forgetfulness of Existence'. Gabriel Marcel was also preoccupied with the 'rediscovery of the immediate' that has been lost in abstract thought, but tried to link his thought with traditional metaphysics.

By this time – the mid-1920s – existentialism was in the air of the century; it is present in the poetry of Rilke and Eliot, and in James Joyce's determined rejection of the 'novel of ideas'. In another way, it was present in the later novels of H. G. Wells, where he attempted to use his scientific training in a painfully honest attempt to analyse the problems of his own existence. It is present in all the novels of Hemingway, with their 'return to the immediate' and rejection of intellect, and in a great deal of Faulkner. Both Camus and Sartre are closer to the Kierkegaard tradition; they ask again the question of 'values in a universe of chance'.

Existentialism has again placed the question of human existence under the 'language microscope'. And after half a century of analysis, it has also concluded that the wood has no grain, that life is meaningless. 'Man is a useless passion' says Sartre, and Heidegger concludes that man can exist authentically only in the face of death, a conclusion that seems to be echoed by Camus in *L'Etranger*. Camus agrees that life is a rock that has to be everlastingly rolled uphill so that it can roll down again, and yet adds that 'we must imagine Sisyphus happy' because he possesses freedom of spirit. (This is a repetition of the conclusions of Shelley's *Prometheus Unbound* or Byron's *Prisoner of Chillon*, with his 'Eternal spirit of the chainless Mind! Brightest in dungeons' etc.) Faulkner concludes that on the whole his negroes are the most admirable human beings in his doomed county because 'they endure' (which recalls Professor Toynbee's more sophisticated 'Cling and wait'). Finally, Hemingway writes of his old fisherman, Santiago: 'A man can be destroyed but not defeated.' It can be seen that the tone of existentialism is a long way from the self-pity of Dowson and Verlaine. It is a stoical assertion of man's dignity in the face of defeat. If the spirit is free, then man is not truly defeated; he can only be destroyed.

THE SOUND BARRIER

This, then, is the situation as we face it today. The problem is analogous to the entropy problem, as described by Eddington in *The Nature of the Physical World,* where he points out that nature seems to have left no signposts or pointers to reveal any kind of purpose. He says that it is rather like the White Knight in *Alice*:

But I was thinking of a plan
To dye one's whiskers green,
Then always use so large a fan
That they could not be seen.

But entropy (or the random element in nature) *is* such a pointer, says Eddington. The existentialist, unfortunately, has not discovered the philosophical counterpart of entropy. God never seems to drop the fan so that we can catch a glimpse of the colour of his whiskers. The nihilism of Beckett is apparently as plausible as the optimism of Hegel. Under the circumstances, it would seem that Sartre and Hemingway are right, and values *are* 'what you make them'. Man can be destroyed, but not defeated.

Yet it is possible that one might feel a certain objection to being either defeated or destroyed. Is it not possible that someone has made a miscalculation somewhere? The defeat of the romantics was like the exhaustion of amphibians that cannot yet walk on the land. The strange new element baffled them.

And yet there is another parallel which holds out more hope for the situation. It is impossible to examine the nineteenth century without feeling that some strange evolutionary change came over the species. H. G. Wells has a novel in which a comet fills the atmosphere with a gas that destroys the war-like propensities of the human race, so that the brotherhood of man becomes a reality. One could almost imagine that some such comet had struck the earth in 1789. And the new experiment was rather like the experiments that scientists conducted to build an aeroplane that could go faster than sound. The problem of 'the sound barrier' is that when a plane travels at the speed of sound, the air cannot escape quickly enough from in front of its wings, and piles up like a concrete wall. A point comes where the plane has to smash through this 'sound barrier'. All the early experiments were a failure; the planes smashed.

The experiment of romanticism was an attempt to create a man who could go 'faster than sound', who was capable of accepting the responsibility of being a lord of the universe. Most of the men smashed. With existentialism, the experiment seemed slightly more successful; at last it produced a kind of undefeated stoicism instead of the total defeat of the romantics.

The problem of the sound barrier still confronts us. What is needed is yet another assault, an attempt to go deeper than either romanticism or existentialism. This fourth 'assault on the Bastille' needs a new name to distinguish it from romanticism and existentialism, but so far, this name has not come into existence. For the purposes of this book, I shall speak of it as 'the new existentialism' – but recognising that it is only a new existentialism in the rather dubious sense that existentialism was a new romanticism.

The book that follows is an attempt to discern the outlines of the new existentialism.

Chapter 2

THE STRANGE STORY OF MODERN PHILOSOPHY

THE TREASON OF THE INTELLECTUALS

In his study of Rimbaud, Henry Miller wrote: 'Until the old world dies out utterly, the "abnormal" individual will tend more and more to become the norm. The new man will find himself only when the warfare between collectivity and the individual ceases.'

The position expressed here was the starting point of the investigation in *The Outsider*. But in some ways, it is a dangerous half truth. 'Collectivisation' is an obvious and unavoidable consequence of social evolution, and individualists have always kicked against it. But from De Sade onward, most of the rebels have seen it simply as a question of 'the individual versus collective man'; consequently, most of the revolts have been explosions of violence that have ended in defeat or reaction. It is true of Miller as well as of Rimbaud, and it remains true down to the revolt of the Beat Generation and the Angry Young Men. Obviously there is a great deal 'wrong with society', in the sense that it is often unfair to the 'abnormal' individual; still, we have not yet reached Dostoevsky's nightmare of a society that favours mediocrity and destroys genius. Until this point arrives, the problem cannot be reduced to a matter of the individual versus collective man. The real problem is to reconcile the demands of a healthy individualism with those of a healthy society. A healthy individualism could be defined as one that is not neurotic or self-destructive. The same is true of a healthy society; it would aim at a heightening of creative vitality in all its members.

A little thought reveals the fallacy of the Rimbaud-Miller type of individualism. Obviously, a healthy society would be a society of healthy individuals. But more than this it would be a society in which the *gifted* individuals are healthy, since these gifted individuals tend to become the cultural leaders. If the gifted individuals tend to be pessimists who believe that life is futile and man a useless passion, it is not surprising of the cultural atmosphere becomes stagnant. It is a vicious circle; the rebel blames society for letting him down, and turns his back on it. And in condemning the 'sick culture', he is introducing a little more poison into its system. The next generation of rebels find that the situation is still worse, so they again throw the blame on society, and make a hero of the rebel of the older generation – who is actually largely to blame. So it goes on. The rebel is disinclined to believe either that he might play an important part in determining the cultural atmosphere of his society, or that a society's culture is important to its health. He likes to place the blame on those in power – politicians and businessmen – forgetting that these men are only doing their best to support the society he has rejected. So the spiral of degeneration continues.

It is important to recognise the close connection between a society's culture and its general health. Frederick Wilhelm III of Prussia has often been attacked for his part in promoting Hegel and condemning Schopenhauer to obscurity. In fact, he showed a profounder insight than most princes possess. Hegel's philosophy was optimistic, and he recognised the importance of social stability; Schopenhauer's was pessimistic, and his attitude to politics was wholly cynical. An 'officially approved' Schopenhauer would have been the most dangerous man in Europe. Hegel's influence was comparatively beneficial.

It follows, then, that if our own culture is 'sick', we should not throw all the blame on politicians or businessmen; the thinkers and artists of the past two hundred years are equally to blame. Some have been entirely destructive, like Schopenhauer or De Sade. Most of the others have raised problems that they have left unsolved, or only partly solved. (This list includes almost every important thinker from Coleridge onward.) A very small number have thought the problems through to the end and proposed constructive solutions. (These include Hegel, Shaw and Wells.) Such men are never popular with their 'intellectual peers', since their very existence is an implied reproach. The following generation usually condemns them as shallow, and tries to forget them.

The consequence of all this is that the thinker or artist of today finds himself in a room that contains the accumulated rubbish of two hundred years; every occupant seems to have added to the muddle. All the traditions seem to have reached a state of hopeless confusion. The novelist, for example, discovers that Flaubert, Henry James, Proust, Joyce and Robbe-Grillet have backed the novel into a cul-de-sac and overturned it in a ditch. In all likelihood, he hurries away from the mess and writes a conventional novel that might have been written a hundred years ago. The composer finds that Wagner, Mahler, Schoenberg and Boulez have left music in the same situation; he then has the alternative of going a step further than Webern, or being condemned as 'unprogressive'.

But the person who finds himself in the worst situation is the philosopher. And since the aim of the present book is to suggest a basis for a new existentialism, it is important to understand how this came about.

FROM THE GREEKS TO GALILEO

The problem of the human situation is the problem of the clash between man's inner world and the alien world 'out there'. The Greeks solved the problem in a simple manner – by rejecting the world out there. They were intoxicated with the power of thought, with the beautiful certainty of logic and mathematics. But the real world is irritatingly un-mathematical; it is full of violence and uncertainty. So Greek thought declared that the real world is unimportant, an illusion. Reality lies in the world of ideas. Before a carpenter can make a chair, he must have an idea of a chair; consequently, the idea must be more important than the actual chair. One can destroy the chair, and it is easy enough to make another; but if the idea were destroyed no chairs could be made. The idea is like the mould in which all real things are cast. Somewhere behind the façade of reality, according to Plato, there is a world in which these moulds are kept. This real world can be glimpsed behind the everyday world of change if one stares hard enough. The everyday world is like a fence with small cracks between each board. If you apply your eye to the crack, you will see only a narrow strip of the world on the other side. But if you ride past the fence on a bicycle, all the cracks seem to merge together, as if the fence were semi-transparent, and you can see everything that lies behind it. *But speed is essential.* And in the same way, one needs speed in a mental sense – intellectual vitality and curiosity – to see the eternal world of ideas that lies behind the changing face of the material world.

There is obviously a basic truth in this. But Greek thought threw out the baby with the bath water. Since the philosopher spends his life trying to ignore the real world and study the world on 'the other side of the fence', he will achieve final freedom in death. This is the argument with which Socrates comforts his friends on the day of his execution, and the reason he gives for not escaping while he had the chance. He does not explain why, in that case, he did not commit suicide as soon as he decided to be a philosopher.

The world-rejection of Greek thought dominated philosophy for the next two thousand years. In Europe, it happened to fit in very well with the world-rejection of Christianity. Then its weak nesses began to appear. Aristotle was regarded as the great scientist and realist, in contrast to Plato's idealism. But Aristotle, like Plato, felt rather contemptuous of the material world; he was inclined to make assertions without testing them. He declared, for example, that an object dropped from the mast of a moving ship will fall behind the mast; he also believed that heavier bodies fall faster than lighter ones.* He was aware of the theories of earlier thinkers that the earth revolves round the sun, and that it has an axial rotation, but he rejected them in favour of the idea that the earth is the centre of the universe.

The great revolution came nearly two thousand years later, with Galileo. He proved that all bodies fall at the same speed. He invented a telescope and discovered the moons of Jupiter, con-

* See *The Mechanisation of the World Picture,* by E. J. Dijksterhuis, p. 28. O.U.P.

firming the theory of Copernicus that the sun is the centre of our system. He rolled weights down an inclined plane and concluded that a moving body will continue to move unless something stops it. Galileo practised what Aristotle only preached – close observation of nature.

THE SOURCE OF CONFUSION – DESCARTES

Modern philosophy begins with a contemporary of Galileo, René Descartes. Descartes was a mathematician and a scientist, and he asked what he considered to be the fundamental question: What can we *know* for certain? Descartes began with the principle that one must doubt everything, then went on to ask: Can I be certain that I am sitting here in this chair? No, for it is possible that I might be dreaming. What, then, do I know for certain? I know that I exist, because I am thinking.

Descartes' principle of 'radical doubt' was accepted by all subsequent philosophers. It is the application to philosophy of Galileo's principle: 'Test everything.' But the principle had an unfortunate consequence; *it divided science from philosophy*. Science is bound to take the material world for granted; but according to Descartes, we can never be as certain of the existence of the world as we can of our own existence; the scientist studies the physical world, but the philosopher had better study the mind. Only the mind can get to the truth underlying appearances.

Descartes was carried away by enthusiasm for the scientific method, which, after two thousand years, was now revolutionising human knowledge. Science examines the world through a magnifying glass; so Descartes naïvely proceeded to examine the human situation through a magnifying glass, trying to reduce everything to reason. Oddly enough, he did not apply his principle of doubt to his religion, and continued to regard himself as a good Catholic. So it is not surprising that his system should be confused and self-divided, with religious dogma on the one hand, and naïve rationalism on the other. His rationalism led him to decide that animals are complicated machines without a soul. This led to a difficult problem. If animals are really clockwork, how do we know that men are not also clockwork? 'Because', Descartes replied, 'I *know* I have a soul. I think, therefore I am.' But if an animal can go through all the motions of being alive without really being alive, then is there any *need* for a soul to drive the human clockwork? Plainly not. The soul, Descartes said, lives in the brain, and can indirectly influence the body. Descartes' disciple Geulincx saw the inconsistencies in this theory, and took it to an extreme. The soul has no influence on the body at all. It is true that if you want to raise your arm, you can do so; but this is only because the soul and the body are like two clocks that have been synchronised by God. One of them shows the hour, and the other strikes. We imagine that they are connected, but this is an illusion.

Geulincx's 'improvement' of Descartes is typical of modern philosophy. A theory is self-contradictory; but instead of checking the premises, another theorist takes the contradictions to an extreme, and reduces the whole thing to absurdity – but also to consistency. If Descartes had been bold enough, he would have taken his own radical doubt to an extreme and declared that men are also machines, that consciousness is an illusion produced by the body, and that all religion is a product of ignorance. Later thinkers took these steps. Comte founded the school of positivism, that declared religion to be nonsense; Ernst Mach declared that consciousness is merely a series of sensory impressions; the leader of the Behaviourist group of psychologists, J. B. Watson, wrote '... no behaviourist has observed anything that he can call consciousness, sensation, imagery, perception or will'.

Yet another group of philosophers took Descartes' principle of doubt still further, and continued the work of reducing man to a machine. Locke argued that all our knowledge is derived from experience. This was the first total rejection of Plato's ideas. In the *Meno*, Socrates persuades a slave to reason out a geometrical problem, and goes on to argue that the slave already possessed the knowledge *inside* himself; it is only a question of getting it out into consciousness. All knowledge is inside us, Plato argues. Reason and imagination are the instruments of knowledge, and a man who spent his life in a dark room could, in theory, learn everything about the world outside if he used his mind properly. Locke dismissed this idea of 'innate knowledge'.

Bishop Berkeley went a step further. Descartes had already said that we can only know the physical world through the mind. Berkeley asked why, in that case, should we bother to assume that the physical world exists at all? He argues that all the qualities of objects are supplied by the mind. Jam is not really sweet; it only produces a sensation of sweetness; if a man burns the taste buds off his tongue with caustic soda, jam will taste like pork dripping. The sky is not really blue; it only produces a sensation of blueness on the optic nerve. Berkeley ends by suggesting that objects only exist when we are looking at them – or at least, they would, if it were not for God, who is everywhere and is always looking at everything.

It can be seen that, in this final conclusion, Berkeley is as inconsistent as the rest. David Hume, twenty-six years younger than Berkeley, made the usual attempt to push these conclusions to the absurd limit of consistency. He did this by blending together the essence of Descartes, Locke and Berkeley. He began with Descartes' principle of doubting everything, then proceeded to agree with Locke and Berkeley that all knowledge is derived from experience, and that there are no general ideas. Next he denied the 'self' (i.e., the soul), declaring that consciousness is just a flow of perceptions, and that men are bundles of perceptions (psychologically speaking). Finally, he went further than any previous philosopher and denied that cause and effect have any necessary connection. $1 + 1 = 2$ may be a valid example of cause and effect, but in nature, 'every effect is a distinct event from its cause', and 'It could not, therefore, be discovered in the cause'.

After Hume, philosophy faced a blank wall. Descartes at least had left a basis for certainty: 'I think, therefore I am.' Hume replied: 'That does not prove that you exist at all.' Berkeley had got rid of the outside world; now Hume got rid of the mind as well. Reason had proved to be a kind of forest fire that ended by consuming everything. Descartes' principle of doubt left nothing standing.

The task of rescuing philosophy from Hume's total scepticism was undertaken by Kant. Kant, like all the rest, accepted Descartes' premise, and followed roughly the same line of reason as Berkeley and Hume. The main problem, as Kant saw it, was to re-establish Plato's idea that all knowledge can be found *inside* man – not just mathematical knowledge. Kant's aim was excellent, but his means were not entirely honest. And his first step seems to be only another concession to Locke and Hume. Nobody had ever doubted that $1 + 1 = 2$ is a 'necessary' truth, as opposed to a statement like 'It is snowing because it is cold', which is logical enough, but may not be true. Kant declared that $5 + 7 = 12$ is no more 'necessary' than the connection of cause and effect, because the idea of 12 is not 'contained' in the idea of $5 + 7$. At first sight, it may seem that Kant was only giving away more ground to Hume. But this was essential to his plan, for he goes on to propose a theory of the mind which is the reverse of Hume's. For Hume, the mind is almost nothing, a machine set going by perceptions. For Kant, the mind is everything. For not only does the mind embellish nature with colours and textures and smells – not to mention cause and effect – but it also adds space and time. Kant agrees with Descartes that we can never know the external world, but only our impressions of it. In that case, what is the external world like? We can never know. The mind adds practically everything to what we perceive; these additions are divided into twelve categories, which include colour, shape, size, smell and causality. The only way we can understand our impressions is to sort them out into these categories, and arrange them tidily in the order of space and time. The categories are like a pair of coloured spectacles that we can never remove; we can never hope to see the *Ding an sich*, things as they really are. Reality remains unknowable.

It has been pointed out that Kant failed to follow his arguments to their extremes, like Descartes and Berkeley. For why should we bother to postulate a 'reality' out there, if the mind can do so much? Worse still, if my mind can create the whole world, how do I know that it is not also creating other people, and that I am not the only person in the universe? But Kant slips past these objections, and proceeds quickly to less bewildering matters. If the mind creates the world (and we can now see why Kant asserted that $1 + 1 = 2$ is not a 'necessary' truth), then we can no longer dismiss our moral and religious feelings as delusions simply because they are in the mind. In one sweep, Kant had managed to reinstate religion.

The meaning of Kant's achievement can be seen if we view it in historical perspective – and also its inevitability. Galileo had started the process when he talked about primary and secondary qualities. Shape and size and mass are primary qualities which really belong to nature; secondary qualities, such as colour, texture, smell, may be added by the mind. Berkeley went on to argue that even the primary qualities are added by the mind, because a square seen from an odd angle may appear to be a parallelogram. But still, space and time remained stubbornly 'out there'. Kant simply took space and time into the mind. The 'out there' vanished altogether, and everything was simple again – except that Kant's conclusions seemed a dead end. For where could philosophy go from there?

It seems astounding that no eminent thinker simply challenged the premises of Descartes' philosophy – total doubt – or felt intuitively that reason, applied in this sweeping way to the living world, was only producing destruction. In fact, one friend of Kant's *did* feel this, but he was unfortunately not an eminent thinker or a man of influence. This was J. G. Hamann, a passionately convinced Christian, who believed that Kant was leading philosophy into a cul-de-sac. Hamann asserted that the world is far too complex to submit to such clumsy reason, and that to try to apply scientific reason to the human situation is like using a fishing net as a tea strainer. Kant thought Hamann a crank and a dogmatist, and made no attempts to understand his objections. Kant can hardly be blamed; although Hamann published several books about his ideas, he was no thinker; his reaction was instinctive, and badly expressed.

The importance of Hamann, in the present context, is the influence he exerted on a young Danish thinker of the nineteenth century, Søren Kierkegaard, who is generally regarded as the founder of existentialism. This distinction should perhaps go to Hamann.

But there is yet another thinker whose work is, in many respects, an anticipation of existentialism – a man who usually receives only brief notice in the histories of philosophy. And yet, it might be contended, he produced some of the most exciting ideas of the nineteenth century. This is Johann Gottlieb Fichte, Kant's disciple and thirty-eight years his junior.

Fichte accepted completely Kant's view that the mind creates all the laws we know – the laws of nature, the laws of reason and logic. It is, of course, almost impossible for philosophy to go further in this direction. But Kant had proceeded from his examination of pure reason to the study of practical affairs, and concluded that man possesses free will which is more important than any moral laws. Only common sense and social necessity bid us to do unto others as we would have them do to us. (This is the famous 'categorical imperative'.) It was this aspect of Kant that struck Fichte as a way out of absolute doubt and despair. In one of his best books, *The Vocation of Man* (1800), Fichte states the whole problem with a splendid clarity worthy of Nietzsche. It is in three books. The first shows Fichte looking at the universe as a philosopher, and being overwhelmed by the problem of 'values in a universe of chance' (to use Pierce's phrase). Man thinks he is free, but as soon as he examines the problem, he finds that his freedom is an illusion. He can do nothing without a 'reason' from outside; he is a mere penny in the slot machine, and it is nature that puts in the pennies. In the second book, a spirit appears to him (probably inspired by Goethe's *Faust*, of which the first fragment had been published a few years before) and expounds to him Kant's philosophy – that nature itself is a figment of his brain; the mind creates everything, including the 'laws of nature'. This plunges the philosopher into even deeper despair. What is to prevent him from falling into total solipsism – believing that he is the only person in the universe?* 'You yourself have the answer to that' says the spirit, and disappears. And in the third book, Fichte addresses himself, and recognises that, indeed, he *does* hold the answer. The answer – which is of

* A view expressed with tremendous dramatic force by – of all people – Mark Twain, in his story *The Mysterious Stranger*, which is recommended as a kind of summary of all the philosophical problems of the nineteenth century.

considerable importance for existentialism – is that philosophers make the mistake of supposing that their only task is *to know* the universe; but just as important as knowing is *doing*. 'Not for idle contemplation of yourself are you here, not for brooding over devout sensations – no, for action you are here; action, and action alone, determines your worth.'

At first, this might sound a somewhat disappointing conclusion. It is important to grasp the spirit behind it. Descartes sat in his armchair and wondered what he could know. Philosophy accepted his way of propounding the question, and stayed in its armchair, until Hume managed to doubt the whole world out of existence. Then came Kant, and reversed the procedure. The mind, he said, creates the universe and its laws. True, there is an unknowable reality 'out there' – the *noumena*, but it is unknowable precisely because it does not need to obey our laws, and so cannot enter our perceptions, or even our reason. Now Fichte plunged into the next stage. Why bother about the *noumena*? he asked; let us forget about it. *What is left is Man in a universe of his own creating.* Here a minor problem arises. Can I 'create' the universe, and yet not be aware that I am doing so? Well, Kant said so, and his arguments sound convincing. So there must be *two* 'me's'. One of them is Descartes' 'I think', which sits in its armchair. And plainly, there is a subconscious 'me' that does the work of creating – behind the back, as it were, of the other 'me'.

The full implication of Fichte's argument can now be seen. In Book One, the philosopher despaired because it seemed that he had no free will, only consciousness. In Book Two, the spirit showed him that what he thought was 'implacable nature' was actually his subconscious 'I' busily creating the world and its laws. This is a situation rather like the one in Chesterton's *The Man Who Was Thursday* where the detective who is spying on the anarchists finally discovers that all the anarchists are detectives who think they are spying on anarchists. The enemies are friends after all. A certain problem remains, as Chesterton saw. Who created the confusion? Who is responsible for the practical joke?

Fichte is not concerned about this; he is too delighted by the realisation that the enemy has turned out to be a friend. Man can stop worrying. We are cautious animals who basically distrust the world, and the philosopher is perhaps the most cautious of all. That is why Descartes decided to sit in an armchair and think. Now we have thought ourselves beyond mistrust we can go and act in the certainty that it will turn out all right.

Fichte had stumbled upon the most important single insight of the nineteenth century. But he was not aware of it. He had solved the basic problem of Cartesian philosophy – or rather, pointed out that Kant had solved it. But no one noticed his solution, and it has gone on troubling philosophy down to our own day. In a fundamental sense, Fichte had seen deeper than his master (who later repudiated Fichte). For Kant only believed that he had resolved the Cartesian dualism by reducing everything to mind. (And in fact, Kant really kept the dualism, for he kept the *noumena.*) Fichte perceived that he had done something more momentous: destroyed the dualism *and replaced it with a tri-alism.* Instead of the contemplating mind ('I think') looking out at alien nature, there is a far more interesting situation. There are two I's; one is the 'I think', and the other the 'transcendental ego', the ego behind the scenes, the cinema projectionist who is projecting 'nature' out there. This metaphor of the cinema describes the situation precisely. For if you are sitting in a cinema watching the screen, you assume that what you are watching is happening in front of you. But in a far more fundamental sense, *it is happening behind you*, in the projection room. If the film breaks, or the projectionist decides to go home, the screen will go blank. Descartes was only aware of the 'I' sitting in the cinema; Fichte pointed out that there is another 'I' in the projection room. The left side of the mind doesn't know what the right side is doing.

It cannot be said that Fichte developed this insight in any important way. If his inspiration had held out, he might have gone on to ask: 'How can the "I" sitting in the cinema find out more about the "I" in the projection room?' This question might have led him to create the science of phenomenology a century before Husserl. As it was, Fichte only went on to anticipate the philosophy of Jean-Paul Sartre; for he went on to declare that philosophy is incomplete unless it leads to action, to commitment. (He was also a strong influence on the pragmatists.) Like Sartre, Fichte allowed philosophy to lead him into politics. He roused German youth with his *Addresses to the German Nation*, an attempt to incite resistance to Napoleon, and never afterwards retreated from his conviction that the most important thing about philosophy is its ethical and political consequences, which should lead to social reform. Because of the *Addresses*, he is now largely regarded as a kind of proto-Nazi; while his philosophy of the Ego is often interpreted as a mere anticipation of Nietzsche.

On the whole, one cannot be surprised that Fichte failed to grasp the meaning of his own thought. He swallowed Kant lock, stock and barrel – if we except rejection of the *noumena* – and consequently believed that there is nothing 'out there'. He failed to see that this is a self-contradiction; for even in our metaphor of the cinema, there is at least a screen 'out there'. Simply to posit an 'out there' is to posit a third member of the tri-ality.

So Fichte came to be rejected as a muddled and self-contradictory thinker by later generations. So he was; but his single insight was more important than whole systems of later philosophers.

There was another reason that Fichte lost influence; another, and more exciting star, was rising in the first decade of the nineteenth century: Hegel. Hegel seemed to promise all that previous philosophers had been unable to achieve. He began, like Fichte, by brooding on the problem of religion and revelation. On this subject, Hegel was a true existentialist, for he decided that 'historical truth' can never be as important as subjective truth, the eternal truths of the reason. Whether a man called Christ really existed is beside the point.

But while in this early sceptical stage, Hegel had his own sudden flash of insight; it may well have been a mystical vision of some kind. He saw the 'idea' as the ultimate reality, the absolute, from which all things derive: logic, Nature and Spirit (or mind). All the world as we know it is made up of sub-divisions of these categories.

To grasp the essence of Hegel's achievement – and to ignore its illogicalities, self-contradictions and moments of downright absurdity – we have to recall for a moment the basic attitude of Greek philosophy: the rejection of the real world in favour of the world of reason and ideas. (Plotinus, for example, refused to allow any pictures of himself to be made, or to give any biographical facts, for he claimed that the 'real' side of himself was not only supremely unimportant, but a contradiction of his true self, the spirit striving after the absolute idea.) World rejection has entered deep into philosophy; it can be seen even in Descartes' tendency to stay in bed all day. Eastern and Western philosophy show the same basic pattern: the man of thought and the man of action are fundamentally opposed – except for the occasional enlightened king.

Hegel's temperament rejected this dualism. Something healthy and optimistic in him wanted to be allowed to accept the real world – but in a profounder sense than its usual kind of acceptance by practical men. (It is typical that Hegel was delighted when Napoleon won the battle of Jena – even though it meant that Hegel was out of a job; there was something cheerful in him that could not help approving of vitality.) Therefore it was necessary, as it were, to be a super-practical man, far above both the shallow world-accepters and the pessimistic world-rejectors. And this 'synthesis' on a higher level is the fundamental movement of all Hegel's thought. Hegel did not spend his life arguing in terms of thesis-antithesis-synthesis; this is one of the myths promulgated by people who have never actually read Hegel; it was a purely instinctive movement of his thought.*

If he was to justify this world-acceptance, it would require arguments and reasonings that would make all previous philosophising seem dilettantism. To some extent, he succeeded. But it must also be admitted that this desire of his – a certain element of the actor in him – also led directly to his worst feature: his incomprehensible style. It is impossible to doubt that his obscurity was a part of his technique for being impressive.* Whether

* According to G. E. Mueller and Walter Kaufmann, it is mentioned only once in the twenty volumes of Hegel's works.

* Brand Blanchard has a delightful passage which sums up the case against Hegel's style: 'To say that Major André was hanged is clear and definite; to say that he was killed is less definite, because you do not know in what way he was killed; to say that he died is still more indefinite, because you do not even know whether his death was due to violence or to natural causes. If we were to use this statement as a varying symbol by which to rank writers for clearness, we might, I think, get something like the following: Swift, Macaulay and Shaw would say that André was hanged. Bradley would say that he was killed. Bosanquet would say that he died. Kant would say that his mortal existence achieved its termination. Hegel would say that a finite determination of infinity had been further determined by its own negation'. (*On Philosophical Style*, p. 30.)

this is regarded as a particularly serious charge against Hegel depends on the view one takes of the writer's responsibility to be as clear as possible. What seems to be generally acknowledged – Karl Popper is one of the few violently dissenting voices* – is that in spite of his atrocious style, Hegel has a great deal more to say than most other philosophers of the nineteenth century.

In view of this refusal to be a 'world-rejector', it is not surprising that he eventually became the official philosopher of the Prussian state. For Hegel's philosophy is essentially an immense attempt to 'justify the ways of God to man'. It has one important distinction: it is the first clear attempt in the history of philosophy since Plato, to refute the idea that the world is evil or meaningless, and that the philosopher is better off dead. Hegel's philosophy of history has been the most frequent target for the jeers of anti-Hegelians – for he attempted to show that all history is moving steadily towards the ultimate self-expression of spirit – but for all its absurdities and over-simplifications, it is a philosophy that believes in evolution, and refuses to accept that history is a 'nightmare'.

One might criticise Hegel by saying that his philosophy is not true philosophy at all: that although he begins by talking about perception, consciousness, logic, he has actually broken with the Cartesian tradition of closely connected reason, and is really writing a kind of monstrous novel or epic poem about 'Spirit'. There is some truth in this, but it could be argued about endlessly. Could a completely 'logical' philosophy – without vision or intuition – ever arrive at 'truth'? At all events, Hegel stands next to Goethe as one of the greatest creative minds of the nineteenth century.

Hegel's greatest achievement was his recognition – purely intuitive – that the old dualism must be somehow transcended. If he had been a far greater man, his influence might have been more decisive; he might have written in clearer language, and have shown far more definitely that there was a fallacy in Descartes' dualism. As it was, he became the father-figure of a British school of idealism, and over the next fifty years gradually ceased to exercise any active influence on philosophy.

* *The Open Society and Its Enemies*, Vol 2, a brilliant but unfair attack.

But, strangely enough, it was the philosophies of violent reaction provoked by Hegel's thinking that came to exercise most influence on post-Hegelian thought, and that still dominate philosophy in the twentieth century. The first of these was the positivism of Auguste Comte; the second, Kierkegaard's existentialism.

Comte was one of the first of the great worshippers of science of the nineteenth century. History, he says, proceeds in three stages: superstition, metaphysics and science. The first stage is one of total ignorance; when men are dominated by fear. In the second stage, men know enough to reject the idea of a universe populated by gods and demons, but are still inclined to connect up their facts with vague theories about the 'absolute', 'essences', and so on. Finally, with the coming of science, history enters its final stage; the sun of knowledge rises, and the millenium is in sight. All knowledge can now be verified by observation and logic.

To men of the twentieth century, this view sounds harmlessly optimistic, but naïve. In its own time, it exercised a considerable influence, particularly on the British school of philosophers led by Mill and Herbert Spencer.

The other major philosopher to oppose Hegel must be considered at greater length. Although Kierkegaard remained unknown outside Denmark during his lifetime, and was forgotten for more than half a century after his death, his influence on twentieth century thought has been enormous, and has extended to thinkers with as little in common as Jaspers, Heidegger, Marcel and Sartre.

With Kierkegaard, as with Hegel, one must understand his temperament if one is to go to the heart of his thought. Hegel was fundamentally a kind of Shavian optimist; he experienced despair in his youth, but went beyond it. Kierkegaard never went beyond despair; he never trusted life. He was the son of old parents, and was always physically weak; he was also crippled in one leg. His father was an imaginative neurotic who encouraged the child's intelligence and stunted his development as a normal boy. Kierkegaard inherited his father's emotional immaturity and instability, and when he became engaged to an attractive girl, found it necessary to destroy the relationship as a spoilt child smashes a toy. He went to Berlin, and heard Schelling – a friend and admirer of Hegel – lecture; as a consequence of which he developed an intense dislike of Hegelianism based upon incomplete understanding.

There was, of course, a fundamental difference of temperament between Hegel and Kierkegaard. Hegel reminds us in many ways of Wordsworth. (Their portraits even make them look rather alike.) He had Wordsworth's fundamental vision of universal harmony; but apart from this, his character was pedestrian, and his life orderly, stable and dull. His marriage to a girl many years his junior was uniformly happy. Like Wordsworth he became a pontifical reactionary, somewhat conceited; but none of this detracts from the value of his vision. And he had little patience with the excesses of the *Sturm und Drang* movement. Kierkegaard, on the other hand, was volatile, witty, thin-skinned and unstable. The neurotic oversensitivity bequeathed him by his father gave him endless trouble.

Add to this that Kierkegaard's acquaintance with Hegel's work was all at second-hand, and that he was totally unaware that the young Hegel had been something of a religious visionary, and it can be seen that Kierkegaard's 'Hegel' was a stuffed dummy that he set up for target practice.

Kierkegaard's neurosis did not prevent him from producing work of genius; and if he had been a poet it would hardly have been worth mentioning, except for its biographical interest. But philosophy aims at objectivity, and it must be recognised that, in spite of his genius, Kierkegaard was not ideally equipped for being objective.

His complaint – understandable enough – was that, as far as he was concerned, Hegel's system was *not* a key to the universe. The reaction was primarily emotional, or even physical – like a man with a hangover shuddering at the thought of breakfast. In another respect it was not at all unlike the reaction that W. B. Yeats felt towards Bernard Shaw. Kierkegaard mistook Hegel for something he was not, a heartless rationalist, a kind of gigantic calculating machine offering a 'solution' to the universe. His response was the standard response of the anarchist to authority – to shake his fist and shout defiance.

This is not to say that his rejection of Hegel was entirely a matter of temperament and immaturity. There was a certain valid perception that philosophy since Descartes had become too detached and abstract – precisely Hamann's objection to Kant. Kierkegaard was a man of religious temperament, and he felt that the purpose of seeking truth is to 'exist in it', not to think about it. 'To exist under the guidance of pure thought is like travelling in Denmark with the help of a small map of Europe on which Denmark shows no larger than a pen-point.' (*Unscientific Postscript.*) This is only to say that he was intensely aware of the hidden component in man, the concealed self that is not the detached 'I think', but a struggling and purposive force. But instead of trying to correct the fallacy that had crept into philosophy with Descartes, he chose to reject all philosophy in the name of religion – a paradoxical and pessimistic religion of his own. According to Kierkegaard, to be a Christian means to recognise that the closer you keep to God, the worse it will be for you. 'For in a strict sense, being a Christian means to die to the world, and then to be sacrificed.' (*Journals*, 1851.) This recalls Kafka's remark: 'In the struggle between the world and yourself, always take the world's side.' Kierkegaard's chief desire, it seems, was to be the Anti-Hegel. Instead of being reasonable, and taking what was good in Hegel – and previous philosophers – and then modifying it to suit himself, Kierkegaard rejected it wholesale in a thoroughly emotional way, cutting off his nose to spite his face. Hegel was a professor; so Kierkegaard denounced professors and exalted suffering poets; Hegel thought that history was part of the divine plan; Kierkegaard rejected history as an irrelevancy; Hegel believed that thought could be constructive; Kierkegaard set out to show that, in the paradoxical light of eternity, destruction is constructive. So Kierkegaard's philosophy – or theology – is a curious mixture of valid insight and special pleading. In an attempt to escape the implication that he was an unstable and neurotic personality (which was continually levelled against him by Copenhagen society) he dragged up the business of his jilting

Regina Olsen, and compared it to Abraham's sacrifice of Isaac, implying that it had been some 'higher' motive than mere fickleness that led to his action; he even wrote a whole book showing that the sacrifice of Isaac was the paradoxical symbol of his own anti-philosophising.

In fact, with Kierkegaard the pendulum had swung back to the ancient Greek dualism, Kierkegaard's religious 'paradox' is only a slightly disguised form of Socrates' assertion that the body is the enemy of pure thought, and therefore the philosopher's highest aim is death. Philosophy had merely come a full circle: there had been no evolutionary movement of thesis, antithesis, synthesis; instead, Kierkegaard merely repeated Plato's thesis in a new key.

AFTER HEGEL

Kierkegaard was the major influence on twentieth century existentialism; and since I have already dealt with Comte, who might be regarded as the founder of the other major school of modern philosophy, logical positivism (or logical empiricism), this chapter might well be brought to an end at this point. But for the sake of completeness, it may be as well to speak of some minor developments.

Perhaps it is hardly accurate to speak of the philosophy of Nietzsche as a minor development – particularly since he is often regarded, together with Kierkegaard, as the founder of existentialism. But Nietzsche's work was essentially incomplete; he went insane before he could bring it to fruition. If Nietzsche had stayed sane, he might well have effected the great Hegelian synthesis in philosophy, rising above the simple pessimism of the Greeks and the simple optimism of Hegel. For he was Hegel's successor in one important respect: he did not put the world of thought and the world of history into two separate compartments. Although he began as a pessimistic romantic and disciple of Schopenhauer (who believed that the basic choice was: Happy animal or suffering god?), his natural mental vigour soon rejected Schopenhauer's crypto-Buddhism. He was less of a weakling than most romantics, and his nature was resilient: 'I have made my philosophy out of my will to live ... Self-preservation forbade me to practise a philosophy of wretchedness and discouragement.' Like most romantics, he was inclined to go too far in his opposition to the things he disliked, and his glorification of the military man or the 'blond beast' sometimes sounds a note of sheer absurdity. (In practice, Nietzsche lost no opportunity to sneer at the Prussian tendency to militarism.) But on the whole, his philosophy is remarkably balanced, remarkably free of imprecision and overstatement. Darwin's theory of evolution provided him with the basic concept he needed for his new romanticism: the superman. 'Not mankind, but Superman, is the goal.' As an analyst of the weaknesses and pockets of decay in contemporary thought, he was unrivalled. He speaks of the 'smell of defeat' in contemporary thought, and declared with sheer inspiration that 'the nineteenth century goes in search of theories by which it may justify *its fatalistic submission to the empire of facts*'. He captured the objection to Descartes in a single phrase when he jeered at 'the idea of will-less contemplation as the road to truth' (*Will to Power*, 95). Like Hegel, Nietzsche had experienced a vision in his teens, on the top of a hill called Leutch,* as a consequence of which he wrote: 'Pure will, without the confusions of intellect – how happy, how free!' This vision, of total life-affirmation, transcending the mere animal will to live and the doubts of the intellectuals, was always the mainspring of his thought, and is far more important than the casual aspects of it that are sometimes selected for criticism: his glorification of the Ego, his occasional anti-rationalism, his contempt for 'the herd'. Under slightly different circumstances, Nietzsche might easily have become the officially approved philosopher of Germany at the turn of the century. But there were obstacles. Like Kierkegaard, he had inherited feeble health from his father, and this was made worse when he contracted syphilis in a brothel. His feeble health was an obstacle to sustained intellectual effort, so that his books are written in brief disconnected fragments; unlike Hegel, he was incapable of out-Kanting Kant. (And perhaps the fact that Hegel

* See *The Outsider*, chapter 5.

had already done it, discouraged him.) Finally, his fluctuating health emphasised the inner-inconsistency of his philosophy, so that the exaltation of free will is immediately countered by *amor fati*, and the idea of the superman is contradicted by the notion of Eternal Recurrence. Nietzsche had chosen a task – or rather, his temperament had chosen it for him – that was too great for a sick, poverty-stricken man who had no stable domestic background. And yet even so, his life gives us a feeling of a near miss. His sanity collapsed at just about the point when he was becoming a European celebrity. His death in a mental home must have struck many would-be artists as a warning that 'you can't win', that life and spirit are irreconcilably opposed.

Apart from Nietzsche, European philosophy continued in the rut selected for it by Descartes. The work of Comte was continued by Ernst Mach (1836-1916), a scientist-philosopher who became alarmed at the way that metaphysical ideas were infiltrating into physics, and who attempted to remedy this by creating a materialistic philosophy of science. 'Concepts have meaning only if we can point to objects to which they refer.' In Mach's time, there were bewildering developments in science – in physics, mathematics, psychology – and scientists were becoming increasingly prone to use concepts that seemed to belong to philosophy. Mach, in the expressive words of H. D. Aiken, 'proposed a radical therapeutic regimen that would strip the physical sciences to their fighting weight'. Consciousness, for example, became simply a stream of sensations, not the 'something' in which sensations occur. (Hume, of course, had taken the same view.) For Mach, 'sensation' is the key word.

Mach's chief importance is that he was a major influence on twentieth century thought; for he not only influenced Carnap, the founder of logical positivism, but also the young Albert Einstein, who used his ideas as the philosophical basis of the theory of relativity.

Logical positivism (sometimes called logical empiricism or scientific empiricism) is one of the most influential philosophical movements of the twentieth century. It is an attempt to remove the contradictions of the nineteenth century philosophy by applying

Mach's principle: sticking to the *observable*, or to that which can be verified by logic. The founder of the 'Vienna school' of logical positivists, Moritz Schlick, believed that philosophy should be confined to an attempt to clarify meanings by the use of logic; anything that cannot be reduced to logic can be dismissed as meaningless. This view clearly stems from the same impulse that induced Marx to explain history in terms of economic conflict, or that led Freud to reduce religion to the need for a father figure. It is an emotional gesture of despair in the face of complexity. A more recent form of positivism affirms that the business of philosophy is the logical analysis of language; it works upon the assumption that thinkers like Kant and Hegel managed to deceive themselves by their unconscious misuse of language. For this school, philosophy is a science, and has no business to concern itself with human life. The Cartesian dualism vanishes because mind is reduced to that which is observable.

Logical positivism is related – emotionally at least – to another doctrine that attempts to resolve the Cartesian dualism by violent methods: pragmatism. Pragmatism was foreshadowed by Fichte, with his impatient declaration that if the *noumena* is unknowable, then we had all better forget about it. C. S. Pierce and William James apply the same kind of test to the confusions of philosophy. What are the respective merits of Kant's *noumena* and Hegel's absolute idea? Can it possibly make any difference to practical conduct? No? Then they mean the same thing. James himself was by no means a sceptic – as his *Varieties of Religious Experience* makes clear – but his way of resolving the problems of belief has an air of convenient over-simplification. There is no final way of knowing whether a religious or moral belief is true or not. So James follows Fichte in saying: Truth is relative to the individual. If belief in God works for you, then it is true – for you. Belief is better than scepticism because the believer *may* be right, whereas the sceptic, suspending his judgement, is neither right nor wrong. James's idea of belief obviously has a certain humorous casualness about it, like filling in a football coupon with the help of a pin and a blindfold. It can be seen that both pragmatism and logical positivism are forms of relativism. Truth is not 'absolute'; in one case, it is relative to human psychology (and conduct), in the other, to the laws of science and language.

All this will have made it clear that my simile of the untidy room is hardly adequate to describe the state of philosophy in the twentieth century. If the concern of philosophy is to understand the universe and man's place in it, then it seems that there has been no advance since Descartes. There is not a single statement by any philosopher since then that cannot be immediately contradicted by another statement from another philosopher – or sometimes from the same one. It might seem that it would require the synthesising power of a Newton to create a unity out of this chaos. And yet again, the problem can be approached with common sense, and certain basic 'truths' begin to emerge.

To begin with, it is clear that Descartes was responsible for much of the confusion by introducing a fallacy at the very beginning. The fallacy was not a logical one; rather it was psychological. Descartes assumed that the philosopher is a thinking machine who can solve the problem by pure thought. He reminds us of Poe's Dupin, who solved the mystery of Marie Roget while sitting in an armchair with the blinds drawn. Fichte stumbled on a glimpse of the truth. Descartes was wrong to assume that all the problems are 'out there', and that the machine can be trusted completely. Admittedly, Fichte expressed his question in a somewhat extreme form, which prevented his immediate successors from perceiving its fundamental good sense. 'Can I create the universe and yet not be aware that I am doing so?' Probably not; but I can do a great many things without being aware that I'm doing them. When I think something or perceive something, it is not a simple mechanical process; thousands of interior valves flicker into life; my whole being takes part in the process. For example, someone may whistle a few bars of music and say: 'What is that?', and I reply immediately, 'The opening of Beethoven's fifth symphony.' He asks: 'How did you know?', and after a moment of baffled silence, I shrug and say: 'But it was obvious.' It seems an extremely simple process; but to explain it fully would require a combination of scientist, psychologist and musician, and explanations about logarithms of frequency ratios and their effect on the cochlea, as well as of the selective action of memory. We are like a man who thinks that cars are simple mechanisms because he knows how to drive one, even though he has never looked under the bonnet. Descartes was almost certainly right in believing that nature will finally be entirely explainable in terms of logic and science; but he was mistaken in assuming that the laws of the mind are the laws of logic and science.

From this simple Cartesian fallacy sprang all the subsequent confusion. Descartes declared that the key to philosophy is simplicity; so Locke, and Hume aimed for simplicity, even if it meant assuming that man is a machine and can therefore have no possible use for truth. Comte and Mach certainly achieved simplicity; so did Kant and Hegel, in a different way; so have the logical positivists. But simplicity is not the key to philosophy or nature. Newton's *Principia* explains the movements of the heavenly bodies, but no one would call it simple. The basic simplicity of Newton lies in his unifying principles; this constitutes his superiority over earlier astronomers. Before philosophy can be meaningful, it needs a similar set of unifying principles.

This analogy with astronomy perhaps explains the nature of the Cartesian fallacy most clearly. It seems both simple and common sensible to believe that the earth stands still and the heavens revolve; but when astronomers tried to explain the motions of the heavens on this principle, they discovered that it led to complications that defeated them. It seems simple and obvious to assume that the universe will finally be understood if the mind looks on in an attitude of scientific enquiry. *But making the 'I think' the centre of gravity of philosophy is like making the earth the centre of the universe.*

These complications vanish at once if we make another hypothesis: that the centre of gravity of philosophy should be the recognition of the 'I' behind the 'I think'. The starting point is still the 'I think', the questioning intelligence. But instead of looking out at the universe from its armchair, it now needs two faces, one to look out, one to look inward towards the 'hidden I', the transcendental ego. But at the same time, it should be recognised that this is not a true 'tri-ality', any more than that a person who sleep-walks is truly two people. Although the 'I think' seems self-evident, it is actually an abstraction, a single aspect of the transcendental ego. (I am borrowing Kant's phrase for the 'hidden I' at this point, because it will have to be brought in again later in discussions of Husserl.)

Chapter 3

THE NEW FOUNDATIONS

WHITEHEAD PROPOSES A SOLUTION

At this point, the problem becomes somewhat more difficult to present. So far, I have been able to present it historically, showing the unfolding of science, philosophy and romanticism. If twentieth-century philosophy could be represented as a steady advance, this would be the ideal way to continue. Unfortunately, it cannot. Two of the most important thinkers of the century have been curiously uninfluential – Whitehead and Husserl. Both of them took important steps towards solving the problems posed in the last chapter. Whitehead has had no followers; Husserl has had many – the most important being Heidegger, Sartre and Merleau-Ponty. But in both cases, the essence of their solutions has been ignored.

Whitehead's contribution is simple, but of incalculable importance. It is stated in one of his least known books, *Symbolism, Its Meaning and Effect*, and takes the form of a criticism of Hume. Whitehead simply points out that when we talk about the problem of perception, we are forgetting that *there are two distinct ways of perceiving the outside world.* These Whitehead calls, somewhat ponderously, 'presentational immediacy' and 'causal efficacy'.

If I am getting bored in a dentist's waiting-room I am aware only of objects. I may stare at my finger-nails, become aware that my left foot itches, find myself listening to every sound from the street. Now suppose that I see an article in a magazine that interests me. I cease to be aware of sounds and sensations; if I am interested enough, I may even forget an aching tooth. My attention is still focusing on minute particulars – the words on the page – but something else has come into play. When I was bored, my attention was only aware of minute particulars; apart from that, my mind was a blank. Now another kind of perception has started in my brain: a *perception of the meaning of the article*. This is like a great bracket that holds together all the individual perceptions of words.

Now observe what happens if I turn from this article to an article which I find very difficult to understand. My mind tries to grasp the meaning of the sentences, and slips, as if I have tried to get a foothold on ice. It can no longer grasp the meaning of a whole page or paragraph; it finds it difficult enough to make sense out of individual sentences. Finally, if the article continues to baffle me, I become aware only of individual words on the page, and have to read a short passage two or three times to give the words any connection. The meaning-perception has gone; I am back to my perception of 'immediacy'.

Hume would say: 'There is nothing strange in this. You know the meaning of the individual words; you simply add these meanings together to get the meaning of the sentences and paragraphs.' You might object: 'But that is not true; I am very bad at adding up figures, and my perception of the meaning of the article is nothing like adding up sums.' Hume would reply: 'No, it is only that it takes place so quickly and naturally that you are not aware of it as a process of adding up. A trained office girl can feed figures into a calculating machine at such a speed that you might suppose the machine was inspired and leapt to the answer in a flash; but it is not true; for every figure, a key had to be pressed. The meaning (i.e., the answer to the sum) was the result of several tiny steps. And *all* meanings can be analysed down into steps.'

This might seem convincing until one reflects on the sense of beauty. I look at a scene and say: 'That is beautiful.' This is the 'answer' to the sum of one's perceptions of the scene. But how can I analyse this sense of beauty into its constituent parts? I can analyse the scene, but the analysis will not include the 'beauty'. The scientific approach would be to examine it with a magnifying glass; but this is like trying to locate the beauty of a lake by swimming in it or drinking it. Yeats expresses this idea in the poem *Towards Break of Day*, speaking of a waterfall 'that all my childhood counted dear':

> I would have touched it like a child
> But knew my finger could but have touched
> Cold stone and water. I grew wild,
> Even accusing Heaven because
> It had set down among its laws:
> Nothing that we love overmuch
> Is ponderable to our touch!

The sense of meaning is what Whitehead calls 'causal efficacy'. Whitehead admits that Hume is right about cause and effect – if the only mode of perception is *immediacy*. Hume's meaning could be made clearer by an analogy with space. One is in a dark room, and is asked to examine the room carefully by the sense of touch, and afterwards make a drawing of the inside of the room. This seems easy enough; but the room is large, and the darkness total. One discovers that there is a table in the middle of the room – at least, you think it is probably the middle of the room by pacing from the table to the walls. There are also several chairs and other pieces of furniture disposed around the room. Some of them are so close to the table that you can place one hand on the table and the other on the chair, and judge the distance between them and their relative position. But where a chair is too far from other objects to use this method, it is more difficult; one has to rely on less immediate methods.

Now Hume would object that unless you can place one hand on the table and the other on a chair, you have no right to make a positive assertion about their relative position. You might be deceived in the darkness; when you think you are walking in a straight line, you might have made a slight turn, and so on.

Whitehead would agree, but would say: There is a simple answer: 'turn on the light'. Hume would deny that this is possible. There is no light, only the sense of touch, and the sense of sight is really the sense of touch aided by logical inference. We might reply indignantly: 'Nonsense, sight is something quite different from touch!' 'No,' Hume would reply, 'they are the same thing;

sight is only the sense of touch at a distance. Instead of your hand encountering a book, a ray of light bounces off the book and then bounces off your eyeball, and you infer the presence of the book.'

This simile of the room also helps to explain why it is that science is a product of the western mind, and that the East has produced so little science. If a blind man and a man with sight were led into the same room, and both told that, after ten minutes, they would be led outside and asked to describe it in detail, which of the two would be able to offer the minutest description? Clearly, the blind man, for it would cost him far more effort to get to know the room. He would be forced to take a tape measure and first of all measure the exact size of the room, then to note the position of all objects along the walls (bookshelves, tables, etc), then to pace out distances across the floor and measure the distance of other objects from the walls. Because of the sheer *effort* of all this, he would have a closer acquaintance with the room than the man who possesses sight, for the latter would probably wander around casually, taking a vague mental inventory of the objects he saw, confident that he would remember them later because their impact is so immediate. And, like a man who says he will remember a telephone number, he would probably forget half of what he has seen.

Western man is in the position of the blind man; his meaning-perception is so limited that he is forced to rely on his intellect and upon symbolism to give him a grasp of meanings. A Chinaman or a Hindu would not dream of doing anything so boring as rolling a weight down an inclined plane or dropping weights from the leaning tower of Pisa; they naturally possess far more meaning-perception than a westerner; so, like Aldous Huxley under mescalin, they are inclined to sit passively, absorbed in the sheer meaningfulness of reality.

The issues can now be seen clearly. For Hume – as for all thinkers from Descartes onward – there is only one mode of perception, which we might compare to the sense of touch. For Whitehead, there are two modes, which always accompany one another: immediacy-perception and meaning-perception. Neither is of much use without the other. Immediacy-perception shows us the 'reality' of things in the sense that a microscope shows the reality of a piece of cheese. But the reality of the cheese as seen through a microscope is not its only reality. A man who eats the cheese knows quite another reality. Only a man who has seen the cheese through a microscope as well as eating it can be said to know the reality of the cheese.

But if meaning-perception is really a separate mode from immediacy perception – and not just an inference from it – how have ten generations of philosophers come to overlook it? The answer would seem to be: Because our faculty of immediacy-perception is so much more developed than that of meaning perception. We look at the world; meaning hangs around it as a dim aura, rather as the luminosity hangs around the figures of a watch. We might be forgiven for noticing only the figures, and not the luminosity, for the luminosity illuminates nothing but the figures; it is not strong enough to read by, for example. If the luminosity suddenly became stronger, until it glowed from the face of the watch like an aurora borealis, then we would soon notice that we could perceive the light *without* perceiving the figures – for example, if the watch happened to be on a table at the other side of the room.

In short, what is wrong with post-Cartesian philosophy is the fallacy inherent in the scientific approach. In its early stages, science is not concerned with meaning-perception, but with 'facts'. In science, nature is presumed guilty until she has proved herself innocent. Science is based on the principle of verification, on examining nature through a microscope. In *Symbolism,* Whitehead points out that 'immediacy-perception' is definite, clear cut, while meaning-perception is vague, imprecise. Man is in the position of a painter painting a gigantic canvas. If he is close enough to be able to work, he is too close to see it as a whole. If he stands back to see it as a whole, he is too far away to use his paint-brush. The natural solution for the painter would be to move back and forth as often as possible. But the scientist would feel that such conduct was unscientific. He keeps his nose to the canvas, and creates 'theories' to unify his facts. Science begins with facts, proceeds to theory, then returns to the facts to verify or disprove the theory. The scientist has no use for meaning-perception – at least in theory. In fact, any good scientist or mathematician will admit that imagination is as indispensable to the scientist as to the poet; still, one will find no mention of this in books on scientific method.

The scientific method – the method of doubt and verification – is indispensable to science. But it was never meant to be applied to philosophy. Philosophy is concerned with the question of the universe *and* human life. One can learn a certain amount about the universe by examining it through a microscope, just as one can learn a certain amount about Leonardo's paintings by studying the texture of the paint. But an art critic who was concerned only with paint texture would miss the whole point. To change the simile slightly, the philosopher could be compared to the music critic, whose task is to interpret difficult works to a musically unsophisticated public. From the critic's point of view, a symphony has two aspects: the emotions the composer wanted to convey, and the techniques he uses to convey them. If the critic confined his explanations to the technique – 'Here the main theme is repeated a semitone higher' – he will fail in his task of *interpreting* the music. And if he began a book about the quartets of Beethoven by saying: 'We must start by doubting everything', the book would soon become as confused and gaseous as nineteenth century philosophy.

It will be seen, then, that Whitehead's 'answer to Hume' is also an answer to Descartes. For Descartes' philosopher, sitting in his armchair, there is only one type of perception – looking at what is at the end of his nose. All knowledge has to be *inferred* from this immediacy-perception. But if immediacy perception is the perception of the 'I think', then what aspect of consciousness deals with meaning-perception? It is something broader, more intuitive, than the 'I think'. It stretches away into the penumbra of consciousness. Descartes was intoxicated with the scientific method, this ability of the human mind to concentrate a searchlight beam of consciousness on particular problems, and solve them by logic. He assumed that this method would eventually be able to take in everything in the universe; that all our feelings, emotions, beliefs, could ultimately be translated into this beautifully clear language of immediacy and logic. What he forgot was that a searchlight beam pays for its intensity with a certain narrowness, so that it can only focus on one thing at a time. And Hume, in a way, reduced the whole thing to absurdity by asking how we could be sure there is any necessary link between the different objects the beam picks out. Hume's criticism – his attack on causality – should have made philosophers realise that there is something wrong with Descartes' dream – and consequently with the way they were doing philosophy. Instead, Hume's absurdity was solemnly accepted, and philosophers brooded on the problem of how to incorporate it in the structure.

The revolutionary implications of Whitehead's 'two modes of perception' will become more apparent after Husserl's contribution has been outlined. But it should be noted here that Whitehead's criticism of Hume is a part of his general attack on what he calls 'the bifurcation of nature', the scientist's tendency to treat the world as if it could be comprehended in terms of logic or mathematics. When Galileo divided nature into primary and secondary qualities, the primary qualities being 'really there', and the secondary qualities (colour, smell, etc) added by the senses, he assumed that nature is 'really' a 'dull affair ... merely the hurrying of material, endlessly, meaninglessly'. So there was no need for a second mode of perception, meaning perception, because the meaning was added by the human mind. There was no meaning to perceive,* for meaning is inferred, not perceived. (Sir Charles Snow's more recent plea for a closer liaison between 'the two cultures' is a re-statement of Whitehead's complaint about the bifurcation of nature.)

Whitehead has also added another valuable term to the discussion. Instead of talking about perception, he prefers to speak of 'prehension'. When the mind perceives, it does not merely see something; it actively *grasps* and digests; the process is active, like the stomach digesting food, not passive, like receiving a slap

* It will now be seen why I have preferred to speak of 'meaning perception' rather than using Whitehead's phrase 'causal efficacy'. Whitehead was aiming at Hume, and stating that we *do* possess a faculty that perceives cause and effect. But Galileo was the real culprit.

in the face. A man staring out of a train window and about to fall asleep may be perceiving passively; but the moment the consciousness wakes up and takes stock of its surroundings, it begins an act of appropriation, of grasping. The importance of this concept will also be seen after we have spoken of Husserl.

ORIGINS OF PHENOMENOLOGY – BRENTANO

Husserl's master was a theologian-turned-psychologist called Franz Brentano. Brentano (1838-1917) was concerned with the chaos of nineteenth century philosophy, and wondered how it might be untangled. It seemed to him that this might be done by starting from human psychology. The same reflection led thinkers like Mill and James into 'psychologism'. Psychologism is a tendency to declare that metaphysical absolutes (or logical absolutes) can be translated into terms of psychology. (In the same way a biologist might declare that philosophy and logic have no independent existence, but can be reduced to terms of the body and its workings; such a philosophy would be a 'biologism'.) But Brentano found himself unable to take this conveniently simplifying step, for he was unable to agree with the psychologists about fundamentals. Since Galileo and Locke had left philosophy in such confusion about what the mind 'adds' and what it merely sees, psychology had involved itself in contradictions about such questions as sensation and imagination. According to Berkeley, there is no real difference between riding a horse and thinking about riding a horse; but even without taking this extreme attitude, we can see that physical and mental phenomena are mixed up in a most complex manner. For example, I may be blindfolded and told that I am about to be burnt with a red hot iron; if someone then touches me with a piece of ice cold metal, I may cry out, convinced that it is red hot. In this case, a physical phenomenon is 'adulterated' with a mental one. Again, in the case of a musical chord, it could be argued that the chord is not a physical phenomenon; since it is a mere vibration of air *until I hear it*; here again it is a question of where the mental begins and the physical ends.

Brentano proposed what seemed to him a satisfactory way of

distinguishing mental from physical phenomena. A mental phenomenon, he said, is *directed at an object*; mental phenomena 'include an object intentionally within themselves'. The important word here is *intentionally*. Consciousness focuses like a searchlight beam, or, to use a simile closer to Brentano's mode of expression, it encloses its 'object' in the way that a fruit encloses its stone. (For this reason, Brentano spoke of 'intentional inexistence' meaning intentional existence *in* consciousness.)

Brentano's influence on Husserl was enormous. But more important than any specific idea or theory was Brentano's attitude to life and philosophy. He started as a theologian; his ultimate aim was to write about the problems of God and human destiny; and yet he spent his whole life *preparing* to write about them, laying the foundations. Husserl was later to remark: 'No man is too good for foundation work.' (Many of Brentano's philosophical papers are still unpublished, so it is impossible to know how far he got beyond the foundations.)

The aspect of Brentano that became the starting point for Husserl was his assertion that 'the true method of philosophy is none other than that of the natural sciences'. At first sight, this may seem to be identical with Descartes' premise. But although Descartes was a scientist, his method was not scientific; he sat in an armchair and proceeded to theorise. The true scientist – like Galileo – begins by dropping weights off a tower or rolling them down an inclined plane; that is to say, *he begins by collecting his data*. With his discovery of the intentionality of consciousness, Brentano had stumbled on a starting point that was far more fundamental than Descartes' idea of doubting everything. Science is the attempt to be completely objective about 'the facts'; but if the scientist's instruments are inaccurate, objectivity is impossible; he must begin by examining his instruments. The philosopher's basic instrument is not logic; it is observation – that is to say, consciousness. So the starting point of philosophy, according to Brentano, should be the checking of the instrument of consciousness.

INTENTIONALITY

Before describing Husserl's application of Brentano's idea of a 'scientific philosophy', I should perhaps attempt to make clear what is meant by 'intentionality'.

The basic activity of consciousness is prehension – to use Whitehead's word. This is what Brentano meant when he spoke of mental states as 'including something as an object' within themselves. Consciousness may be described by two analogies. It is a beam of attention, like the 'eyebeams' that Donne mentions in one of his poems. Or it could be described as a hand, grasping objects within its continuum. If I look at a table-top covered with assorted objects, and then look away, I shall remember certain of the objects and forget others. But I can also remember something of the relation of the objects to one another and to the table-top; my attention somehow grasped the situation as a whole, even though it cannot remember all the individual parts.

Why did my attention select certain objects to remember rather than others? The reasons are not important; what is important is that my consciousness *selected* its objects. This act of selection is a form of intentionality.

I reproduce below three figures that illustrate this selective activity.

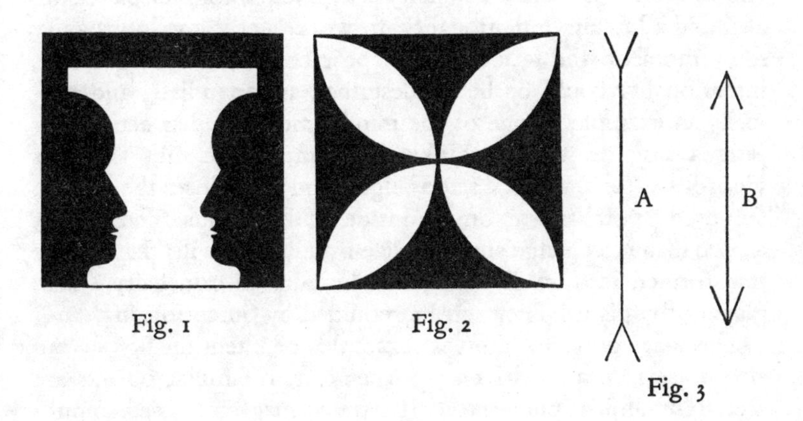

Fig. 1 Fig. 2 Fig. 3

Figure 1 can be seen either as a vase or as two faces looking at one another, depending upon whether one looks at the white area or the shaded area. Figure 2 may be seen either as a Maltese cross (shaded) or a white four-leaved clover. Figure 3 (known as the Müller-Lyer illusion) shows two lines of equal length; the 'forked twig' A appears longer than the double-headed arrow B because the eye continues the movement of A along the forks. In the first two examples, it will be observed that the attention can be trained to see first one aspect of the figure, then the other; but no matter how quickly the mind can make the leap from faces to vase, from Maltese cross to four-leaved clover, *it can never see both aspects at the same time*. The attention has to grasp the picture in a particular way, as the hand might grasp an object to pick it up; but the hand cannot simultaneously hold the object in two different ways. In the Müller-Lyer illusion, the mind can, with considerable effort, see the two lines A and B as being the same length, but to do so has to make a mental act of excluding the arrow heads or forks; if the attention slips and 'sees' the arrow-heads, the lines immediately change length. In looking at these figures, we can catch the attention in its act of selectivity.

Other examples of this working of intentionality are the faces we see in the fire or on the moon. A face seen in the fire can be endowed with as much personality as a good photograph by staring at it and allowing 'intentionality' to work. Yet if one looks away for a moment, the face may disappear completely. In this case, intentionality could be better described as 'prejudice', and provides an example of one of the mind's more familiar activities – rationalising or wishful thinking. Again, if one rubs the eyes vigorously, (or stares at a strong light) and then closes the eyelids, coloured 'spots' appear on the inside of the eyelids. These spots can be made to change shape or size by an act of will; they can be transformed into an elephant, a mountain, an armchair, a man playing the piano. They can be moulded by 'intentionality'.

These are only the simplest examples of intentionality. It can also be seen in a negative way when certain familiar objects are seen in unfamiliar perspective. Illustrated magazines used to publish photographs with a caption 'Do you know what this is?', perhaps showing the Eiffel Tower photographed from underneath or a man's hat held at a curious angle to the camera. These examples baffle the selective faculty' by offering it only the elements that it would normally ignore or exclude.

The world as normally seen, then, is not at all the world as it 'really is', any more than the word 'mountain' is the same thing as a mountain. Attention has to be economised, and so attention works on the same principle as language. Language takes a piece of knowledge and turns it into symbols and formulae, so that it can be stored and handled more conveniently. Consciousness treats the physical world in the same way; it does not bother to examine each object; it writes down its formula. A book is a 'rectangular red object', a clock a 'round ticking object', and so on. Sherlock Holmes once told Watson that he didn't care whether the sun went round the earth or vice versa, because his mind could only store so many facts without forgetting others; like an attic, it could receive only so much lumber, and a point came where another piece of lumber meant forgetting something he already knew. Holmes's principle of mental economy is practised by the human mind. But the human mind is unaware that its view of the world is strictly selective; it sees the world from its 'natural standpoint', and assumes that the natural standpoint is the whole truth.

HUSSERL'S DEVELOPMENT

The mention of the 'natural standpoint' brings us to Husserl, for it was his starting point.

Born in 1859, Husserl studied mathematics under Weierstrass and Kronecker, then developed an interest in philosophy after he had heard Brentano lecture. His earliest reading in philosophy was the British empiricists, from Locke to Hume. Their question: How far does the mind influence what we perceive? became the basis of his phenomenology. (Until the end of his life, Husserl recommended the British empiricists as the best introduction to phenomenology.) Husserl, then, had returned to the sources of European philosophy before the stream became hopelessly muddied by Kant and Hegel. He then moved into the problems of mathematics and logic, and in his early work *Philosophy of*

Arithmetic, tried to derive the foundations of mathematics from psychological acts – that is to say, he began his career as an exponent of 'psychologism'. This soon began to dissatisfy him, and he turned to philosophy to resolve some of his problems – only to experience complete disillusionment when he discovered that philosophy has even less certainty than mathematics. With considerable optimism, Husserl set out to reconstruct philosophy from the foundations, starting out with only one basic idea; that every statement should be carefully analysed for any kind of preconceptions or prejudices. Nietzsche once remarked contemptuously that philosophy is only the autobiography of individual philosophers. Husserl recognised the truth of this, but felt that it should not be true. Philosophy should begin by merely trying to describe things without prejudice. And since everything depends on man's subjective states, then it should be, to begin with, *a descriptive analysis of subjective states.*

The question in which Husserl was basically interested was: Why does the consciousness select in a certain manner? True to his scientific approach, Husserl did not propound the question in these terms. According to the scientific method, 'Why?' often demands an unnecessary amount of theorising, but 'How?' can be observed by anyone who goes to enough trouble. What Husserl did in his major work, *Ideas* (1912) was to suggest a certain method for observing the workings of intentionality. The basis of this method was the technique that he called 'bracketing'. (However, later phenomenologists, including Husserl himself, have tended to drop this bracketing ritual.) Bracketing consists in disconnecting the attention from the object under examination, attempting to outwit the 'natural standpoint' by treating it as completely alien. An example might make this clearer. I am writing a letter to a man who might employ me, and I write it frankly and without attempting to conceal anything. Having finished the letter, I now re-read it *as if I am the man I am sending it to.* I try to suspend all that I know about myself, pretend that I am a total stranger reading the letter for the first time, trying to understand how it will strike the reader. I treat the letter 'purely as a phenomenon'. This is bracketing, the temporary suspension of the natural standpoint.

An objection will be seen immediately. It is true that I can, with an effort, put myself outside myself and treat the letter purely as a phenomenon. And yet even if I am a total stranger reading the letter, I am still applying *some* preconceptions to it. I know it is written by a human being, and I know various things about human beings in general. If I withdraw myself too far from the letter, it will become merely a white sheet covered with signs. The next stage would be to close my eyes and become totally unconscious of it.

Plainly the simple act of reading the letter is not as simple as it seems on the surface. How far can we sort out the different *layers* of preconception as we read it? This is the task that Husserl sets himself. For if we can learn how to read a letter without prejudice, then we are prepared to start reading the universe without prejudice – to start philosophising, that is.

I am not concerned at this point to analyse Husserl's complicated system of *epochés* (as he calls the act of bracketing) and 'reductions'. What is more important is to grasp the essence of his method, which attempts to analyse the act of perception. Its first object is to force us to study consciousness more closely. The history of art provides an illuminating parallel. The ancient Greeks had no idea of perspective. If you asked a Greek artist to sketch you a house, he would have drawn a square with windows and a door. You might have pointed out: 'But we can also see the other wall.' The artist would have added another square to the first. At this point, you might say to him: 'But observe closely. Does that second wall appear to us as a square? We know it *is* a square? But how does it appear to you?' By pointing out to him that it appears as a parallelogram, you would have taught him the essence of perspective. The lesson would have been a simple illustration of phenomenology. 'Do not tell me what it is; suspend your belief in its real existence and only tell me *what you see*.'

Cezanne had grasped the essence of phenomenology years before Husserl formulated the method; he expressed his approach to painting in the words: 'An eye, a brush.' Cezanne was a phenomenological painter; this is the reason that he appeals as a purist.

In some ways, painting provides the simplest illustration of

Husserl's approach. Consider the work of a literary painter whose picture tells a story, like 'When did you last see your father?' Such a painting requires a human level of interpretation as well as the pure attention that would be brought to Cézanne. If we wished to consider it purely as painting, then the story level would have to be 'bracketed out'. Even so, we cannot yet consider it purely as a painting, because it contains human figures, and even if we feel no curiosity about their story, there is another level of curiosity about the figures – whether they are attractive human beings or not. This level can also be bracketed out, leaving only a series of shapes on the canvas. Now at last we are ready to analyse the workings of 'intentionality'. We know about our emotional response to the story, we know about our interest in the human shapes. But why do we feel certain responses to the forms and colours when these extraneous responses have been bracketed out? We are now analysing our response to an abstract design. (We can even bracket out our awareness of the colours, and consider the painting purely as architecture.)

Phenomenology, in short, is *the study of the way that consciousness perceives objects.*

Now it can be seen that Husserl's method has an immediate application to the problem stated earlier in this book. The world appears to have 'no grain', to be poker-faced when interrogated about its relation to human aspirations and destiny. It most carefully conceals the colour of its whiskers behind a fan. Phenomenology provides a new starting point. When I stare at the world in an attempt to see some meaning in nature, it seems to me that my static consciousness is confronted by a poker-faced world. Husserl has shown that my consciousness is not as static as I thought, and the poker-faced world is not the real world at all, but a world of symbols. The world seems to be wearing a mask, and my mind seems to confront it helplessly; then I discover that my consciousness is a cheat, a double agent. It carefully fixed the mask on reality, then pretended to know nothing about it.

It can now be seen why Husserl gave existential philosophy a new impetus. Kierkegaard called himself a philosopher, but Mach would never have admitted his right to this title at all; in the eyes of a scientist, existential philosophy was only another name for autobiographical rambling. Now Husserl had provided existentialism with a scientific method: the description of consciousness and the way it apprehends the world.

What use Sartre and Heidegger made of this method – or failed to make – will be described in the next chapter. But the next point to be made is one on which he parts company with most later existentialists. Husserl wrote that the task of phenomenology is the examination of types of intentional experience, 'learning thus what is the nature of the physical, and comprehending the being of the soul'. Hume once said that when he looked inside himself for his 'I', he only stumbled across different perceptions. Husserl emphatically disagrees with this. Like Kant, he feels that there is an 'I' presiding over consciousness. He believes that this 'I' can be reached through a rigorous process of bracketing, and he uses Kant's term to describe it, the 'transcendental ego'.

It will be seen that Husserl's phenomenology is not at all unlike Kantian philosophy, except that the 'categories', those coloured spectacles through which we have to see the world, are called 'forms of intentionality'. And we might at this point recall Fichte's question about Kant: Can the mind create the world and yet not know that it is doing it? Husserl's intentionality is a less extreme concept than the categories, for Husserl never really doubts that there is a real, solid and knowable world 'out there'. But it can be seen that the same question might be applied to Husserl. The 'I' of the natural standpoint is distinct from the 'transcendental ego'; man contains two 'I's'. Husserl's philosophy, then, as much as Whitehead's, leads to an 'answer to Hume' and Descartes and Galileo, and the answer is the one that was suggested in the last chapter. Philosophy made its mistake by starting with a duality, and then devoting itself to somehow reducing this to a unity. But when Descartes set the stage for western philosophy – with himself seated in his armchair confronting 'the world' – he left out the most important actor: the transcendental ego. He should have started with triality, not a duality.

This notion of a triality should not be taken too seriously. It may seem only to add a complication to the problem. In fact, when one starts from the Husserlian 'triality' instead of from the

Cartesian duality, the whole problem begins to resolve itself in a different way, as will be seen later.

HUSSERL'S LATER DEVELOPMENT – THE LIFE WORLD

There is something curiously unsatisfactory about Husserl's development after the publication of *Ideas*. Like Brentano, he spent his life on the threshold of philosophy, laying the 'foundations'. To some extent, this unsatisfactoriness is inherent in the nature of the task. Husserl was a metaphysician by temperament; he felt that philosophy should be concerned with the 'nature and destiny of man'. Yet he could never quite bridge the gap between his scientific foundations and the metaphysical superstructure he was anxious to build on them. His dream was to 'uncover the secrets of the transcendental ego' – an aim which, expressed in this way, sounds almost Freudian. In a different way, Freud was also concerned to reveal the 'intentional structure of consciousness' (if consciousness is here taken to include the 'subconscious'). Freud's best known illustration – of a man leaving behind an umbrella at a house he wants to re-visit – is a perfect example of subconscious intentionality. But Freud assumed that the contents of the subconscious mind reveal themselves in dreams, and can be discovered through a system of symbol interpretation. This is an assumption of the kind that Husserl could never have allowed himself, since it cannot be confirmed by the descriptive method.

During the last ten years of his life, Husserl was preoccupied with the idea that links him with Whitehead. (His death in 1938 probably saved him from the Nazi gas chambers.) This was the notion of the 'Lebenswelt', or world of lived experience, from which the world of science is an abstraction. It must be faced squarely that Husserl's later philosophy tends in the direction of mysticism, and the seeds of this mysticism were present from the beginnings of his career. For Brentano, intentionality meant only 'reference to a content', the 'directedness' of consciousness; for Husserl, it became increasingly a means of penetrating the apparent meaninglessness of the 'given world' and discerning the hidden meanings. He often spoke of the task of phenomenology as being the approach to 'the mothers', the keepers of the key of the ultimate sources of being (alluding to the 'mothers' of part two of Goethe's *Faust*).

The 'life-world' may be defined as the world of our living experience, as distinguished from the world of abstractions with which science deals. This life-world is not the world as seen from the natural standpoint, since this world is, as we have shown, largely a world of abstractions of a different kind. But the life-world is more primitive than the world seen from the natural standpoint; it can only be separated from this world by a certain reduction, a suspension of science, an attempt to see the world without categories of logic or mathematics. The work of Heidegger and Sartre is a development of this idea of the life-world; Heidegger's *Sein und Zeit*, of which I shall speak in the next chapter, is an attempt to present the life-world in all its complexity, before our human tendency to familiarise and simplify can get to work on it.

This outline of Husserl's phenomenology will help to clarify one of the most obviously baffling features of Whitehead's 'two modes of perception'. We find it very difficult to believe that 'immediacy perception' is not the most basic mode of perception. When we are bored, we find ourselves stuck in a world of objects, a meaningless world, whereas when we are excited by ideas or by music, our 'meaning perception' seems to expand. Surely, in that case, most animals would possess immediacy perception without meaning perception – not vice versa, as Whitehead suggests? An animal's world must be rather boring, by our standards (which is no doubt why we use the phrase 'a dog's life'), and an animal, certainly, has no capacity for getting carried away by ideas or art.

But consider for a moment what science teaches us about the 'reality' underlying our perceptions. When I look at green fields against a background of blue sea, my eyes are actually registering the impact of two different wavelengths of light, and passing on this information to my brain. When I hear the sound of birds or the bleating of sheep, my ear is receiving vibrations in the air. When I press down on the table, the pressure of the table against my hand is actually the bombardment of millions of electrons. Although I do this automatically, my senses have had to learn to distinguish colours and sounds, just as a musician has to learn to pick out the various instruments of the orchestra. Although it seems so natural to me, this ability to distinguish red from blue is a far more astonishing feat than a mathematician's ability to understand the complicated page of symbols at a glance. It has taken millions of years of evolution to develop this ability to see wavelengths as colours, or to hear vibrations in the air as distinct sounds. The process was rather like what happens when a child learns to read and write, but far more complicated. We do not really 'see' colours; we *read* them, but the reading has become so automatic that it has become seeing.

It will now be seen why presentational immediacy is a 'higher' form of perception than causal efficacy. All the immense concentration and mental effort that goes into seeing and hearing is done by us subconsciously; we are born with it. When a man yawns in a dentist's waiting-room and says 'I am bored', he does not realise that his boredom – that seems the cheapest and most common thing in the world – has been purchased by millions of years of effort; as a commodity, it is more expensive than radium. This universe around is a vast chaos, buzzing with an uncountable number of energy vibrations; and yet life, instead of being overwhelmed and bewildered by all this, has learned to sort them neatly into pigeon-holes and to make an 'orderly universe' out of it all. We make the mistake of supposing that boredom is an 'animal state' because it reduces us to a level which we mistakenly suppose to be animal. This ability to play a searchlight beam of attention over objects is a late evolutionary development; we can observe this when our attention becomes exhausted, and we simply cease to notice things. The bored man in the waiting-room can dissipate his boredom in a few seconds by drinking a quarter of a pint of whisky, which will plunge him into a state that is closer to that of his dog. Time ceases to matter; objects no longer seem 'really there'; vaguer, bigger meanings seem to hover on the edge of consciousness; the world itself is again suffused with meaning – but at the expense of his ability to concentrate on minute particulars.

This may be the reason that animals and primitive peoples so often seem to possess certain telepathic abilities, even 'second sight', and leads one to speculate that telepathy may not be a matter of 'brain waves', but simply primitive 'meaning perception'.

Berkeley wrongly supposed that we 'add' the colour to nature, and all subsequent philosophy has been built on his error. We most certainly *interpret* nature, but that is a different matter. We also interpret a newspaper as we read it, but we are not creating the meaning of what we read. It will be seen at once that Whitehead and Husserl have overturned the foundations of western philosophy, and then laid a new and unshakeable foundation.

In the present day, neither Whitehead's philosophy of organism nor Husserl's later phenomenology can be said to exercise any great influence on philosophy. This is understandable, particularly in the case of Whitehead, who speaks bafflingly of 'eternal objects' of which the natural world is a selection, with God as a 'principle of concretion' which determines the selection. But their basic criticisms have created new possibilities in philosophy. Both were scientists and mathematicians, who were concerned that science not only has no connection with the world of values, but actively denies the world of life-values, explaining them away in terms of mechanism. Their criticisms restored the notion of meaning and value to philosophy, and indicated the possibility of a science that strengthens and supports man's sense of purpose instead of sapping it.

It would, then, be no exaggeration to say that Whitehead and Husserl together reversed the trend of European thought since Galileo. If the superstitions of the mediaeval church are regarded as the thesis which evoked its antithesis – the reign of scientific materialism – then the revolution of Whitehead and Husserl can be regarded as the synthesis of both.

But the strangest thing of all – or so it may appear to some historian of philosophy in a future age – is that this counter-revolution had no immediate effect on philosophy, which continued exactly as before. Admittedly, it could be argued that Husserl gave a new impetus to existentialism; and yet existentialism continued to be pessimistic and Cartesian. How this came about will be examined in the following chapter.

GESTALT PSYCHOLOGY

At the same time that Husserl was formulating the method of phenomenology, a number of psychologists were formulating a psychology that was also a kind of 'answer to Hume'. This chapter would be incomplete without an outline of their views.

In 1890, the German thinker von Ehrenfels pointed out that though the ear can analyse a musical sound into a tone and various partial tones, these are heard in a note of certain pitch, and the pitch does not correspond to the sum of its tones. This is rather as if the eye could see the colours of the spectrum in a beam of white light (without the aid of a prism), but recognised that no arithmetic will make red, orange, yellow, green, blue, indigo and violet add up to whiteness. He also pointed out that when one remembers a melody, it is *as a whole,* not as a number of notes. To reverse it would be to destroy it. If a child hums a familiar tune, he may transpose it into another key, altering all the notes, yet still remember its 'shape'. Most people will also observe that if they strive to remember a half-forgotten tune, it at first presents itself as a shape before its details become clear. In the case of a child transposing a tune, it might be objected that the notes remain constant, but that is not true either, for the relations can be altered – as when a semi-tone is substituted for a whole tone – without altering the melody.

Gestalt psychology was first clearly formulated in 1912, in a paper by Max Wertheimer; the other two names most frequently associated with the theory are those of Kurt Koffka and Wolfgang Kohler. In fact, their views had been anticipated in the previous century by the English psychologist James Ward, who revolted against the mechanistic psychology of Mill and Bain, declaring that psychology is the science of *individual* experience, and that consciousness is a whole because it is somehow 'chosen' by a purposive subject. (The similarity to Brentano's views will be noted here.) Ward's method was the analysis of attention; he insisted that the flow of the 'stream of consciousness' is purposive, not due to a mechanical association of ideas. His most important English disciple, G. F. Stout, also emphasised that the basic character of psychological life is purpose and effort. Stout carried Ward's 'attention analysis' even further, and aimed at a careful and detailed description of how things are seen and grasped.

In 1924, Wertheimer outlined the ideas of gestalt psychology to the Kant society in a way that emphasises its affinity with the views of Whitehead and Husserl. He began by stating that when we turn from the 'everyday world' to the world of science, we hope that we are gaining something, going deeper; in fact, we are also losing something. Science teaches that analysis is the answer to problems, but no amount of analysis can explain what happens when we suddenly 'see the point' of a statement; the mind simply makes a leap of understanding, and grasps the statement *as a whole* (although it may formerly have grasped all the separate parts without seeing their connection). Koffka points out that a baby can recognise its mother's face at two months, and can distinguish between a friendly and an angry expression at six months, although it cannot distinguish colours until sometime later. One would suppose that the difference between red and green would be far more striking than the difference between two human faces.

Gestalt psychology asserts, basically, that we grasp things as wholes before we grasp their constituent parts. This is only another way of saying that causal efficacy, the meaning faculty, is as important as presentational immediacy.

The basic action of the human mind is similar to the baby's tendency to touch whatever attracts its interest and if possible to convey it to its mouth. The mind never lies open and passive; it wants to separate and isolate whatever it perceives. It is like a man with agoraphobia who likes people in twos or threes in a small room, but cannot bear them in crowds outside. Or, to use another analogy, it is like a man who cannot bear to look at a view with his naked eyes, but has to use a telescope so that he will only see a small area surrounded by a circle. In the old associationist psychology, it was believed that learning began with vague chaos; then various elements separated themselves out and became clear; then finally, those bits were joined together to form wholes. Gestalt psychology denies this, and states that the mind is never interested in parts until it has first grasped the whole. It is like a criminal who will not go out into the street until he has carefully surveyed it through a crack in the blind.

All this is to say that the human mind is not a passive receptacle, receiving stimuli as a slot machine receives pennies, and then responding. *It seems to operate on a basic hunger for form.*

What is being created here is a new idea of the nature of science. The scientist of the 'age of reason' regarded the scientific method as the reverse of that of religion, since religion starts from faith (preconceptions). He would argue that science is the natural flow of the living mind: that when a baby reaches out its hand to touch a bright object, it is becoming a scientist, investigating. Gestalt psychology replies, in effect: No, science is a temporary reversal of the natural flow of the living mind. The scientist never merely 'observes'; it is not true that he looks first and judges later; *he would see nothing if he did not judge first*. This is not to say that the mind pre-judges in the ordinary sense of the word; the results of its observations may cause a complete change of attitude; but the new factors are introduced into the 'whole' to form a new whole. But the whole has to be there in the first place.

In *The Varieties of Religious Experience*, James wrote: 'We have a thought, or perform an act repeatedly, but on a certain day, the real meaning of the thought peals through us for the first time, or the act has suddenly turned into a moral impossibility. All that we know is that there are dead feelings, dead ideas, and cold beliefs, and there are hot and live ones; and when one grows hot and alive within us, everything has to recrystallise about it. We may say that the heat and liveliness mean only the "motor efficacy", long deferred, but now operative, of the idea; but such talk is only a circumlocution, for whence the sudden motor efficacy? And our explanations then grow so vague and general that one realises all the more the intense individuality of the whole phenomenon.'

There are echoes of Ward here (particularly in the last sentence); but it was not until 1912 that James's inspired intuitions were supported by experiment. (James had then been dead for two years.)*

Since 1912, there has been much discussion and controversy over gestalt theory, and certain modifications have had to be made. For example, when congenitally blind people have their sight restored by an operation, they do not recognise the difference between a square and a triangle spontaneously, as gestalt psychology would affirm; they have to count the corners. But considerations such as these have not affected the basic assertion of gestalt psychology, which Wertheimer expressed as follows: 'There are wholes, the behaviour of which is not determined by that of their individual elements, but where the part processes are themselves determined by the intrinsic nature of the whole.'

* In the same way, William Blake anticipated gestalt psychology when he wrote in 1788: 'Man by his reasoning power can only compare and judge of what he has already perceived', and 'Man's perceptions are not bounded by the organs of perception; he perceives more than sense (though ever so acute) can discover.'

Chapter 4

HEIDEGGER AND SARTRE: THE QUESTION OF BEING

Husserl's most brilliant follower – and perhaps the most influential German philosopher of this century – was Martin Heidegger. Accounts of Heidegger's thinking are generally prefaced with the statement that he is the most difficult of modern philosophers. This is true; but not in the sense that is usually intended. Admittedly, his language and mode of self-expression are even more difficult than Whitehead's. But this is partly a kind of clumsiness, and partly his way of utilising Husserl's concepts. Acquaintance with Husserl, and the use of a certain amount of intuition, can overcome this barrier. The real difficulty of Heidegger is of another kind, closer to the difficulty presented by the work of William Blake. Even more than Husserl, he is a poet or a mystic trying to express his intuitions in the language of philosophy. But no amount of study can make a connected 'system' of his work. Sometimes he arrives at the goals that he has announced in advance; sometimes he arrives at quite different goals than the ones he announced; but most often, his works remain signposts pointing towards goals that he seems unable to reach. He is at once the most rewarding and the most exasperating of existentialist thinkers.

Heidegger was prevented from studying under Husserl by financial difficulties, but he became Husserl's assistant in Freiburg in 1916; his major work, *Being and Time* (1927) was published in Husserl's *Phenomenological Yearbook. Being and Time* was planned in two parts, each with three chapters; only the first two chapters of part one have appeared. Subsequently, Heidegger has published many books; but all have been small (with one exception – an analysis of Kant), and the style usually aphoristic, not unlike that of Heraclitus, whom Heidegger admires. A great deal of hostility was aroused when Heidegger became chancellor of Freiburg university under the Nazis in 1935 – particularly as Husserl's work was condemned by the Nazis – but there is no real evidence that Heidegger was ever a Nazi sympathiser.

In spite of his use of the phenomenological method, Heidegger derives from Kierkegaard rather than Husserl. It is therefore to be expected that he should be a figure of controversy. His followers regard him as the most important thinker of the past century; his opponents – Professor Walter Kaufmann, for example – regard him as a pretentious mountebank, a pseudo-philosopher. Heidegger's manner of philosophising provides such opponents with ammunition. He speaks of himself as the philosopher of Being, attempting to restore the question of Being to its primary importance in philosophy. His opponents object that Being is the one thing that cannot be philosophised about; we cannot go deeper into a thing than to say 'it is'. Certain linguistic analysts have objected that the whole of Heidegger's philosophy is based upon a misunderstanding; a thing possesses attributes – it can be round, blue, warm, etc – but it is not true to say it possesses 'being'; Being is simply the sum of all the other attributes.* It has also been objected that Heidegger's thought has shown no real development since *Being and Time*; Heidegger meets this objection by agreeing, and declaring that this is one of the most important characteristics of his thought; like Being itself, it is static. It can be seen why Heidegger's name is a red rag to many of his colleagues, and why he has never achieved the widespread recognition that his followers believe to be his due.*

Being and Time is a lengthy and careful analysis of 'the human situation', using the techniques of phenomenology. There can be no doubt about the depth of many of the insights – again, it is Blake who comes to mind – but one might have many doubts

* I heard A. J. Ayer maintain this position in a lecture in 1956.

* One would have supposed, for example, that Heidegger would have been an obvious choice for Northwestern University's *Library of Living Philosophers* series; but although a dozen or so volumes have now been issued (1964) including one on Jaspers, there is still no sign that Heidegger's name is being considered.

about the language in which they are expressed. In an attempt to place his observations on a 'scientific basis', Heidegger invents a battery of terms that make Hegel seem lucid by comparison, including several different shades of the meaning of 'existence' or Being. (In later books, he even writes Existence with a cross through it to indicate yet another level of meaning.) The complexities of philosophers (or scientists) can usually be defended as an attempt to drag out their meanings into the daylight – and ultimately to penetrate deeper; where Heidegger is concerned, a grasp of his central ideas leads one to wonder whether he might not have done better to stick to the language of intuition. One sometimes suspects that he is concerned to 'sound like a philosopher', to disguise the fundamentally intuitive and poetic nature of his thought from disapproving colleagues.

Being and Time begins with the assertion that philosophy must return to the question of Being, forgotten since the Greeks. He will begin, Heidegger says, by considering a specific kind of Being – human existence, which he calls *dasein*. *Dasein* would be used to throw some light on Being itself; in the second part, Being would be used to throw light on human existence. The second part was, of course, never issued (although Heidegger declares that it was written, but that he kept it back because it was too obscure).

In spite of the obscurity of the presentation, Heidegger's major ideas are clear and vital, and remind us of Kierkegaard, or even of Pascal. Pascal was concerned with 'inauthentic existence', the way that people waste their lives in amusements or trivialities. (Eliot asked: 'Where is the life we have lost in living?') Heidegger also talks about 'Being that degrades itself in the mediocrity of everyday life.' These are the words of a poet rather than an academic philosopher, and his development of this notion confirms it. His whole philosophy seems to be based upon a fundamental insight – the feeling that the basic problem of human beings is their 'forgetfulness of Existence'. Husserl was preoccupied with man's ego, pure consciousness; Heidegger writes: 'Man alone of all existing things ... experiences the wonder of all wonders – *that things exist*.' (*What is Metaphysics?*, 1934.) This expresses the fundamental difference between the two thinkers. For Heidegger, there are two fundamental states of existence for man, authentic and inauthentic. When man takes his social existence for the whole of life, when he is preoccupied with trivialities and living in the eyes of other people, then he is in a state that Heidegger calls 'living-in-the-midst-of-the-world'; he also calls it 'fallenness'. But there is another way of living-in-the-world; we can rise from inauthentic existence through knowledge or through poetry, and apprehend another world of a purer kind of Being.

Heidegger is obviously restating a problem that has been recognised since the Greeks. Wells meant exactly this in the passages from the *Autobiography* and *The Undying Fire* that were quoted in chapter one; there is a higher kind of existence than mere preoccupation with everyday things.

What causes inauthenticity? To some extent, language is to blame. It gets worn out, and 'spreads untruth', causes man to forget the real existence of the things it refers to. But in any case, man is strongly disposed to inauthenticity by another of his inventions: society. Here Heidegger's analysis has affinities with that of David Riesman in *The Lonely Crowd*; Riesman's 'other-directedness' (keeping up with the Joneses, etc) is inauthenticity; his 'inner-direction' is authenticity.* Heidegger's analysis of language and society leaves no doubt of the basic moral preoccupation of his thought. Language degenerates into chatter or gossip; man uses his mind to get to know the contents of the latest books – usually from reviews – and uses these in the social game. Serious discussion, the attempt to burst through this dead language to urgencies, is regarded as bad taste. There are times when Heidegger seems to be writing a more serious version of Stephen Potter's books on One-Upmanship. (They could certainly be used as ideal illustrations of what he means by inauthentic existence.)

How can man escape inauthenticity? There are two ways. First of all, one must live constantly in the face of death, recognising it as the ultimate necessity. (Gurdjieff had also declared that man could escape from his fallenness if he had an organ that made him constantly aware of the date of his death.) Heidegger

* This notion was also discussed in my *Age of Defeat*. I have been told since that Riesman fails to see the connection between his ideas and those of Sartre and Heidegger.

goes further than the biblical idea of 'remembering the last things'; he takes over Nietzsche's idea of an active acceptance of death, willing it as one's ultimate fate, *amor fati*.

There is another way – and to this Heidegger has devoted most of his work since *Being and Time*. Poetry and myth can bring man closer to the realm of pure Being. Heidegger is fascinated by the poetry of Hölderlin, and has published several essays analysing it. The Greeks felt that the alternative to the messy real world is the world of ideas; Heidegger prefers to believe that it is the realm of poetry or spirit. He sees the conflict between 'the world and holiness' as the fundamental characteristic of Hölderlin's poetry. He also symbolises the world of holiness in the Greek gods; he seems to mean by these what Husserl meant by the Mothers, the 'keepers of the keys of Being'. So to some extent, the rift between Heidegger and Husserl begins to vanish when one compares their later work.

It would not be true to say that Heidegger's final position is pessimistic, even though his idea of 'existence-towards-death' dominates his philosophy. His attitude to death is stoical rather than pessimistic; but his belief that poetry is a key to authenticity has a definite note of optimism.* But perhaps more important than any of this is his fundamental insight: that the cause of the decline and crisis in human history is due to forgetfulness of Being. This must be examined further after the analysis of Sartre.

There is a central objection to the work of Heidegger, which also applies to Kierkegaard, Marcel, Jaspers and Sartre. Language, as Heidegger points out, tends to obscure Being (or truth). This is particularly true of the abstract language of science and philosophy. So it is a contradiction to talk about 'existential philosophy'. The Zen masters sometimes found it necessary to kick a pupil downstairs to free his mind from its bondage to ideas and make him grasp the essence of reality. So in a sense, it might be said

* This aspect of Heidegger can best be studied in the two essays on Hölderlin included in Dr Werner Brock's anthology *Existence and Being* (Vision Press, 1949.)

that the philosopher who attempts to 'unveil Being' in a ponderous analysis is like a man who digs a hole by throwing each shovelful of earth over his shoulder, so that it simply falls back in the hole. A piece of music or a painting would stand a better chance of conveying the essence of reality than a philosophical treatise; the chances of a play or a novel are somewhat higher. But this is not an ultimate objection. An idea is not *necessarily* the antithesis of reality; a vital mind could train itself to absorb ideas without blunting its sense of Being. But it must be admitted that Heidegger's fondness for ten-syllable German words is likely to blunt all but the strongest minds.

SARTRE

Sartre was strongly influenced both by Husserl and Heidegger. The influence of Kierkegaard is also clearly present.

As with Heidegger, there is an element of self-contradiction about Sartre's thought. There is a note of optimism in his constant emphasis on the idea of freedom; and yet the overall tone of his philosophy is rationalistic and pessimistic. I have analysed the literary aspect of his work elsewhere,* so I shall confine this analysis, for the most part, to his philosophical ideas.

As soon as one examines Sartre's most fundamental idea, one sees why pessimism and defeat are unavoidable. He is a Cartesian; he rejects the whole notion of the 'unconscious mind', and believes that consciousness must mean something which is aware of itself. Inevitably, then, he finds himself tangled in the problems that baffled philosophy for two centuries.

It seems ironical that Sartre was a follower of Husserl, and yet failed to accept the most important aspect of Husserl's work. And yet his first book, *The Transcendence of the Ego*, written in 1936, is simply a denial of Husserl's concept of the transcendental ego. Admittedly, this attitude is foreshadowed in Brentano, who, when he said 'No love without something loved, no hate without something hated' etc, might also have been implying that mental states are thus dependent upon their objects. But for Sartre,

* In *The Outsider* and *The Age of Defeat*.

consciousness cannot be regarded as 'intentional' in the sense of possessing motives of which it is not normally aware. It is a mere 'wind blowing towards objects', an emptiness, a kind of eternal observer with no power to do anything but observe. Husserl had transformed Brentano's concept of intentionality into something far more active; now Sartre restored its passivity. Consciousness, said Sartre, *is* intentionality. It is also freedom.

Why did Sartre do this? His motive, it seems, was rationalistic. He wanted to restore phenomenology to its old simplicity, to the state where there was a clear division between subject and object. Descartes had based his philosophy on this clear division; he was 'in here', the world was 'out there'. Berkeley, Kant and the rest had betrayed philosophy into solipsism, total subjectivism. Husserl seemed to have rescued it from this state; once again there was a clear division: objects out there; consciousness in here (but directed at objects). Then Husserl placed the transcendental ego in charge of consciousness, and we were once again not sure of which was the object and which was consciousness. For intentionality, according to Husserl, performs its work on data (or *hyle* – stuff – as he preferred to call it), and the consciousness knows this, not the object itself.

Sartre would seem to feel Heidegger's distrust of subjectivity – the stifling little inner-world furnished with ideas and worn-out language – and wants to turn to a real world of objects for relief. Hence this strange anti-subjectivism.

Two of the best boks on Sartre – by Iris Murdoch and Mauric Cranston – have pointed out this strong anti-emotional tendency, and also the curious puritanism of Sartre's disposition, his constant reference to the physical world in terms of disgust. His rationalism – the desire to reduce the world to straight lines and clean surfaces – is a kind of passion. Hence this rejection of the subconscious. The rationalism is a reaction against the disgust; it seems to be an attempt to impose a logical order on a disturbing world. Under different circumstances, one feels that Sartre would have been a follower of Comte or Mach, and been glad to see the world in terms of a simple materialism.

And yet at this point, there is another paradox. Earlier 'realists' had felt that the real existence of the external world is something to be pleased about. Bertrand Russell, for example, describing his own early mental development, wrote: 'Bradley argued that everything common sense believes is mere appearance; we reverted to the opposite extreme and thought that *everything* is real that common sense, uninfluenced by philosophy or theology, supposes real. With a sense of escaping from prison, we allowed ourselves to think that grass is green, that the sun and stars would exist if no one was aware of them.' But this real external world disgusts Sartre as much as man's confined subjective world; he seems to seek relief in Plato's world of ideas.

This becomes apparent in one of Sartre's earliest and most interesting books, the novel *Nausea*. It concerns a man called Roquentin who is living in a French seaside town and writing a history of an eighteenth-century diplomat. He is overwhelmed by sudden strange insights. The first happens when he picks up a stone to throw into the sea. 'I saw something which disgusted me; I no longer know whether it was the stone or the sea.' And the roots of a tree in the park become 'a knotty mass, entirely beastly'. What has happened is that Roquentin has somehow lost the defence of inauthenticity that keeps man away from Being; suddenly he realises that things exist in their own right.

Sartre was not aware of it, but Whitehead had dealt with precisely this problem in *Symbolism*. For example, Whitehead writes:

'As William Pitt, the Prime Minister ... lay on his death bed ... he was heard to murmur: "What shades we are, what shadows we pursue". His mind had suddenly lost the sense of causal efficacy, and was illuminated by the remembrance of the intensity of emotion that had enveloped his life, in its comparison with the barren emptiness of the world passing in sense presentation.' Whitehead comments: ' ... in some tired moments there comes a sudden relaxation, and the mere presentational side of the world overwhelms with a sense of its emptiness'. Whitehead recognised that the new vision of emptiness is not a glimpse of reality; the reality is the world of causal efficacy. What has happened to Roquentin is that his faculty of 'intentionality' has slipped, leaving him in a universe divested of meaning.

Sartre himself can find no answer to these problems. Roquentin has many experiences of 'nausea', when the world is seen as meaningless; yet he also has other experiences of the reverse. A record of a negro woman singing 'Some of these days' causes the nausea to vanish. 'Suddenly it was almost unbearable to feel so hard and brilliant ... ' He experienced the same sense of meaning in the dusk of a Sunday evening. But there is an essentially static quality about the book. All that Sartre can do is to present these two opposed states, and make his hero realise that he has been living inauthentically. But there is no real solution; for all we know, Roquentin goes off to kill himself at the end of the book.

Always in Sartre's work there is this feeling of the two 'realities' contradicting one another. At times – particularly in the early work – there is a strong note of optimism. If man can stop deceiving himself, Sartre implies, he can express his freedom. He must recognise that 'God is dead', that man is alone in an empty universe. But there is a feeling of courage about this. Orestes, in *The Flies,* refuses to make himself responsible to Zeus, and when Zeus demands 'Who created you?', replies: 'You did, but you made one mistake: you created me free.' It was this aspect of Sartre that made him such a powerful influence on the younger generation after the war. His world might be harsh, but it contained the possibility of freedom, of moral responsibility. But as time went by, it began to seem that this Sartre was partly a creation of the war. (*The Flies* was a veiled protest against the German invaders.) Sartre's philosophy became at the same time more practical and more pessimistic. The novel *Roads to Freedom* revealed a strong nostalgia for the dogmas of communism which emphasised the emotional undertow in his rationalism. Sartre showed an increasing tendency to reduce the problem of man's 'salvation' to a matter of economics and class war. The novel *Roads to Freedom* is significantly left unfinished; as with *Nausea,* he could find no adequate resolution of the problems. The play *Altona* is more pessimistic than anything that has gone before; the central character, who was a Nazi killer, finds refuge from his conscience in self-delusion, and has to commit suicide when this collapses. It is not made clear in what fundamental sense his guilt differs from that of Orestes.

But the full consequences of Sartre's denial of the transcendental ego appear in his most famous work *Being and Nothingness* (1943). The world that Sartre creates in this is a world completely without meaning.

Being and Nothingness resembles Heidegger's *Being and Time* in that it is an attempt to describe the human condition using the phenomenological method; it is written more clearly than Heidegger's work, although there are times when Sartre seems wilfully to imitate the German's ponderousness.*

There are, according to Sartre, three kinds of being. Objects have being 'in-itself' (*en soi*). People have being 'for-itself', because consciousness exists for itself (whereas objects do not). Finally, there is being-for-others, which means that we all exist in the eyes of other people, and our estimate of ourselves comes from what other people think of us. Consciousness for-itself is an emptiness (a nothingness, Sartre calls it – hence the title); a man left completely alone would not be aware of his psychic existence. (Conrad's *Heart of Darkness* might be taken as a parable illustrating this attitude.) The gaze of other people makes me exist for myself, and my gaze makes other people exist. If my gaze is contemptuous and dismissive, then its recipient will exist less; if it is admiring, he will exist more. So all relations between people are a form of conflict. Real love is an impossibility, for what I really want from you, is for you to give me more existence by admiring me. Since the same applies to you, love is at the best a bargain, and at the worst a conflict; there can be no real exchange. Hatred, sadism and masochism are subjected to the same kind of analysis, and proved to be just as frustrating. It is not surprising that Sartre ends with the famous conclusion: *L'homme est une passion inutile.*

This doctrine of existence only in the eyes of others (which, like the categories of for-itself and in-itself, Sartre has adapted from Hegel) is a natural consequence of the denial of the transcendental ego and of causal efficacy. If consciousness is an emptiness, it follows that it can only become a 'somethingness' by having things imposed on it – that is to say, inauthentically. At first sight, Sartre's views seem to be supported by our common experience.

* In an article on Sartre quoted by Maurice Cranston, Mme de Beauvoir remarks that young Sartre was never so happy as when he could not understand what he was writing.

It is true that if I am caught looking through a keyhole, I feel myself suspended on the end of the other's gaze, stained with guilt; it is true that flattery gives me a sense of importance. This is to say that for a large part of the time, my consciousness is purely passive. But what of the sudden moments of intensity when my inner being seems to light up, or to harden into reality? What of Roquentin's experience listening to *One of these days*? If Sartre is inclined to dismiss these as illusion, then he is advancing a view that amounts to a new Watsonian materialism, with consciousness as a mere reflection of matter.

But in fact, Sartre has never faced the implication of Roquentin's moments of reality, of anti-nausea. The constant refrain of *Nausea* is the phrase 'There's no adventure'; yet at the end of the Sunday when he becomes aware of the poetry of the external world, Roquentin writes: 'Then I felt my heart swell with a great feeling of adventure', and says 'For a moment I wondered if I were not going to love humanity' (which recalls Greene's 'I was discovering in myself a thing I thought I had never possessed: a love of life'). But Roquentin hastens to add: 'But after all, it was their Sunday, not mine.' The meaning, the 'adventure' of which Roquentin became aware, *came from outside*. Yet according to Sartre, the world has no meaning. Man has freedom – consciousness – and this means that he is free to choose his own meanings and live by them. What Roquentin experienced was not merely freedom (which, according to Sartre, is empty), but *meaning*. According to *Being and Nothingness*, this is an impossibility.

One of the most revealing things that has been written about Sartre appears in Mlle de Beauvoir's *The Prime of Life*, the second volume of her autobiography. About a year before the writing of *Nausea,* Sartre took mescalin. Mlle de Beauvoir says: 'He had not exactly had hallucinations, but the objects he looked at changed their appearance in the most horrifying manner; umbrellas had become vultures, shoes turned into skeletons, and faces acquired monstrous characteristics, while behind him, just past the corner of his eye, swarmed crabs and polyps and grimacing Things ... I was wearing a pair of crocodile skin shoes, the laces of which ended in two acornlike objects; he expected to see them turn into gigantic dung beetles at any moment. There was also an orang-utan ... which kept its leering face glued to the window.' A few days later: 'His visual faculties became distorted; houses had leering faces, all eyes and jaws, and he couldn't help looking at every clockface he passed, expecting it to display the features of an owl – which it always did. He knew perfectly well that such objects were in fact houses and clocks, and no one could say he *believed* in their eyes and gaping maws – but a time might well come when he *would* believe in them; one day he would be really convinced there was a lobster trotting along behind him.'* Significantly, she mentions that Sartre was in a state of deep depression when these things were occurring, and believed he would go insane.

Compare this with the account in *Nausea*: 'And then, all of a sudden, there it was, clear as day: existence had suddenly unveiled itself. It had lost the harmless look of an abstract category; it was the very paste of things; this root was kneaded into existence. Or rather the root, the park gates, the bench, the sparse grass, all vanished; the diversity of things, their individuality, were only an appearance, a veneer. This veneer had melted, leaving soft monstrous masses, all in disorder – naked with a frightful, obscene nakedness.'

The word naked recalls Aldous Huxley's use of it in describing his own mescalin experiences in *Doors of Perception*. But there is here a curious difference. What Huxley saw was 'what Adam saw on the morning of his first creation – the miracle, moment by moment, of naked existence'. It would also seem that mescalin delivered Huxley from the world of inauthenticity: 'mescalin had delivered me (from) the world of selves, of time, of moral judgements and utilitarian considerations, the world ... of self-assertion, of cocksureness, of over-valued words and idolatrously worshipped notions' – in short, from 'forgetfulness of Existence'. Like Roquentin, Huxley became aware that things existed in their own right, but the realisation was entirely pleasant. Huxley uses

* English ed. p. 169.

the word *istigkeit* to describe it: 'is-ness'. His bookshelf is filled with 'red books, like rubies; emerald books; books bound in white jade; books of agate, of aquamarine, of yellow topaz; lapis lazuli books whose colour was so intense, *so intrinsically meaningful,* that they seemed to be on the point of leaving the shelves to thrust themselves more insistently on my attention' (my italics). A chair also seemed to 'thrust itself into existence' like Van Gogh's famous chair.

All this makes it evident that mescalin had helped Huxley to achieve Heidegger's ideal, some kind of perception of pure existence, had stimulated the faculty of 'causal efficacy' so that all the underlying meanings of existence became clearer.*

Huxley goes on to mention that mescalin may have one of two effects; it may plunge the drug-taker into heaven or hell, depending on his state of mind or nervous constitution. A man who feels a basic dislike or distrust of life will probably find himself in 'hell'. Mescalin also removes the mind's usual checks and inhibitions, so that a man who had suppressed the irrational part of his nature by intellectual aggressiveness would find his 'hidden self' snapping its controls. Mescalin has the effect of sweeping away the 'thought riddled nature', so that reality is seen as if through a magnifying glass. The effect is like that of waking up suddenly on a train and finding a stranger with his face thrust within an inch of one's own. A nervous person would scream; a baby would probably smile, since it would associate this kind of proximity with its mother. It is clear from *Doors of Perception* that Huxley's attitude towards the world was basically one of trust. (It is equally clear from Mme de Beauvoir's account of Sartre's relationship with other women – with strong elements of jealousy and aggressiveness – that Sartre's attitude was the opposite of trust or 'abandonment of selfhood'.

These experiences take on altogether new meanings in the light of Whitehead's book. Whitehead calls 'causal efficacy' 'the sense of controlling presences', and gives as an example the fears we sometimes feel in the dark. He points out that 'most living creatures of daytime habits are nervous in the dark'. If Hume is

* My own experiences of mescalin are described in Appendix One.

right, the sense of meaning ought to vanish in the dark and increase in the daylight, not vice versa. 'This the sense of unseen presences in the dark is the reverse of what should happen.' It might be objected that the sense of unseen presences in the dark is illusion, a remnant of the fear felt by our distant ancestors, listening for wild beasts. But Huxley suggests another reason. 'Experimental psychologists have found that if you confine a man to a "restricted environment", where there is no sound or light, nothing to smell, and if you put him in a tepid bath, with only one almost imperceptible thing to touch, the victim will soon start "seeing things", "hearing things" and having strange bodily sensations. He explains the mescalin effect by saying that it interferes with the enzyme system of the brain. By starving the brain of sugar, 'it lowers the efficiency of the brain as an instrument for focusing the mind on the problems of life on the surface of this planet. This lowering of what may be called the biological efficiency of the brain seems to permit entry into consciousness of certain classes of mental events which are normally excluded, because they possess no survival value'. The effect of mescalin on Huxley was to remove all desire *to do* anything; a world in which everyone took mescalin would have no wars, but it would have no civilisation either.

Huxley quotes a theory of C. D. Broad to the effect that the nervous system is not designed to let things in but to keep them out. The brain contains a filter to prevent the mind from being swamped with useless knowledge and experience, and mescalin puts this filter out of action. (*See also Page* 151)

In the light of Husserl's ideas, we know that there is no need to posit a particular filter or reducing valve; man trains his mind for survival – and also for evolution; the function of intentionality is mainly eliminative.

From all this, we can begin to grasp the fundamental difference between the existentialism of Heidegger and that of Sartre. Heidegger's basic intuition is closer to that of Huxley; the possibility of the real existence of objects outside himself strikes him as a form of salvation; hence his emphasis upon the 'forgetfulness of Existence' as the fundamental (if necessary) evil of the modern world, and a nostalgic looking-backward to a simpler state of things in Ancient Greece – or in the nature poetry of Hölderlin.

Sartre, like Greene, seems to see the world from a lower energy level; his 'indifference threshold' is wider; consequently the external world is usually seen in negative terms, and his internal world provides no effective escape.* The alternative is to take up an aggressive attitude towards the external world, to see it as something upon which categories or ideas – or social reforms – must be imposed.

THE ULTIMATE OBJECTION TO SARTRE

To summarise: it will be seen that both Heidegger and Sartre recognise, in their different ways, that the fundamental problem for existentialism is the problem of the 'St Neot margin'. As expressed in Chapter One, it is the problem of human purpose – or rather, lack of purpose. Man's strongest impulses are negative: revulsion from death or pain, the need for security. This is the heart of the mystery. One would expect that a creature with such strong negative impulses would have equally strong positive ones, that the power of his revulsion from death would indicate a profound sense of purpose, an equally powerful appreciation of life. Yet the lives of these creatures are wasted in trivialities. They are like spoilt children who kick and scream when they are told it is time to go to school, and yet who are bored and listless at home. It is not surprising that many nineteenth century materialists refused to recognise an evolutionary urge in man. Everything he has created has been created for negative reasons – fear of discomfort and of death. He thinks in terms of 'freedom from' this and that, but never of 'freedom for' some ultimate purpose. Roquentin observes with a kind of stupefaction of his landlord: 'When his café empties, his head empties too'. These paradoxical vegetables hate death and yet cannot be said to love life. The ones among them who have a deep hunger for life – the poets, artists, explorers and reformers – are regarded as a little eccentric.

* The publication of the first volume of Sartre's autobiography *Words* (1964) seems to confirm the above speculations; the parallel with Greene becomes even more striking.

Heidegger places his faith in the poets and philosophers; he himself is a 'philosopher of solitude'.* Sartre, on the other hand, seems to prefer engagement, involvement in politics, in writers' conferences, in schemes for legal reform. Like Fichte, he seems to feel that the only escape from solipsism lies in action. Both solutions have a certain validity (although Sartre is having some difficulty making the transfer from his philosophy of meaninglessness to his new 'existentialised' Marxism). And yet the careful study of their works reveals that both lost all possibility of breaking from the closed circle of romantic defeatism when they abandoned Husserl's fundamental principle: the study of phenomena to uncover the hidden patterns of intentionality.

What strikes one as most strange about the situation is that both Sartre and Heidegger came so close to creating a truly post-Husserl existentialism. For the objections to Descartes have been obvious for more than a century now. Tolstoy expresses the most fundamental one in a story called *Memoirs of a Madman*. The essence of this story is that the 'madman' – an ordinary landowner, tied up in his personal little affairs – suddenly has an 'awakening' one night when he is on a trip to a distant province to buy more land. It is partly the question of death that strikes him – the realisation that this anxiety to add to his land is irrational in the face of the inescapable fact of death. But his awakening goes further than that; he realises that all the things he has been taking for granted – his home, background, etc – constitute *his identity*; and he finds himself asking the question 'Who am I?'

Now this recognition came to a great many people in the nineteenth century. (*The Outsider* quoted many such documents.) William James himself experienced it – and came close to a mental breakdown – as a consequence of seeing a mindless idiot in an asylum. The man to whom this realisation comes is like a sleep-

* According to Stefan Schimanski, Heidegger's way of life seems to be consistent with his ideas. For more than a quarter of a century now, he has spent most of his spare time in a small skiing hut in the mountains of the Black Forest, the main item of furniture in which is a complete edition of Hölderlin. Heidegger was born nearby (in 1889), and his later philosophy lays emphasis on the importance of 'soil' and familiar things.

walker who wakes up and finds himself balancing along a high wall. It was the kind of revelation that was hardly likely to come to pre-Newtonian man, who might be compared to a child who has been told that there are many things he will not understand until he is grown up – and so can somehow take mysteries for granted, certain that *someone* knows the answer. The rationalist of the nineteenth century was in the position of a man who has been given a number of specious answers to the problems that troubled him as a child, and convinced that everything is now solved – and who suddenly wakes up in the middle of the night and realises that nothing is solved, that the mystery is deeper than ever.

This awakening to the question of meaning and identity reveals the untenability of Descartes' position. For Descartes, the questioning consciousness could face the unknown universe, and the situation had a beautiful simplicity about it. The universe might be a matter for doubt, but consciousness could take itself for granted: *cogito ergo sum. When Tolstoy's madman asked 'Who am I?', the falseness of Descartes' position was revealed.* This falseness had never struck Descartes himself, for his universe, in fact, was not dualistic at all. There was a third behind the scenes – God. In all essentials, Descartes was a pre-Newtonian man. It was the task of mind to interrogate the universe – but he could never forget that the ultimate mysteries could be known only to God. The death of God came after Descartes; but for a while, no one noticed that it affected the Cartesian definition of science. Most men are so wrapped up in their everyday affairs that they need nothing else to give them a solid sense of identity. This applies particularly to the scientists and philosophers of the nineteenth century, who were too absorbed in their vision of progress to notice that anything was wrong. Only a few of the more sensitive ones became aware that there was something fundamentally wrong with the Cartesian outlook as applied to a godless universe. Jouffroy was one of these, and William James quotes the passage in which Jouffroy described his own attempts to 'doubt everything'.

I shall never forget that night of December in which the

veil that concealed from me my own incredulity was torn. I hear again my steps in that narrow naked chamber ... Anxiously I followed my thoughts, as from layer to layer they descended towards the foundation of my consciousness, and, scattering one by one all the illusions which until then had screened its windings from my view, made them every moment more clearly visible.

Vainly I clung to these last beliefs as a shipwrecked sailor clings to the fragments of his vessel; vainly, frightened at the unknown void into which I was about to float, I turned with them towards my childhood, my family, my country, all that was dear and sacred to me; the inflexible current of my thoughts was too strong – parents, family, memory, beliefs – it forced me to let go of everything. ... I knew then that in the depth of my mind, nothing was left that stood erect.

This moment was a frightful one; and when towards morning I threw myself on my bed, I seemed to feel my earlier life ... go out like a fire.

Descartes doubted everything, but not God; therefore his disbelief had a firm foundation; he never knew the sense of shipwreck and desolation described by Jouffroy, and experienced by so many other sensitives of the nineteenth century.

Now this feeling, which is described by Jouffroy and by Tolstoy, was one of Sartre's earliest philosophical insights (according to Mme de Beauvoir). He called it 'contingency', man's recognition that something he assumed to be stable and permanent is dependent on something else, and therefore might or might not exist. It might also be described as relativism; it is the recognition that human existence is not an absolute, but can come to an end at any moment. 'Contingency', if experienced strongly enough, could lead to insanity, for it removes all possible basis for acting, or even thinking; it means an ultimate sense of insecurity about existence. Heidegger also recognises contingency in his attitude towards death – that it is inescapable, and that there is no immortality, personal or otherwise.

The sense of contingency is the outcome of accepting the simple Cartesian attitude – that consciousness is passive, a 'wind blowing towards objects'. It can mean one of two things; that life *is* so fundamentally insecure and meaningless that there is no point in even thinking; or that Cartesianism is an error. The first can hardly be called an alternative, for the result of total acceptance of it would not be an 'attitude', *it would be pure terror*; man would look at the universe around him with the feelings of a rabbit facing a snake. The second alternative is the only one possible to human beings. The first one, properly faced, amounts to hurling oneself into a furnace.

We can only conclude, therefore, that neither Sartre nor Heidegger *did* face it completely; it would have led them into the state of mind of Tolstoy's madman – from which it is hardly possible to write books of philosophy. And yet Sartre has continued to declare that he is basically a Cartesian, and that he cannot accept that consciousness is anything more than an 'emptiness', an observer.

It should now be clear what are the implications of the attitude of Husserl and Whitehead when applied to science. For better or worse, Descartes' God vanished. All that was left of the Cartesian position was the feeling that it was quite right that consciousness should confront the unknown universe; after all, it had the methods of science to help it investigate. Then Tolstoy stumbled on the objection. 'But who am *I*? Never mind about the unknown universe – that can wait. No amount of unveiling the secrets of geology, astronomy, biology, will penetrate the mystery *inside* me.' Socrates' 'Know yourself' did not mean know your faults and tendencies to self-delusion; far more profoundly, it meant what Tolstoy meant: 'Who am I?'

Husserl and Whitehead did not provide an answer; but at least they provided something that could save the philosopher from plunging into the despair of Tolstoy's madman: the recognition that 'Who am I?' is not a lightning-flash that destroys all man's pretensions, but a reasonable question that can be investigated like any other scientific problem.

The consequences of the rejection of Husserl followed inevitably; both Sartre and Heidegger found themselves becalmed before they had properly begun their philosophical voyage. Their situation could be compared to that of astronomers who refused to accept Galileo's idea that the earth goes round the sun; the complications remained insoluble, and the way was closed to further developments. Even Newton would have remained unknown if he had not begun by accepting Galileo's hypothesis. Logic and brilliance are not enough to endow a human mind with the 'power of flight'; its premises must be correct, or it is trying to fly in a vacuum.

Chapter 5

THE CHANGING VISION OF SCIENCE

At this stage, the wider significance of the Whitehead-Husserl revolution may not be clear. It may well seem to be no more than a family squabble among philosophers. But a moment's consideration will show that the implications go far beyond philosophy. Our culture is permeated with a nihilism, a defeatism, that is generally agreed to be the outcome of the rise of science; it is aggravated by the sense of insignificance that is bound to be felt by most individuals in a highly mechanised civilisation. Too many of our days amount to psychological defeat, and there is no sense of a *background* of real values of the kind that mediaeval man possessed, to make us feel that our individual defeat is unimportant.

Man, as described by science, is passive, a product of a process of mechanical evolution, a blind will to live conditioned by natural selection. This 'passive man' has become one of the most important characters in modern literature. His passivity may be a kind of metaphysical agony, like Roquentin's nausea, a sense of being a creature of illusions, negated by the overwhelming reality of 'things'; it may be simply the boredom and bewilderment of Beckett's two tramps, feeling that there is 'nothing to be done' because ultimately nothing is worth doing. There develops the sense of meaninglessness and pointlessness that is expressed in *The Waste Land* or a film like *La Dolce Vita*.

It must be understood that, in a certain sense, this is a religious crisis; and yet this is not to say that its solution would be a religious answer. Professor W. T. Stace of Princeton has analysed the problem brilliantly in an essay called *Men Against Darkness*, and it may be worthwhile to quote his essay here in order to see the problems quite clearly in perspective.

Stace begins by quoting the Catholic Bishops of America to the effect that the chaotic state of the modern world is due to man's abandonment of God. Stace comments: 'For my part, I believe in no religion at all; yet I entirely agree with the bishops.' He quotes Sartre and Bertrand Russell on the 'death of God', and agrees that this is due to the rise of science. It is not due to some particular discovery, like Darwinian evolution or the revelations of geology, but to the basic attitude of science, which is not interested in purposes but in *causes*. This disappearance of purpose from the universe is the greatest of all revolutions.

Stace dismisses the notion that there can be a return to religion; those who believe this fail to realise that the crisis is unique in history. When the religions of Greece and Rome collapsed, Christianity took their place; if Christianity had not been available, Mithraism would have served the purpose. But all religion depends on man's feeling that he is a creature and the universe has a purpose that goes beyond his understanding. Science has destroyed all possible basis for religion in our civilisation. Stace feels that ultimately this is not a bad thing, for religion is the Great Illusion, 'the idea that the universe is moral and good, that it follows a wise and noble plan, that it is gradually generating some supreme value'.

But as to the answer, Stace has no definite ideas. He rejects the notion, put forward by Russell and Dewey, that man should turn to science itself for 'salvation'. 'This seems to me to be utterly naïve.' But Stace's own conclusion is somewhat joyless. There is no reason why men should give up the minor illusions that keep them happy, the illusions connected with love, fame, glory, money, social superiority. But they must learn to live decent civilised lives without the Great Illusion. If Hume, Mill and T. H. Huxley could live moral lives without religion, there is no reason why the rest of us shouldn't learn to. (Stace is forgetting that these men lived in an age of national optimism, when it seemed that 'freethinking' might provide man with a substitute religion of progress.) 'That such a life is likely to be ecstatically happy I will not claim. But that it can be lived in quiet content, accepting resignedly what cannot be helped, not expecting the impossible, and thankful for small mercies, this I would maintain.' Stace predicts that if man cannot learn to do this, he will sink back to a 'humble place among the lower animals'.

This states the problem clearly, and it obviously provides no answer, unless a rather joyless and resigned stoicism be regarded as an answer. As Stace puts it, there are no other alternatives.

Implicit in the ideas of Whitehead and Husserl is the possibility of another alternative. The scientific view of the universe is the Cartesian view – man's conscious mind probing unknown nature, the known confronted by the unknown. Husserl has demolished this view of passive consciousness, and therefore – without fully grasping the implications of his own revolution – demolished the epistemology of science.

WHAT IS HAPPENING TO MODERN SCIENCE?

Let us consider this question of the scientific outlook more closely – first of all, in biology, which in certain fundamental respects, seems to disagree with physics. For example, in a famous passage in *The Nature of the Physical World*, Eddington speaks of the primacy of the second law of thermodynamics ('Energy can only flow from a higher to a lower level'), which 'stands aloof from all the other laws of nature'. This law is sometimes called the law of entropy, and it states that entropy must always increase. (Entropy is the element of disorder in the universe; if I drop a pack of cards, I have increased its disorder; but if I carefully sort them out again, I have still increased the *total* disorder in the universe, because I have dissipated energy in doing so.) Eddington says: 'If someone points out to you that your pet theory of the universe is in disagreement with Maxwell's equations – then so much the worse for Maxwell's equations. If it is found to be contradicted by observation – well, these experimentalists do bungle things sometimes. But if your theory is found to be against the second law of thermodynamics I can give you no hope; there is nothing for it but to collapse in the deepest humiliation ... The chance against the breach of the second law ... can be stated in figures that are overwhelming.'

And yet as far as we can see, evolution has been ignoring the second law of thermodynamics since the beginning of time. Sir Julian Huxley, for example, had written five years before *The Nature of the Physical World* appeared: 'We assume, on fairly good although indirect evidence, that there has been an evolution of the forms assumed by matter; that in this solar system of ours, for instance, matter was once all in electronic form, that it then attained to the atomic and the molecular; that later, colloidal organic matter of a special type made its appearance, and later still, living matter arose. That the forms of life, simple at first, attained progressively to greater complexity; that mind, negligible in the lower forms, became of greater and greater importance, until it reached its present level in man.'* This is nothing less than a flat denial of the law of entropy. The universe of physics is running down; the universe of evolution is winding up, and seems to have been doing so steadily for a thousand million years. (Man has appeared only in the past million.) Biology, then, contradicts flatly the nineteenth century materialism that regarded mind as some kind of emanation of matter as alpha rays are an emanation of radium. Eddington once said that an army of monkeys strumming aimlessly on typewriters would eventually write all the books in the British Museum according to the laws of chance; but for the kind of 'chance' that produced man, a thousand million years is far too short.

Biologists, then, are in general agreement in accepting the organising principle called life. They may disagree about how this principle works; but about life itself, there is at least no disagreement.

* *Essays of a Biologist*, 1923, p. 241. This is not to say, of course, that the 'build up' of inorganic matter – carbon atoms – contradicts the law of entropy, since the active agent here is the sun. (See Oparin's *Origin of Life*, 1957. Huxley has written: 'The fact that the origin of life and its subsequent evolution is anti-entropic in the sense of creating higher organisation of complexification, does not contradict the second law of thermodynamics, since it depends on energy received from the sun. It merely means that *on this planet* the second law of thermodynamics is now not working, and of course opens up the possibility that there may be agencies operating in the universe supplying energy which would enable the whole cosmos to behave in an anti-entropic manner.' (Letter to the writer, February 26, 1964.)

But having said this, we now confront certain fundamental disagreements, which must be explained at some length.

According to Darwin, species change by 'natural selection', which favours the strongest. There is no need to posit an 'evolutionary force' whose *purpose* is to build up higher forms of organisation. For example, Huxley cites the case of the Japanese *Heike* crab, whose back has a design that so resembles the face of an angry warrior that the Japanese will not eat it, believing it to be inhabited by the spirit of one of a tribe of warriors who committed suicide in 1155 by leaping into the sea. There is obviously no question of the crab *knowing* that it will not be eaten if it can learn to resemble a warrior. What has happened is that the crabs that least resembled warriors got eaten; the others mated, and so on – natural selection 'polishing up' the resemblance until today it is uncannily precise.* There are far more unfavourable mutations than favourable ones; but it is the favourable ones that survive – hence evolution.

Now even Darwin was slightly worried by this picture of a mindless and purposeless evolution; towards the end of his life he expressed strong misgivings about it; for if mind was an accidental product of nature, how could it make value judgements? How could one even rely on its opinions about natural selection?

But Darwin was not entirely a 'mechanist'. Some years before, the naturalist Lamarck had expressed what then seemed to be a common sense point of view: that species change because they want to. Lamarck's most famous example is that of the giraffes; he believed that giraffes developed long necks because they wanted to reach the tender shoots on top of trees; possibly also because in a time of food shortage, it was necessary to stretch the neck to the higher leaves. Darwin accepted that Lamarck was probably right to a limited extent; for him, natural selection did not completely rule out Lamarckian evolution, although he thought that its effects were probably very slight when compared to those of natural selection.

In the second half of the nineteenth century, a monk called the

* *New Bottles for New Wine*, 1959, p. 137.

Abbé Mendel made certain experiments concerning the growing of peas, and when their results eventually became known, they seemed to deliver a killing blow to the Lamarckian theory. To explain the way in which certain distinctive characteristics of the peas reappeared in later generations, Mendel postulated particles in the reproductive cell that carry these characteristics. The existence of these 'units of heredity' was later confirmed; they were called 'genes'. The gene is a kind of biological atom. All living organisms, from fungi to human beings, depend upon genes. Each gene determines some tiny characteristic – perhaps the colour of the eyes, the shape of the nose. In the simplest organisms, only a few genes are necessary to determine their characteristics. In a complex organism such as man, the number is uncountable. In recent years, it has been discovered that the element in the genes that actually carries the hereditary characteristics is nucleic acid – the so-called DNA and RNA, and progress is being made in investigating the 'gene code'.

Mutations are due to changes that take place in the genes. We now know that radiation affects the genes and can cause mutations. Since all living organisms are under a constant bombardment from outer space, it would seem that we need look no further for the reason that species change.

It will now be seen why the work of Mendel destroyed the possibility of Lamarckian evolution. According to Lamarck, an animal changes some fundamental characteristic because it wants to – or has to if it is to survive; this change is then passed on to the children. Let us suppose that a pair of crocodiles find their way into some northern lake, and manage to survive the cold.* According to Lamarck, we could expect their children and descendants to be born with thicker skins, larger bodies – or whatever characteristic the crocodiles had developed to resist the cold. According to Mendel, the young crocodiles would be exactly like their parents, and would have to develop similar powers of resistance on their own; the same would be true of the thousandth generation of crocodiles, unless some chance mutation had happened to occur. The genes cannot be affected by the

* As a single crocodile is actually supposed to have survived in Loch Ness, according to Commander Gould.

will of the individual; therefore there can be no inheritance of acquired characteristics.

The alternative to this mechanistic principle had been first advanced by Georg Ernst Stahl in the seventeenth century – the notion called 'vitalism' – that the body is not governed by physical and chemical laws, but by the action of a soul or vital force; even in our own time, a form of vitalism was held by the biologist Hans Driesch.* This form of vitalism has become something of an Aunt Sally to modern biologists and psychologists.

Shaw and Bergson were both vitalists in another sense; that is to say, they believed that evolution is not a purely mechanical process, but is the result of a force, more or less purposive, which Shaw called the life-force, and Bergson the *élan vital.* Samuel Butler had attacked Darwinian evolution on the ground that it 'banished mind from the universe', and pointed out that it would be almost impossible to *prove* Darwin right or Lamarck wrong, since it would be very difficult to devise an experiment that would force a living creature to will a physical change that would enable it to survive. On the other hand, Butler pointed out, social workers every day see weak youths developing strength or agility in competition with others of their age.

Shaw was apparently unaware of Mendel's existence. He wrote a preface to *Back to Methuselah* in which he stated the two hypotheses – Darwin and Lamarck – and came down in favour of Lamarck, and of a purposive evolution of the spirit of man towards godhead. His idea was that spirit (or will) would come to pervade the universe eventually. This basic notion was expressed with great clarity by T. E. Hulme:

> The process of evolution can only be described as the gradual insertion of more and more freedom into matter ... In the amoeba, then, you might say that the impulse has manufactured a small leak through which free activity could be inserted into

* This type of vitalism tends to be dualistic – to believe that the body is a machine operated by a ghostly soul that is in some way the exact counterpart of the body. The arguments applied by Gilbert Ryle in *The Concept of Mind* to the Cartesian body-soul dualism also apply to this vitalism.

the world, and the process of evolution has been the gradual enlargement of this leak. (*Speculations,* p. 208.)

Shaw, unfortunately, affirmed his belief in the inheritance of acquired characteristics, which had the effect of discrediting the whole Shavian notion of evolution. This is a pity, since the kind of evolution predicted by Shaw could take place without the inheritance of acquired characteristics.

New complications were introduced into this controversy in the 1930s when the Russians suddenly decided to adopt Lamarckism as part of the official policy of Soviet biology. The reason for this is obvious. Soviet ideology was optimistic, and emphasised the importance of the will. If acquired characteristics could be inherited, then the educated peasant could pass on his advantages to his children in a biological as well as a social sense.

A horticulturalist called Michurin was the patron saint of the neo-Lamarckian movement. Michurin claimed that the heredity of plants can be altered by certain experiments – mainly by a process called 'shattering', a kind of shock treatment – and that this new heredity will be transmitted to all future generations. An Austrian biologist named Kammerer had made a spectacular claim to have demonstrated the inheritance of acquired characteristics in toads and salamanders; but it was discovered that certain of his specimens had been faked. Kammerer declared that someone had tampered with them to discredit him, but he was generally disbelieved, and committed suicide.*

Michurin died in 1935, his views favoured by Stalin, since they seemed to demonstrate that environment is the all-important factor – a view that obviously fits in closely with Marxian

* Kammerer claimed to have demonstrated the inheritance of acquired characteristics with midwife toads – a variety in which the male carries the female's eggs on his legs until they hatch. Several generations were raised under abnormal conditions, some entirely out of water, some in water with islands that were kept too hot to afford anything but temporary rest. He claimed that the male toads raised on land lost their egg-carrying habit, while the water toads developed horny pads on the thumbs, possessed by ordinary frogs to hold on to their mates in the water. Dr G. K. Noble noticed that the 'pads' were actually injections of Indian ink under the skin. Many biologists, including Sir Julian Huxley, are inclined to absolve Kammerer himself from any part in the 'hoax'.

materialism and its dialectic of history. In the same year, Trofim Lysenko published a book, on which he had collaborated with the philosopher Prezent, attacking Mendelianism – or at least, the aspect of it that declared that the genes cannot be affected by human will or environment.

Unfortunately, the whole controversy developed into a highly unpleasant business. (It is described in detail in Sir Julian Huxley's admirable little book *Evolution, East and West*.) Mendelian biologists were victimised, and there is reason to believe that some of them were 'liquidated'. (For example, the biologist Vavilov was accused of being a British spy, and died of hardship in Siberia.) Again, in 1948, at a Soviet Congress of Genetics, Mendelianism was proscribed, and Lysenko revealed in a speech that his own views had the support of 'the greatest scientist of our age, Comrade Stalin'. A few harassed Mendelians, who had been tricked into expressing their views in a literary gazette, with the understanding that the subject was again a matter for reasonable public debate, were denounced as traitors to the people, and ruthlessly dealt with. Lysenko had a temporary eclipse after the death of Stalin, but at the time of writing (1964) is back in favour.

One of Lysenko's chief claims concerned the vernalisation of wheat – treating it so that wheat that would normally be sown in the autumn could instead be sown in the spring. Lysenko claimed that his treatment of wheat (involving moistening and keeping at a low temperature) could not only produce vernalisation, but could make the vernalised wheat go on producing generations of similar wheat. Sir Julian Huxley states that these claims are false – at least, that no other scientist has succeeded in duplicating the experiments.

It is difficult to know whether Lysenko was a fraud, a madman, or simply a bad scientist. (That he was a good agronomist is beside the point.) What matters here is that the disproving of Lysenkoism seems to have destroyed all possibility of a revival of Lamarckism.

Let us summarise the situation so far. Lamarck believed that species change because they want to. Lamarckian biologists were, in general, vitalists; that is, they believed that evolution can be explained in terms of an *élan vital* driving life up the evolutionary ladder. (Sir Julian Huxley retorted that we can no more explain evolution in terms of *élan vital* than we can explain the motion of a train by saying it possesses an *élan locomotif*.) Darwin's discovery of the mechanism of natural selection meant that no force was necessary; nature favours 'complexification'; therefore, evolution could be the result of 'accident'. There was no need for God, or 'universal purpose'. Post-Mendelian biology has confirmed the Darwinian position. Waddington and Huxley have shown that inheritance of acquired characteristics is unnecessary – in fact, downright undesirable, since degenerative characteristics would also be heritable. It is now clear that evolution is a far more complicated process than Darwin realised, and that simple 'mutationism' is a long way from being able to explain it. Environment *does* affect the genes, but by a process of what Huxley calls 'cybernetic feedback', not in a simple Lamarckian way.*

It might seem, then, that we are back in the 'mindless' universe of nineteenth century materialism. In fact, this is not so. The development of biology in the past fifty years has demonstrated that Shaw was wrong to assume that the only hope for true evolutionism lies in the inheritance of acquired characteristics. To begin with, no biologist today holds the view that living matter is fundamentally indistinguishable from inorganic matter – that is, that life is some sort of an emanation of matter, a by-product of the 'running down of the universe'. Even if natural selection is the only method of evolution, life is a force that takes advantage of every possibility of evolution. It may not be able to create changes, but it can seize upon them as soon as they appear.

And yet it is not even true to say that life cannot create changes. On the level of mind, man is able to take his evolution into his own hands. Through civilisation, he is able to create, and then perpetuate, evolutionary changes. The only power that is not in his hands is to pass on changes directly through the genes; but he can pass them on by an equally effective method – education.

* For a simple and clear discussion of the modern vision of evolution, see Huxley's *Evolution, the Modern Synthesis,* which, although twenty years old, is still in many ways the best summary of the subject. A summary of more recent advances can be found in George Gaylord Simpson's *This View of Life,* while C. H. Waddington's *Strategy of the Genes* gives a fuller but more technical approach to the subject.

(He may even learn how to affect the genes directly when he understands enough about the 'gene code'.) Man holds the power of evolution in his own hands.

All this is expressed with great force by Sir Julian Huxley, an uncompromising neo-Darwinian. In an essay, 'Man's Place in Nature', he writes: 'All nature is a single process. We may properly call it evolution, if we define evolution as a self-operating, self-transforming process which in its course generates both greater variety and higher levels of organisations'.* He goes on to say that there are three levels or processes in nature: the inorganic, the biological and the human. On the inorganic level, 'complexification' is limited and slow. On the biological level, with the aid of natural selection, the tempo is faster. On the human level, the change seems to be accelerating all the time.

The full significance of this can be seen by reconsidering the passage from the opening of Wells's *Experiment in Autobiography* (cited on page 33). In effect, Wells says that an animal cannot have a purpose that is not connected with its basic biological needs: food, security, dominance. This has also been true for most men throughout history. And yet, Wells says, he is in the strange position of not wanting to live at all unless he can satisfy *another* appetite – an appetite than no animal has ever possessed before, and that has appeared very rarely in human history. All this can be summarised in a single phrase: *Man is a purposive animal* – the first really purposive animal. An animal's needs are limited to its body. Without physical stimulus, an animal will sit and stare straight ahead. This is also true of men – truer than most men would like to admit. 'When his café empties, his head empties too.' Sartre's phrase describes something fundamental about human beings; purpose comes from outside, so it cannot be called real purpose; it is mere 'challenge and response'. A cigarette machine serves a purpose; but it does not *have* purpose because it produces a packet of cigarettes in exchange for a coin. Most animal activities are equally un-purposive, no more than mechanical reactions. Man – at least, 'Wellsian man' – possesses a conscious hunger for 'complexification', for evolution. All this is to

* *New Bottles for New Wine*, p. 43.

say that the 'human level' is quite different *in kind* from the animal level, and possesses the potentiality of a new freedom. Man – and again I must add 'Wellsian man' – is a purposive animal. He is still an amphibian trying to learn to live on land, but he is approaching a condition when he will cease to be a creature of biological motives – security, sex, dominance – and will regulate all his activities by a primary motive – evolutionary purpose, self-change. He cannot be contented with purposes that come from outside; he hungers for an *inner drive.*

Huxley states his biological credo in a remarkable essay called *Transhumanism,* that opens his book *New Bottles for New Wine.* From this, it can be seen that the discrediting of Lamarck and Lysenko makes no real difference to the evolutionist vision; there is no danger of a lapse into the mechanistic outlook of the nineteenth century.

Huxley begins by stating: 'As a result of a thousand million years of evolution, the universe is becoming conscious of itself, able to understand something of its past history and its possible future. This cosmic self-awareness is being realised in one tiny fragment of the universe – in a few of us human beings.' 'It is as if man had been suddenly appointed managing director of the biggest business of all, the business of evolution. ... ' 'The first thing that the human species has to do to prepare itself for the cosmic office to which it finds itself appointed is to explore human nature, to find out what are the possibilities open to it (including, of course, its limitations).' 'The great men of the past have given us glimpses of what is possible in the way of personality, of intellectual understanding, of spiritual achievement, of artistic creation. But these are scarcely more than Pisgah glimpses.' 'Up to now, human life has generally been, as Hobbes described it, "nasty, brutish and short" ... We are already justified in the conviction that human life as we know it in history is a wretched makeshift, rooted in ignorance; and that it could be transcended by a state of existence based on the illumination of knowledge and comprehension.' This can be done by improving the social environment, and by making men aware that beauty is indispensable to our existence. Huxley rightly places considerable emphasis on the importance of art in the process of human evolution. 'The human species can, if it wishes, transcend itself – not just sporadically, an individual here ... and there ... but in its entirety, as humanity.' To this belief, Huxley gives the name 'transhumanism', and ends: ' "I believe in transhumanism"; once there are enough people who can truly say that, the human species will be on the threshold of a new kind of existence, as different from ours as ours is from that of Pekin man. It will at last be consciously fulfilling its real destiny.'

The non-scientific reader might well feel somewhat bewildered at this point. The Russians, who profess to be materialists, enemies of philosophical idealism, apparently support a view that leaves the way open for Shavian evolutionism; Sir Julian Huxley, a neo-Darwinian, holds that man has become the 'managing director of evolution', and yet does not believe in a universal purpose, an *élan vital,* that makes for evolution. In *The Science of Life* by Wells and Huxley, the authors dismiss the idea of a purpose in nature or in living things, and conclude: 'Human purpose has arisen as a product of the mechanical workings of variation and selection. But now that consciousness has awakened in life, it has at last become possible to hope for a speedier and less wasteful method of evolution, a method based on foresight and deliberate planning instead of the old, slow method of blind struggle and blind selection.' (Book IV, Chapter 9). This view is more or less consistent with the view that Wells expounded fourteen years earlier in *God the Invisible King,* that 'God works through men ... He is the immortal part and leader of mankind. He has motives, he has characteristics, he has an aim ... The finding of him is salvation from the purposelessness of life.' Wells' God began to exist through man, but did not exist before.

This is not as paradoxical as it may seem at first sight. (One is at first inclined to ask how a belief in evolution and in a 'God within man' really differs from Shaw's views.) Dead matter can obey only natural laws; it might be said that water possesses 'purpose' in flowing downhill, if purpose is understood simply as a movement towards a certain end. An animal possesses purpose when it goes in search of food, but it has a wider range of choices than a stream flowing downhill; it is incapable of purposes beyond a certain range of instincts. What Wells is contending is that, in man, purpose exists on a new level, beyond ordinary biological appetites; man has a choice of a purpose that cannot exist for animals.

This view leaves open certain questions that seem unanswerable in purely scientific (anti-theological) terms, and that carry us into the country of existentialism. Man has a choice; he can devote himself to evolutionary purposes, or confine himself to his everyday animal purposes. But if he has a choice, presumably the purpose lies in some sense outside himself, or at least beyond his ordinary conscious self? Wells, like Huxley, rejects the Cartesian mind-body dualism on the same kind of grounds that Ryle outlines in *The Concept of Mind*; Huxley also rejects the use of such terms as 'universal purpose' or 'evolutionary intentionality', and prefers to speak of 'teleonomy', which implies movement towards an end without a necessary purpose. T. E. Hulme's view of life as the insertion of freedom into matter – so that the amoeba is seen as a small 'leak' and man as a large 'leak' – obviously retains the dualism that Ryle and Huxley object to.

But phenomenology removes the simplicity of this new monism, and raises against it the same objection as against Sartre's identification of consciousness with intentionality. We 'uncover' intentionality by phenomenological analysis. Wells objects to Shaw's notion of evolutionary purpose because it is impossible to ascribe 'even rudimentary foreknowledge to a tapeworm or a potato'. But the kind of intentionality uncovered by phenomenological analysis is not purpose in the sense of foreknowledge, but in the sense of drives of which the individual is not consciously aware. Some of these drives have come from 'outside', have been built up by consciousness and passed on to the realm of instinct – my ability to type, for example. But this cannot be said of the sexual impulse. Wells and Huxley would say that in man, the 'drift' of evolution (due to natural selection) is at last able to become a conscious evolutionary *drive*. The phenomenologist might object that, from his point of view, it is as reasonable to speak of an evolutionary *intentionality* at last becoming conscious in man as to say that man is turning the 'evolution drift' into evolutionary purpose. The main advantage of the Huxleyan point of view is that it does away with the Cartesian dualism of mind and body.

But phenomenology has its own way of dealing with the Cartesian dualism, as I have tried to show, and it is fundamentally different from Ryle's method (which argues that mind and body are a unity, and that the tendency to separate them arises from a misuse of language). And if we once posit that the sexual urge, like man's drive to broaden his knowledge, is a part of an 'evolutionary intentionality', then it immediately becomes arguable whether this intentionality has to be limited to the human phase.

For the biologist – and for the evolutionary humanist – these questions are not important; they might be dismissed as 'metaphysics'. From the point of view of existentialism – particularly of the kind of 'positive existentialism' with which I am concerned in this volume – they are of enormous importance; in fact, they are key questions, and must be considered more closely.

The central objection, then, to the Huxley-Wells notion that evolution has so far been mechanical, and that it is only now becoming purposive (in man), can be summarised in two words: Carpenter's monkeys. Let us imagine a mechanist of the old Watsonian school, who feels that Huxley and Wells are allowing their idealism to get the better of their scientific training, and who believes that man, like all animals, is a machine pure and simple – a machine with consciousness, but no will. This man will argue that there is no evidence at all of a 'break' between biological material and human material. He will, of course, agree with Huxley about the origin of life due to the action of sunlight on carbon suspended in water, and on the action of natural selection in bringing life to its present stage. He will go on to argue that man is simply a higher form of monkey, that his art and religions prove nothing to the contrary, since they can be accounted for in Freudian terms. As to what we night call 'Wellsian man', the mechanist will have little difficulty demonstrating that he amounts to wishful thinking. Wells says that he does not wish to live unless he can devote his life to satisfying an appetite for intensification of consciousness – which we have cited as evidence that man possesses a kind of appetite unknown to any animal. But Wells had gained his position in society – his dominant position – through the use of his mind; (he was, of course, born into a working-class background). Dominance is a fundamental animal appetite, almost as fundamental as the need for food, and Wells is only revealing his urge to continue to develop the instrument that has gained him his dominant position. No doubt Carpenter's monkeys also thought that their love of offspring revealed a 'higher nature', until Carpenter's experiment showed that it was less deep than the need for an established territory. If Wells had ever been placed in a situation where he had to struggle for basic necessities – like the prisoners in Auschwitz, for example – he might have discovered that his 'evolutionary appetite' was less fundamental than he thought.

All the activities of man – our devil's advocate might continue – can be summarised in terms of basic animal appetites; the need for food, territory, sex and dominance. If he were more honest, he would admit that his idealism is really self-flattery. He is completely incapable of an unselfish action – that is, an action which is not directed at satisfying one of the above mentioned appetites in himself. And so, our mechanist would conclude, evolutionary humanism is no more scientific than Shintoism or the worship of idols.

From the Huxley-Wells position, this is unanswerable. This position depends on the notion of a break between 'biological material' and 'human material'. Wells might argue that no animal has any appetite for knowledge for its own sake, but the mechanist would immediately reply that knowledge has always given human beings a dominant position – particularly in primitive society, where the intellectual automatically becomes the priest, and sometimes the king as well.

Now only one possible argument is left open to Wells; it is a 'subjective' argument, but it also has the advantage of being true. He might say: 'But the one thing I know about my appetite for knowledge is that it is *not* selfish in the sense you have defined.' Any boy who has experienced, at the age of twelve or so, what Shaw calls 'the awakening of the moral passion', the sudden marvellous discovery of the world of poetry, or science, or music, knows perfectly well that this appetite is quite unlike the urge that made him strive to become captain of the football team or the head boy in his form. It is a discovery that knowledge can open up new potentialities *in himself* – not potentialities for dominating his friends, but for becoming a higher type of creature, no longer confined in the child's world of petty selfishness. Dominance *may* be a by-product of this awakening. But the most significant thing about it is that it may drive a man in the opposite direction, against his will, as it were, and can overcome his animal and social appetites, turning him into an outcast or 'outsider'. This is what happened in the case of Van Gogh, Rimbaud, Nietzsche and T. E. Lawrence. This is the real significance of the 'outsiders'. By the mechanist's standards, they can only be dismissed as misfits and neurotics. They are the most powerful evidence of the reality of a new phase of evolution.

But this argument leads to an undermining of the Wells-Huxley position on evolution in favour of the phenomenological view I have outlined (i.e., for an evolutionary 'intentionality' rather than a 'teleonomy'.) If man can say that this appetite for knowledge and consciousness is not selfish in the way that the appetite for food or sex or dominance is selfish, then he is saying that it points to something beyond himself, outside himself if we use 'self' in the ordinary personal sense. Wells would not hesitate to agree that this 'something beyond' is the evolutionary appetite. And now the contradiction of the Wellsian position becomes apparent; he wants the best of both worlds; he is a Shelleyan idealist as regards man's future, but a scientific materialist as regards his past. He can write irritably of Shaw's 'life force': '(It is) a pantomime giant ... Lamarckism in caricature ... Mr Shaw's Life Force does not exist.' But his own 'God the invisible king' bears suspicious resemblances to Shaw's life force – except that Wells insists that this God has been born in man, and never existed before. This brings to mind Descartes' belief that animals had no souls; in fact, seems to be another example of a man trying to keep his science and his religion in different compartments.

I would suggest that existentialism, guided by the phenomenological method, can offer an 'evolutionary humanism' altogether more consistent than the strict Wells-Huxley version (although it goes without saying that it does not differ profoundly from that of Wells and Huxley). Huxley has used a version of Ryle's monism as his metaphysical foundation. Gilbert Ryle is concerned with the paradox implied in the statement that man 'has' a body and a mind, the body being in space and being subject to natural laws, and the mind not being in space and not being subject to natural laws. If man 'has' a body and mind, it follows that he is somehow their *owner,* and separate from them. Ryle compares this error to a visitor being shown the university of Oxford, and after seeing all the separate buildings, asking, 'Yes, but where is the university itself?' *The Concept of Mind* argues brilliantly that all statements about man can be made without implying the Cartesian dualism. One of Ryle's chief arguments is that the mind's activities are physical activities that take place in space, like the actions that result from them (if, that is, my thinking leads me to action). 'To talk of a person's mind is not to talk of a repository which is permitted to house objects that ... the physical world is forbidden to house; it is to talk of the person's abilities, liabilities and inclinations to do ... certain things ... ' (Chapter 7, Foreword.)

This is a brave attempt to make the human world subject to simple logic; but it is doomed to the same kind of failure as the attempt to explain light either in terms of waves or particles or, for that matter, as Sartre's attempt to reduce Husserl's phenomenology to Cartesian terms, to which Ryle's position might be compared. Science has shown that man lives in a universe that can only be described in terms of a multi-dimensional mathematics that is beyond the conceptual grasp of the human mind; any attempt to eliminate 'curved space' in favour of Newtonian space is bound to fail. Man also inhabits a complex mental universe that cannot be described in terms of the body-mind dualism, even with the Freudian 'ego-id' dualism thrown in. Ryle's book is completely valid in its criticisms of the Cartesian 'ghost in the machine', but its monistic solution of the problem is a half-measure.

But where evolutionary humanism is concerned, this is unimportant, for the Husserl-Whitehead criticism of Descartes and Hume is just as deadly as Ryle's, and is less open to the criticism of over-simplification. Its 'tri-alism' is only apparent, the first stage in an argument that leads towards a position closer to Whitehead's 'organism'. It undoubtedly finds the Bergson-Hulme notion of life manufacturing a 'leak' in matter more consistent with its approach than Huxley's monism. (And one might point out that Huxley's description of evolution as a single process involving all matter, animate and inanimate, has a Whiteheadian ring.)

It is interesting in this connection to consider Sir Julian Huxley's introduction to Teilhard de Chardin's *The Phenomenon of Man*. Teilhard was, of course, a Jesuit, and therefore committed to a purposive view of the universe. His great achievement was to unite a religious vision and the evolutionary vision. Before Teilhard, it could be alleged against 'evolutionary' thinkers like Wells and Russell that they lacked any profound sense of man as a spiritual creature, and against religious thinkers like Eliot or Simone Weil that they were too obsessed with original sin, and lacked the capacity for bold constructive thinking. Teilhard's vision is as fundamentally optimistic as Shaw's, and as religious as Eliot's. The chief allegation to be made against him is that he failed to recognise – or did not want to recognise – that his evolutionary vision was not consistent with his view of Christ as the universal redeemer, and that no matter how much symbolic truth there may be in Christianity, its identification of Christ with God is a remnant of superstition. But on the positive side, Teilhard provided a precise account of the 'three stages' (dead matter, biological matter and human material), backed with the kind of precise observation that Darwin brought to *The Origin of Species*. Wells had compared man to an amphibian trying to leave the water and learn to live on land; Teilhard invented terms for these two spheres, calling the water the 'biosphere' and man's new element the 'noösphere' – the sphere of mind – and described the process that Huxley calls 'psycho-social evolution' as 'hominisation' – that is to say, man's process of becoming *more human*. Like Shaw, Teilhard believes that this process tends towards an emergence of divinity, and he sometimes calls the process Christogenesis. At the end of *Back to Methuselah,* Shaw had spoken about the final end of evolution as the time when the 'whirlpool of pure force' becomes a 'whirlpool of pure intellect'. To return to Hulme's simile, it will be the point where the 'leak' has been enlarged to such an extent that matter is entirely submerged by life or consciousness, and the universe will be a single organism. Teilhard calls this 'point Omega', the point to which all evolution is tending. But since Teilhard is a Catholic, he cannot accept Huxley's view that the emergence of human consciousness is the emergence of evolutionary purpose. 'In the beginning' is the 'point Alpha', and the whole process between the two is a process of evolution, purposive evolution, even though its chosen method is natural selection.

Huxley makes it clear that he cannot accept this notion, or Teilhard's term 'Christogenesis' (which, as Huxley rightly points out, comes dangerously close to personifying the nonpersonal elements of reality). But what is most interesting here is to find the neo-Darwinian Huxley willing to go so far with a view that his grandfather, T. H. Huxley, might have described as religious mystification. What is also significant is that a hundred years ago, the brothers Julian and Aldous Huxley would have found themselves on opposite sides of the fence, whereas today the author of *Religion without Revelation* and the author of *The Perennial Philosophy* can both describe themselves as humanists and see no serious grounds for disagreement in their different versions of humanism.

To summarise this stage of the discussion: the views that are common to the evolution of Huxley, Wells and Teilhard de Chardin might be regarded as a contradiction of one of the fundamental ideas of neo-Darwinism: that there is no radical difference between man and the ape. Man must be studied as a phenomenon; he is not unique in the sense that Archbishop Ussher believed, but he *is* unique in that he represents a completely new phase in the history of evolution. Man is a purposive animal. Biological material is not purposive in the sense that it depends completely on external stimuli. Man as he exists at present is a hybrid, a creature whose natural home is the biosphere but who is striving to adapt himself to the noösphere. When man discovers that he is a creature of the noösphere, and that he possesses a supra-personal moral passion, he becomes a purposive creature. For those who have experienced it, the hour of the awakening of the passion for knowledge is the most memorable of a lifetime. It is the moment when it seems self-evident that man needs no religion of divine authority and commandments. Religion in that sense is a need of the animal, who needs it as a dog needs a master. The passion for knowledge replaces the need for faith, and purpose becomes an *internal drive*. In that moment, man glimpses the possibility of becoming truly human, and recognises that the instruments required in this new existence are not weapons or tools, but intellect and imagination. Imagination is the key word. The animal travels through time head first; its life consists of physical experiences. Man has this strange capacity for anticipating his experience, or even evoking experiences that are never likely to happen to him. Man's discovery of these powers of the mind is as startling and momentous as if he had suddenly noticed that he possessed wings. In a moment, he assumes a new status, discovers that he is not in the least what he thought he was, and that neither is the universe what he took it for.

Later on in the individual's development, the problems begin to appear. Like Faust, man realises that knowledge has only a limited power, and that it may still leave him confined in a narrow and unsatisfying life; or he may enthusiastically set sail on the seas of philosophy, and find himself becalmed in the shallow wastes of positivism, or simply involved in self-contradictions that defy disentanglement. But in any case, that early sense of miracle cannot be expected to persist. The noösphere is not yet man's natural home, and the water behind him exerts a strong pull. The sense of purpose evaporates, and man finds it hard to believe that it was not an illusion. He comes back to the realisation that he is an uncomfortable misfit, that the promise of a new kind of existence has not been fulfilled, that he might have been better off without this vision of purpose that has now become his jailer. T. E. Lawrence writes: 'I ... lamented myself most when I saw a soldier with a girl, or a man fondling a dog, because my wish was to be as superficial and as perfected, and my jailer held me back.' This is the 'outsider' phase, a phase of misery and self-doubt. (Nietzsche analyses it penetratingly in 'The Tree on the Mountainside' in *Zarathustra*.) This is the period when the 'outsider' *cannot afford* to believe that life is futile and the universe a vast machine (as Lawrence did). Some kind of belief, some sense of purpose, is an urgent necessity. Evolutionary humanism can at least supply the framework of this sense of purpose.

Fundamentally, the problem is a problem of consciousness, not of mere 'knowledge' ('head-knowledge', as D. H. Lawrence called it). We take our consciousness for granted, as an animal is bound to, for in an animal, consciousness is completely dependent on the environment. But once man has recognised himself as a potential inhabitant of the noösphere, he has also the potentiality of a new control over consciousness. Consciousness can be analysed phenomenologically. If, for example, one has been reading some adventure story merely for the sake of its plot, or watching television because there seems to be nothing better to do, one's consciousness becomes steadily flatter, like a bottle of soda water left open. Take up a volume of philosophy at this point, and the mind shrinks from the effort. Note, on the other hand, the champagne-quality of consciousness when one is excited by ideas, or moved by music; it seems to fizz and bubble with *potentiality*. One can recognise clearly that *consciousness is potentiality*. The problem is that it seems difficult to inaugurate these changes oneself. It would be convenient if we had a kind of volume-control knob attached to the brain, so that we could turn consciousness up or down at will. It is obvious that such a volume-control mechanism *does* exist somewhere inside us, and constant mental effort can generate a certain ability to make use of it. Clearly, this is the next step in human development. Man, as he exists at the moment, is no more than a missing link between animal and true man. The first man to learn the secret of the control of consciousness will be the first true man, wholly in possession of the new dimension of freedom. The phenomenological analysis of consciousness is a first step in this direction.

MODERN PSYCHOLOGY

We can say, then, that in modern biology, the mechanistic hypothesis is no longer regarded as tenable – which is also to say that Descartes' picture of the body as a machine housing a passive consciousness cannot be accepted as an accurate picture either. (It is difficult to see how a science calling itself biology could ever have held the mechanistic view – it would be 'the science of machines-mistakenly-assumed-to-be-alive' rather than the science of life.) What of the other branches of science?

A parallel revolution has occurred in psychology (which I have described at length elsewhere*). Again, the objection to the psychology of the nineteenth and early twentieth centuries is its mechanistic nature. Admittedly, the English psychologist McDougall regarded Freud as a representative of the 'Dionysian' trend in philosophy as opposed to the mechanistic trend (which comes down from Democritus, through Locke, Mill, Spencer, until in our own day it is represented by Russell and positivism). But in a more fundamental sense, Freud is a 'mechanist'; for him, man is passive, a slave of forces that are greater than himself; neurosis is the conflict between these hidden forces and man's social self. At bottom, Freud is deeply pessimistic; man lives in a world of illusions; if these collapsed, it is difficult to say whether man could survive. The idea of 'transhumanism' put forward by Sir Julian Huxley would have struck Freud as some kind of sublimation.

One of the most curious aspects of Freud's psychology is that he revived vitalism in his theory of the libido as the source of all vital impulse; yet the libido, the force of sexual creativity, was a blind impulse to create another generation; it had no ultimate evolutionary end. It is completely consistent with his pessimism that his chief contribution to psychology, apart from the libido, is the idea of the death wish. Obscurely, Freud recognised the need for an aim, an end, and since he could see no purpose in life except a blind, destructive striving, the death-wish was the logical choice. Freud's philosophical outlook is summarised in Eliot's lines: 'Birth, copulation and death. That's all the facts when you get to brass tacks. Birth, copulation and death.'

Although it would be untrue to say that there has been a revolution in psychology comparable to the evolutionist revolution in biology, it has certainly moved a long way from its mechanistic basis since Freud. Unlike Freud, his disciples Jung, Adler and Rank were unable to swallow the Galileo-Descartes world view;

* In *Origins of the Sexual Impulse*, chapters 3 and 8.

they were aware of Tolstoy's question of identity, the question of purpose in human existence. Jung came close to reversing Freud's procedure; where Freud had explained religion in terms of man's needs and strivings, Jung was inclined to explain man's needs and strivings in terms of some ultimate, transcendent religious goal. But Jung's reaction against Freud was rather like Kierkegaard's against Hegel; it was inclined to go to extremes and lose itself in mysticism. Jung never formulated an anti-Freudian theory with the same clarity that Sir Julian Huxley has formulated an anti-Watsonian theory. One feels that the revolt was only half-accomplished in his work.

Perhaps the greatest advance in psychology has been the formution of an 'existential psychology' by Straus, Binswanger, Minkowski, Medard Boss, and others. This is the closest that psychology has come to an evolutionary theory, for existential psychology recognises that neurosis is not the result of man's maladjustment to society, *but to the whole of existence*. This at least removes one of the major Freudian heresies: that somehow a 'socially adjusted' man is the ideal that the psycho-therapist should try to produce, and that nothing more can be expected. It might be said that existential psychology recognises that for man, the only 'norm' can be creativity, some form of self-transcendence. Neurosis is due to a kind of lop-sidedness, like an overloaded car driving with two wheels off the ground. All this is to say that the surest way of becoming neurotic is to believe, like Beckett's tramps, that there is nothing to be done, nothing worth doing. Then man is at the mercy of trivialities and the human tendency to hypochondria and making mountains out of molehills. It might be said that the aim of the existential psychologist is to destroy 'forgetfulness of existence' (since preoccupation in a world of illusions is the same thing as losing touch with existence). Existential psychology recognises that the surest way to destroy a neurosis is to induce a sense of creative purpose, of meaning. Yet again, as with Jung, one feels that the revolt has not yet fully recognised all its own implications, and is only half accomplished.

MAURICE MERLEAU-PONTY

The late Maurice Merleau-Ponty, Husserl's most important follower, has also devoted two of his most important books to an attack on 'mechanistic psychology', and so should be considered at this point. Outside France, Merleau-Ponty is sometimes regarded – wrongly – as a disciple of Sartre; in fact, he is fundamentally opposed to Sartre in rejecting the latter's basic idea of the meaninglessness of the world.

Merleau-Ponty's concern for a broadening and deepening of the scientific attitude is as real as Whitehead's, and is the key to all his work. Like Husserl, he starts from the 'scientific attitude', and attempts to base all his later generalisations on it. He is unwilling to evoke Bergson's *élan vital* or Shaw's life force, still less the 'evolutionary principle'. His first book, *The Structure of Behaviour* (1942) is a fine example of logical induction; he begins with Pavlovian 'behaviourism' and Watsonian reflexology (i.e., the idea that the mind is a machine that works on reflexes), and attacks it on its own ground, attempt to show that only a gestalt interpretation can account for various phenomena connected with the brain. This leads to a section in which Merleau-Ponty attempts to show that existentialism is a logical extension of the conclusions of the previous section, by distinguishing between three 'orders of nature', the physical, the biological and the human, and showing that all can be defined in terms of process or behaviour. The human level is therefore as valid a subject for science as the physical. The book ends with a section on phenomenology as the method of philosophy. (Merleau-Ponty has gone further than Husserl in declaring that phenomenology *is* philosophy.) It might be said that Merleau-Ponty has begun from a basis that would satisfy a positivist, and created a bridge between scientific positivism and existentialism.

His most significant book is probably *The Phenomenology of Perception* (1945). Aein, he begins from gestalt psychology, and uses it to show that materialistic behaviourism is inadequate. The first part of the book then deals with man's experience of his own body, and refutes the mechanistic physiology of the nervous system, using examples like the 'phantom limb' experienced after it has been amputated. He also uses sexual pathology to demonstrate that Freud's mechanistic psychology cannot explain the origin of the sexual impulse. The final section of the first part deals with speech and language; this leads to a section dealing with the 'perceived world'. The book ends with Merleau-Ponty's alternative to the Cartesian opposition of subject and object; in many ways, we are reminded of Ryle's similar exercise in *The Concept of Mind*. For Merleau-Ponty opposes St Augustine's statement 'Turn into yourself; truth dwells only in the inner man' (re-phrased by Kierkegaard as Truth is subjectivity) and declares that there is no such thing as the inner man; man is man, and he is man because he exists in the world and sees his reflection in it.

As with Husserl, there is ultimately something unsatisfactory about Merleau-Ponty's philosophy. What he rejects is clear enough; but when he comes to putting something in the place of the things he rejects, it seems that he is unsure of himself. He insists that the philosopher cannot escape 'ambiguity' if he is honest. He says that man is 'condemned to meaning' – hence emphasising his difference from Sartre, who says that man is condemned to freedom. By this he means that it makes no difference even if a philosopher decides that the universe is meaningless; there is nothing that he can do or say that can follow logically from this denial; even sitting still or committing suicide is doing something meaningful. But if man is condemned to meaning, this is also to recognise that meaning is external to him, not a matter of arbitrary choice, as Sartre maintains.

It should not be assumed from this that Merleau-Ponty takes up a religious position. He declares himself an atheist and a humanist. On the question of human dignity and man's relation to God, he is closer to Antoine de Sainte-Exupéry or Romain Gary. (*Phenomenology of Perception* ends with a quotation from Exupéry's *War Pilot* stating that 'man is a knot of relations').

But it will be seen from this account that there is a certain amount of inner-confusion in Merlau-Ponty's 'existential humanism'. Although he is a follower of Husserl – and finds the later Husserl more important than the earlier – he has still not freed himself from the Cartesian dualism – as the final section of

Phenomenology of Perception shows – and grasped the full implications of Husserl's intentionality. Ultimately, his position comes close to that of Albert Camus: that is to say, he is a kind of existentialist stoic. The chief value of his work undoubtedly lies in his carefully argued refutation of behaviourism and mechanistic psychology in general.

We may say, then, that there seems to be a distinctly anti-mechanistic trend in modern science. There is no sign of a return to a pre-scientific idealism or 'vitalism'; the new tendency is a synthesis, not a return to the old thesis. The scientific method is still regarded as all important. Another sign of this attitude can be found in the present-day trend to investigate scientifically the phenomena of telepathy, 'second sight' and 'psychic manifestations' in general. It is difficult to imagine an American university of the 1880s endowing a research programme into 'parapsychology' as Duke University has endowed Professor Rhine. It is difficult to imagine a 'scientific philosopher' of the 1880s feeling free to write books on psychical research, like Professor C. D. Broad – or like the analytical philosopher Anthony Flew. The dogmatic narrowness has disappeared; but it has not given way to an anti-scientific attitude. It is simply recognised that the old assumptions about the boundaries of science led to self-contradiction.

And yet this revolt has so far proceeded instinctively; *there has been no attempt to revise the philosophical foundations,* nor has the need been fully recognised. This situation cannot continue indefinitely.

A NOTE ON SHAW'S LAMARCKISM

I should conclude this chapter with some comments on Shaw's evolutionism which, for the past thirty years, has been subjected to the contemptuous comment of almost everyone who has written on evolution. (Robert Ardrey even makes the astounding statement that Shaw did not believe in evolution.) And yet it is to be doubted whether many of these writers knew exactly what Shaw believed on the subject.

Shaw accepted Lamarck's statement that living organisms change because they want to, and used Lamarck's illustration of the giraffe's neck. But he was aware of the problem of acquired characteristics, even though he paid no attention to Mendel. Far from believing that acquired characteristics can be inherited overnight, he recognised that they seldom ever are inherited. 'For instance, Raphael, though descended from eight uninterrupted generations of painters, had to learn to paint as if no Sanzio had ever handled a brush before.' 'When your son tries to skate or bicycle in his turn, he does not pick up the accomplishment where you left it, any more than he is born six feet high with a beard and a tall hat. The set-back that occurred between your lessons occurs again. The race learns exactly as the individual learns. Your son relapses, *not to the very beginning, but to a point which no mortal method of measurement can distinguish from the beginning.*' (My italics.) In Shaw's view, then, Lamarckian evolution may well take as long as natural selection, and *accompanies natural selection*. It is not proposed as an alternative.

It can be seen that whether Shaw's view is correct or not, none of the arguments or experiments so far has refuted it. It is true that Shaw states elsewhere in the same preface that the great factor in evolution is use *and disuse*. 'If, like a mole or subterranean fish, you have eyes and don't want to see, you will lose your eyes.' But the experiments with a few generations of *drosophila* flies will hardly prove or disprove this point; it might be disproved if *drosophila* flies could be transported to the dark side of the moon and bred there for five hundred years, and then *still* showed the same tendency to fly towards the light.

On the other hand, the Shavian notion of 'use and disuse' has a disturbing implication that Shaw apparently failed to see. The kind of Lamarckism advocated in *Back to Methuselah* could be described as 'the inheritance of *willed* acquired characteristics'. If disuse is also to determine what characteristics are inherited, then there seems to be no reason why degenerative acquired characteristics should not also be inherited. This means that a man who had acquired a taste for sadism as a guard in a concentration camp would pass some fraction of his taste on to his children. A highly mechanised civilisation obviously produces more factors that make for degeneration (through boredom, lack of purpose) than for evolution, and if Shaw is right, then this degeneration would be passed on in the same way as the 'degeneration' of the appendix or finger nails. To this extent, the purely Mendelian view held by Huxley provides better grounds for an optimistic humanism than Shaw's Lamarckism. Natural selection is a 'safer' method of evolution than inheritance of acquired characteristics. Again, one can only display both sides of the argument, and admit that it is a question that can only be decided by biologists themselves.

To reach any conclusions on the relation of dominance to evolution, it would be necessary to make a study of the factor of will. During the Korean war the Chinese discovered that it was not necessary to expend large numbers of men on guarding prisoners; they merely subtracted the five per cent of 'trouble-makers' and placed them under heavy guard, and left the remaining ninety-five per cent with almost no guard at all. And yet there were no attempts on the part of the ninety-five per cent to escape. The impulse to escape would have come from the other five per cent – the men with the will-power, the 'dominant minority'. Again, it is observable that the communist party in Russia is about five per cent of the total population. It would seem, then, that if biologists ever carried out a series of experiments to establish inheritance of acquired characteristics, they would do well to pick out the dominant five per cent minority, who would almost certainly be the 'carriers'.

Most of the objections to Shaw's Lamarckism seemed to be based on a dislike of his Nietzschean theory of the superman. (This is particularly true of the Eliot-Lawrence generation.) It was a part of the rejection of the nineteenth century ideal of 'Progress'. Now that Sir Julian Huxley's 'transhumanism' has revived the idea of progress on a scientific basis, it is perhaps time to re-examine Shaw's ideas with a less prejudiced eye.

Chapter Six

THE ANALYSIS OF MAN

The problem then, as Sir Julian Huxley has stated, is to redefine man *in terms of possibility and limitation.* It might be said that human history has been working towards such a synthesis. Ancient literature – the Greeks, the Old Testament – felt that life is fundamentally tragic, since man is a creature. The early romantics went to the opposite extreme, and decided that man was born for absolute freedom – that man is really a 'god in exile'. They acted on this belief after the manner of a man who feels that he should be able to fly like a bird by flapping his hands, and tests the theory by leaping off the roof. The impact of reality startled them so much that most of them died of despair. But man is neither a creature nor a god; he is somewhere between the two, and his evolution depends on recognising the precise nature of his limitations. He can occasionally experience the state of mind in which Van Gogh painted *The Starry Night* or in which Nijinsky wrote 'I am God'; but nature refuses to allow man to live in this state for long. It would destroy his usefulness as the evolutionary spearhead. As Aldous Huxley pointed out in *Doors of Perception*, a certain limitation of consciousness is necessary if the work of civilisation-building is to continue.

Let us try to state this problem as clearly as possible:

Man has two possible attitudes towards his experience: passive and active – the animal and the truly human. If I am deeply asleep and the bedclothes slide off the bed, I may grope for the sheet and pull it over me; I shall still be cold, but I do not have to rouse myself from sleep. If I find the cold intolerable, I will wake myself up, switch on the light and (if necessary) make the bed. These are the two attitudes to all living experience. The active attitude is what Whitehead meant by prehension.

Now according to Sartre and Heidegger, the world is meaningless, so it is completely up to me which adjustment I make; it makes no difference to anyone but me. Roquentin's experience of nausea (undoubtedly the result of fatigue) is a tendency to be completely passive in the face of the world. 'Nausea' is a recognition of the meaningless 'is-ness' of reality, a confirmation that Roquentin is right to make no attempt to impose his will on it. And yet Roquentin's other fundamental experience is a sense of meaning and adventure. Merleau-Ponty accepts this as the more fundamental truth when he writes that man is 'condemned to meaning'.

This would seem to indicate that no matter how alien and meaningless life may appear to immediate consciousness, man is fully aware of its meaning on some deeper level. It would be, perhaps, a mistake to speak of this deeper level as 'the unconscious mind'. In the *Meno*, Socrates demonstrates that a slave contains all the axioms of geometry 'within himself'; and yet it would hardly be true to say that the slave knew them subconsciously, using the word in its Freudian sense.

Man is involved with the world on many levels. His beam of consciousness picks out matters for attention as a pocket torch might pick single objects in a dark cave. An enormous area of his own being is inaccessible to the beam of consciousness. There are moments when he becomes aware that he contains a 'god-like chaos', that he is potentially an enormous force. These moments are the opposite of 'nausea', for in nausea man feels isolated in an alien world of objects; in the moments of insight, he becomes aware of a connection between himself and nature – that he is capable of a meaningful relationship with nature.

Sartre found these two experiences irreconcilable; so they are, on the Cartesian-Hume-ian outlook that Sartre accepts. Nausea is only Hume-ian immediacy-perception taken to an absurd limit. *But it was Husserl who really exploded Hume by pointing out that if we are going to object to causality on the grounds that it is 'added' by the mind, then we must object to any kind of perception at all, since it is all intentional, all added by the mind.* Pure perception – with intentionality inactive – cannot exist (unless, as Merleau-Ponty contends, the kind of perception we experience on the edge of sleep is pure). In *Nausea*, Sartre only went on to illustrate Husserl's refutation of Hume with a parable – but misunderstood the meaning of his own parable, assuming it to be a proof of Hume. The two kinds of perception illustrated are Whitehead's two modes, presentational immediacy and causal efficacy, and Whitehead had already presented his refutation of the book in the passage (quoted on page 101) about William Pitt. *Nausea* is a clear demonstration that the Whitehead-Husserl hypothesis must replace the Galileo-Descartes hypothesis; there is no alternative.

To grasp fully the meaning of this, we should note that Whitehead distinguishes a third mode of experience – conceptual analysis. Man not only possesses meaning *perception*, the ability to grasp wholes, causal relationships, etc; he also possesses the power of grasping far greater 'wholes' by means of his intellect which, through the use of symbols, has a larger storage capacity. Hume and Sartre recognise these two modes of experience, but object that they are unconnected, that immediacy-perception *contradicts* conceptual analysis. Whitehead and Husserl have simply pointed out that there is a third mode of experience which connects the two others.

What is clear is that the content of the 'moments of insight' is an evolutionary content, in that it points to further meanings, to 'adventure' (as Sartre calls it) and prompts to action. It is the reverse of Beckett's 'nothing to be done'. Man's 'two counsellors', of whom I spoke at the beginning of this book, are no more than the two advocates of the two modes of perception. If, then, we accept evolution – 'complexification', as Teilhard de Chardin calls it – as the alternative to the 'simplification' which is the law of entropy, then we might, in the most precise sense of the word, speak of intentionality as evolutionary. This is not a leap from philosophy into speculative biology; it is a logical consequence of accepting the Whitehead-Husserl hypothesis as an alternative to the Descartes-Hume hypothesis exemplified in *Nausea*.

We return to the question of redefining man in terms of possibility and limitation. It might be said that these two modes correspond to causal efficacy and presentational immediacy. What has never yet been understood in the course of human history is the relation of the two modes, and the fact that this relation is dynamic and not static, that it can be varied, so to speak, to gain fullest advantage. Romanticism attempted to disconnect 'immediacy' and live in the world of meaning; but in rejecting the world of facts, the romantics only enfeebled themselves. They eliminated themselves by natural selection.

Man cannot, then, live continually in the 'world quivering with meaning' that Aldous Huxley saw under mescalin; the penalty is too great. But this does not mean that he is permanently condemned to a barren world of immediacy. There are two clear alternatives, in no way mutually self-exclusive. He can develop the meaning-faculty, which always accompanies immediacy perception in any case. But he can also, if the intentional nature of consciousness is understood, strengthen the meaning-faculty with conceptual analysis. The second alternative is the one opened up by Husserl; it amounts to phenomenological analysis and the development of language. I shall speak of this in a moment. The first alternative is existential – that is to say, practical. In order to grasp its implications more fully, let me try to summarise the argument so far.

The romantics were the first to bring into clear focus the problem of the meaninglessness of life, of man's lack of an instinct of life-purpose, and of the 'St Neot margin' – the fact that man knows what he doesn't want far more strongly than he knows what he does want. Like the creatures created by Pygmalion in *Back to Methuselah*, the romantics died protesting: 'I am discouraged. Life is too heavy a burden. I am afraid to live.' And yet they had at least stated the problem: *Why does life fail?*

In the twentieth century, this problem was taken up again by the existentialists, particularly Heidegger and Sartre. Sartre's answer is completely discouraging. The hero of *Altona* speaks about 'the basic horror of existence'. Life has no objective meaning; all that stands between man and 'the basic horror' is therefore his own will – and the existentialists are as aware as the romantics of the feebleness of the human will unsupported by illusions.

Heidegger proposed an alternative – the one also proposed by Gurdjieff. Man may lack a positive purpose, but at least his will can be intensified by contemplating that which he objects to more than anything else – his own death. This alternative is certainly effective – Hemingway derives his whole strength from it, and his best work conveys an intense feeling of naked existence. But it is like disciplining a class of lively boys by threatening heavy punishments. It certainly achieves its end – but there is a better way: giving them a sense of purpose, giving them something that keeps them so absorbed that they need no external discipline.

Sartre and Heidegger would reply: this is undoubtedly true: but there *is* no external purpose that is true for all human beings: only individual purposes that are mostly based on illusions.

Blake once said: 'An error must be taken to its extreme before it can be combated.' Twentieth century literature has applied itself to the task of taking this error to its limit. It is the Russians who have gone furthest in stating the notion of universal meaninglessness. It is present in Dostoevsky, but Artsybashev and Andreyev take it to a bold extreme. In the western pessimists – Greene, Faulkner, Hemingway, Mann – even Beckett – the nihilism is only implied; it never comes completely into the open. Sartre is the exception; *Nausea* states the ultimate grounds for his pessimism. But it was Merleau-Ponty, the phenomenologist, who went even deeper than Sartre, and recognised that man is *condemned to meaning*. It is impossible to do anything that is not an acknowledgement of meaning. And it was Husserl and Whitehead who pointed out how this had been overlooked. Man owes his evolutionary primacy to his faculty of immediacy-perception, concentrating a narrow beam of attention on the present. Animals possess so little of this power that it might be said that they exist in only one mode of perception; causal efficacy. Man possesses not only immediacy-perception; he also possesses the power of conceptual analysis and imagination. Inevitably, then, he exists on several levels, and since immediacy perception demands first place, he is chiefly aware of himself as a *passive* consciousness. And the more man develops this faculty of selecting and excluding, the further he retreats from meaning-perception. This is to say that the more highly developed the intellect, and the faculty for focusing attention, the more the world is seen as meaningless.

It was Husserl who showed the way out of this cul-de-sac. For even while man is working in a world that appears to be meaningless – aware of himself only as a passive consciousness – another level of his being is absorbed in the meaning-aspect of the world, and is intensely active. Brentano had pointed out that all consciousness is intentional – which only meant, for him, that a mental act is always clearly distinguished from its object. Husserl recognised that it is intentional in a profounder sense, that the mind is perpetually engaged in what could be called 'subconscious prehension'. On the level of the cogito, all may be silent, apparently purposeless; but then, the cogito is a room at the top of a tower. A few floors below, man's being is like a factory, full of deafening activity. And unlike the White Knight, whose whiskers were invisible behind a fan, 'intentionality' is not inscrutable. Phenomenology – the descriptive analysis of subjective experience – can discern the meanings behind this activity. For example, the phenomenological analysis of sex reveals that the origin of the sexual impulse is not a blind libido, but the same basic impulse that animates the artist, the saint and the social reformer. The phenomenological analysis of imagination reveals that it is not a faculty for creating 'compensatory realities', but a form of intentionality that involves the use of all three modes of experience – immediacy, meaning and conceptual analysis – and as such, is a part of man's machinery of *purpose*.

What is usually called 'mystical experience' is a temporary reversal of the usual order of presentational immediacy and causal efficacy, without the usual weakening of immediacy (that occurs, for example, when 'meaning' is glimpsed on the edge of sleep). But the usual price of these 'mystical' experiences has been the inability to convey their essence in language. (Van Gogh succeeds better in painting.) Phenomenology is a systematic attempt to connect the two realms with language. In the most fundamental sense, Husserl's phenomenology is a psychology; it is a mistake to think of it merely as a philosophical method.

An important point should be made here. I have said that Husserl replaces the Cartesian dualism with a 'tri-ality', and it might seem that identifying Descartes' cogito with presentational immediacy, and 'intentionality' with causal efficacy (or prehension) supports this idea of a triadic structure in the subject-object relation. This would be to oversimplify. We refer to a 'tri-ality' for the sake of convenience, and because immediacy-perception and meaning-perception seem to be alien to one another. But it should also be remembered that imagination and conceptual analysis also seem alien to immediacy-perception, and if we proceed in this manner, we shall soon have human consciousness divided into a dozen different modes. The truth is that these modes are only different aspects of the totality of consciousness in the same way that imagination is a combination of the modes themselves. Sartre is right in a sense; there is no transcendental ego; there is only consciousness. But Sartre's cogito, his 'wind blowing towards objects', is only a single aspect of consciousness; its passive top-layer. Merleau-Ponty and Gilbert Ryle are also right in their criticism of the Cartesian subject-object relation. Body is only another aspect of consciousness. It is convenient to think about man as a combination of 'body and mind', but consciousness – or mind – is a constituent of body, an aspect of body-as-consciousness.

Husserl's phenomenology, then, is an investigation of meaning. Husserl himself apparently failed to realise its deepest implications, since he was a scientist and a logician rather than a metaphysician; there is no evidence that he was ever aware of the problem of 'nausea' or of personal identity. He saw phenomenology as a logical analysis of descriptions that might be compared to Socrates's method of making a slave solve a geometrical problem in the *Meno*. It was merely a question of uncovering 'structures'. But Tolstoy's madman and Sartre's Roquentin presented phenomenology with a kind of ultimatum. Is the sense of meaning, of 'adventure', to be regarded as an illusion? Even Sartre does not go this far; he leaves the nausea and the sense of 'adventure', as it were, in silent opposition. If not, if man is 'condemned to meaning', how far can phenomenology uncover this meaning? According to biology, the world possesses a 'tendency' to complexification; since man is the highest expression of this tendency, it is reasonable to assume that phenomenological analysis of man should uncover it. It may be said, then, that the ultimate task of phenomenology is the study of *evolutionary intentionality*. (Husserl was undoubtedly developing towards this recognition when he spoke of a 'genetic phenomenology' and a 'constructive phenomenology'.)

This uncovering of evolutionary intentionality is the answer to the problem of the 'St Neot margin'; Heidegger's 'death contemplation' is self-defeating (which can also be recognised in the work of Hemingway). A simple example of this uncovering through analysis can be found in the last act of *Back to Methuselah*, in the conversation between Strephon and the maiden who is discovering that she has outgrown him.

> STREPHON: You are maturing, as you call it – I call it ageing – from minute to minute. You are going much further than you did when we began this conversation.
>
> THE MAIDEN: It is not the ageing that is so rapid. It is the realisation of it when it has actually happened. Now that I have made up my mind to the fact that I have left childhood behind me, it comes home to me in leaps and bounds with every word you say.

Here the maiden's attempt to explain what has happened to her – to bring it to consciousness – has the effect of 'fixing' her new development, making it a basis upon which to act and think in future. But in this case, it might be said that the evolution had already taken place; the act of uncovering it required very little self-analysis. Awareness had risen to the surface. The phenomenological 'uncovering' is the act of going in search of the awareness long before it has reached the surface.

The starting point for this uncovering is meaninglessness, as expressed by Sartre or Beckett – or by Wells at the beginning of *Mind at the End of Its Tether*, the sense that man and nature are alien to one another, like two train lines that have run parallel by accident, and are now diverging. The analysis then proceeds in the manner of a mathematical proof that begins by saying 'Let us assume that the proposition is untrue', and then demonstrates that this assumption leads to self-contradiction. Whitehead's philosophy, in fact, began at this point in *The Concept of Nature*, with the problem of the 'radical dislocation' between mind and nature,* and proceeded through the recognition of the two 'modes of perception' to his ultimate 'philosophy of organism' in which man and nature form part of a single organism. Whitehead's philosophy is evolutionary in a sense that Husserl's is not (although the manner of expression is closer to Hegel than to Smuts, for example – whose *Holism and Evolution* expresses similar views).

Whitehead's philosophy of organism is difficult to approach through his early books (its true starting point is his criticism of Einstein in *The Principle of Relativity*), but there is a passage in Aldous Huxley's *Doors of Perception* that seems to present a similar idea:

'Reflecting on my experience, I find myself agreeing with the eminent Cambridge philosopher, Dr C. D. Broad, "that we should do well to consider much more seriously ... the type of theory which Bergson put forward in connection with memory and sense perception. The suggestion is that the function of the brain and nervous system and sense organs is in the main *eliminative* and not productive. Each person is at each moment capable of remembering all that has ever happened to him and of perceiving everything that is happening everywhere in the universe. The function of the brain and nervous system is to protect us from being overwhelmed and confused by this mass of largely useless and irrelevant knowledge, by shutting out most of what we should otherwise perceive or remember at any moment, and leaving only that very small and special selection which is likely to be practically useful.' According to such a theory, each one of us is potentially Mind at Large. But in so far as we are animals, our business is at all costs to survive. To make biological survival possible, mind at large has to be funnelled through the reducing valve of the brain and nervous system. What comes out at the other end is a measly trickle of the kind of consciousness which will help us to stay alive on the surface of this particular planet. To formulate and express the contents of this reduced awareness, man has invented ... languages.'

* See my *Religion and the Rebel*, Part 2, Chapter 9.

In this last sentence, it will be seen how close Huxley comes to the Whitehead of *Symbolism, Its Meaning and Effect*.

Now it is difficult to see how anyone could suggest seriously that man is at any moment potentially capable of perceiving everything that is happening in the universe unless, as Huxley says, man is somehow considered as a fragment of 'Mind at Large' – that is to say, unless we advance a new theory of perception in which each individual is somehow a member of the universe in the way that my fingers and toes are members of my body, and therefore a part of its nervous system. And this is exactly what Whitehead *does* suggest in the philosophy of organism: that in some ultimate sense, man and nature are part of the same organism. It is true that this statement has a disturbing resemblance to the Hegelian form of monism that excited such a strong reaction from Kierkegaard. But its idealistic aspect can, for the moment, be ignored. *All that is really being asserted is that man is in a fundamental sense a dual being, a cogito that functions on immediacy perception and inference, and a deeper self that functions on meaning-perception and a purposive evolutionary consciousness.* A practical example might make this clearer. In his various books on tiger shooting in India, Jim Corbett frequently mentions that he developed a kind of sixth sense that warned him when the tiger was lying in wait for him; on one occasion, he even makes a sketch of his route along a road and across a bridge, showing how he quite unconsciously walked over to the other side of the road before crossing the bridge, and returned to the other side on crossing it; he later discovered that the tiger he was hunting was waiting for him under the bridge, on the side that he had avoided. The usual explanation for this kind of intuition would be that it was 'subconscious observation'. Now according to Whitehead, it would mean simply that he was exercising his faculty of 'causal efficacy'; Corbett was in good health and was 'in tune' with his surroundings; he was a part of the organism that surrounded him.

One may, of course, reject Whitehead's philosophy of organism as 'too metaphysical', and involving too many consequences that are not susceptible of scientific verification. But it should be recognised that (*a*) the philosophy of organism is a logical consequence of the Whitehead-Husserl theory of perception, and that (*b*) gestalt psychology has provided a certain amount of scientific evidence for the Whitehead-Husserl theory. The mescalin experience provided still more evidence in its favour. Some of the implications of this theory could be summarised as follows:

The sense of 'oneness with the universe', although regarded by the mystics as the supreme goal, does not make for evolution. The oriental races have always been more deeply aware of the 'unity of the universe' than the west; but, as Whitehead points out, there is no evidence that China or India would ever have produced a grain of science. The enormous advances made by western civilisation in the past few centuries are due to western man's sense of isolation from the rest of the universe, his feeling of alienation – that is to say, to his faculty of immediacy-perception working in close harmony with conceptual analysis.

But this success has also brought its problems; western man now finds himself in the midst of a period of crisis. Auden expressed an important aspect of this crisis in the lines:

> Put the car away; when life fails
> What's the good of going to Wales?

The 'failure of life' is a consequence of the new emphasis on immediacy-perception; man is 'stuck in the present'; he loses the feeling of wider-implications; he has a sense of rootlessness, lack of purpose, insignificance. Science assures him that man is a biological accident on a fourth rate planet; history tells him that 'decadence' is inevitable, and that our civilisation cannot hope to escape the fate of a dozen others; literature tells him that neurosis is the lot of twentieth century man, and that defeat in some form or another is inescapable; psychology tells him that culture is only skin-deep, and that underneath this, the ape-man is waiting to escape. Philosophy is divided into two camps, one of which assures him that man's fate is inevitably tragic, the other of which declares that even to talk about man's fate is meaningless, since philosophy is mainly misunderstanding due to language.

All this is only to say that man is living in a poisoned cultural milieu. It would seem common sense to begin by attacking this aspect of the problem. I have tried to show that philosophy has failed because it has always carried within itself the seed of its own defeat – the Cartesian fallacy, the notion of man as a *passive* observer of the universe. This means that ordinary 'passive consciousness' is taken for granted, and that if a 'meaning' is to be sought, it must be sought 'out there'. It is true, to some extent, that the meaning is 'out there', as Huxley discovered under mescalin; but it cannot be observed by ordinary passive consciousness. To assume that everyday consciousness will be the permanent basis of man's relation to existence is as false as would be a child's assumption that the world will look the same to its adult eyes. *Consciousness is a variable.* To some extent, man is aware of this. The East has always known how to vary it by means of breathing exercises and concentration. The methods used by western man are in keeping with his notion of himself as a passive being; he has developed many forms of relaxation in which he makes the minimum of effort, from the colour television to alcohol and drugs. But if western man can lose this notion of himself as a passive being, there is no reason why he should not learn control of his own consciousness until he is able to reproduce the mescalin experience at will. The basis of the method has been established by Husserl, phenomenological analysis of consciousness, whose first aim is to 'break up' the natural standpoint in the way that a prism breaks up a beam of light. The workings of intentionality can eventually be observed as clearly as in the experiment of rubbing one's eyelids and making the 'spots' change shape. The notion of the passivity – and therefore the unchangeableness – of human consciousness is largely the outcome of habit; in the same way, the schoolboy cannot really believe that he will one day be an adult.

The problem of the 'failure of life' is the problem of the 'St Neot margin', the old woman in the vinegar bottle. The old woman is at the mercy of the poor quality of her consciousness, so that even a palace cannot maintain her sense of adventure in life. She is a symbol of western man, blinkered like a horse by evolution, unaware that perception can be more than peering through a slit. But the 'blinkering of consciousness' has served its purpose; it has brought man into the daylight of the scientific method, and placed in his hands an unprecedented degree of control over his environment. The next task is to use the scientific method to achieve the same degree of control over his consciousness; without such control, man can never realise his destiny as 'the managing director of the business of evolution'.

But the first step in the process does not involve an acceptance of 'transhumanism', or even of the idea of evolution. It involves merely the investigation of the intentional structure of consciousness. This first step implies a rejection of the Cartesian idea of passive consciousness, from which all else follows. The next step is the investigation of the intentional structure of *all* forms of consciousness – as Whitehead says, 'experience drunk and experience sober, experience sleeping and experience waking, experience drowsy and experience wide awake, experience self-conscious and experience self-forgetful, experience intellectual and experience physical, experience religious and experience sceptical, experience anxious and experience carefree ... experience normal and experience abnormal'.

And yet it would not be true to say that the purpose of phenomenology is to 'remove the blinkers'. Presentational immediacy is as necessary as 'meaning perception'. A painter may work close to the canvas or stand back from it as he feels inclined. The important thing is that he has the choice. At the moment, western man does not have the choice of standing back – or rather, does not realise that he has the choice.

Most fundamental of all is the need to study the problem of life-failure and the 'St Neot margin' by the use of the descriptive method. For twentieth century man, this problem presents itself in a new form – as Wells noted in his autobiography. The 'intellectual worker' dislikes the minor problems of everyday life; he wants to be free to devote himself completely to thinking. Yet although he is quite clear about his impatient rejection of most of the things that *were* life to his ancestors, he is not equally sure of himself when it comes to replacing them. A man such as Wells might rage and storm against the time-wasting aspects of running a home and keeping the bills paid; and yet left completely to his 'originative intellectual work' he finds his vitality running low; it would not be true to say that boredom creeps in; but the appetite for life ebbs lower. Wells explains this by saying that men are still half-fish and half-mammal; but this seems to imply that he may have to wait another million years before he is wholly at home in his new element. In fact, this is the very point where phenomenological discipline could bring about the desired evolution. The problem is analogous to the medical problem of transplanting bodily organs – replacing diseased kidneys, etc. The body has a system of defence which causes it to reject alien matter – germs, etc – and this defence system has to be put temporarily out of action before a new kidney is put in place of the old one – otherwise the patient dies. In the same way, man's consciousness is focused in a narrow beam on the present, and the life-energies respond to the challenges of the present. When the consciousness is disconnected from the present and turns inward, the energies sink; the world of concepts cannot provide the same stimulus as the world of present reality. (This, of course, accounts for the high mortality rate among the nineteenth century romantics.) Heidegger's answer to the problem is the contemplation of death; but I have already pointed out that this is a half-measure. Man must learn to disconnect his consciousness – and therefore his life energies – from presentational immediacy, and discover how to expand or narrow the beam of consciousness at will. The problem is that the intellectual – or imaginative – stimulus is usually so much weaker than the stimulus of 'hard fact'. And yet there are certain departments in which the vital energies respond to imagination almost as readily as to reality – sex, for example. There is no reason why they should not be disciplined to respond to urgency of concepts in the same way. And here again, we face the problem of 'nihilism'. If the world is regarded as meaningless, then imagination is only a form of escape, and ideas can only be 'speculations', devoid of urgency. If the idea that man is 'condemned to meaning' is accepted, then ideas become ploughshares, cutting into the soil of the mind, attempting to establish man's direct relation to evolution as a living reality instead of an abstraction.

Without powerful intellectual preoccupations – that is, without ideals – man is the victim of triviality and the 'St Neot margin'. In the past, religion played this role (and it is no accident that the sufferings of the crucifixion occupied a central place in Christianity –

providing, as it were, a standard against which to judge the petty irritations of everyday life). But most of the great religions have been as 'Cartesian' as science; that is, man is envisaged as a simple consciousness confronting the world and God, fundamentally passive. Science destroyed the notion that there is any point in searching for meaning 'out there', and left man in an apparently meaningless universe, with no fundamental value to redeem him from the banality of everyday life. And yet science and philosophy have gradually replaced what they destroyed, since science has demonstrated the reality of evolution, and phenomenological philosophy has shown that man is not the passive consciousness he assumed himself to be. In fact, although it is not yet fully realised – except by a few men such as Sir Julian Huxley – science has replaced religion with a set of ideals and values that are as profound as those of the old 'Cartesian' religion, and assign man an altogether more responsible role than has been granted to him by any religion – with the possible exception of Hinduism.

It may be objected that man has known about evolution for a long time now, and there is no sign that the idea of evolution can replace the values of Christianity. This is because evolution seems to be an impersonal idea. According to Christianity, every sinner matters to God as much as if he were the only one. Evolution acknowledges that the part played by the individual is unimportant – each one is a single grain of sand on a beach.

But this is not quite the whole truth. Religion has so far been irreplaceable because it enables the individual to participate in a uniquely satisfying way in the sense of a meaningful scheme of things. Science can offer no equivalent to prayer and worship. Science has always objected to 'particularising' the individual; it deals with generalities. When a poet – like Yeats – wishes to believe in individual destinies, he has to first of all state his fundamental opposition to all science. (When Yeats was young, his bugbears were Tyndall and T. H. Huxley.) In so doing, he placed his intuitions outside the serious consideration of science. But this 'bifurcation of nature' (into 'scientific truth' and 'artistic truth') was exactly what Whitehead spent his life opposing; his philosophy of organism was an attempt to create a continuum where the opposition would vanish. And if Whitehead's organism and Husseıl's phenomenology are to form the basis of a 'new existentialism', this problem must be faced. Art and religion are concerned with the individual. Philosophy and science are concerned with generalities. So the very idea of an 'existential philosophy' seems to be a contradiction.

There is only one way to escape this contradiction: to make the idea of evolution the basis of existentialism, to recognise, as Sir Julian Huxley says, that man is on the brink of an evolutionary change that could make him a *direct and conscious agent* of evolution instead of a grain of sand, a mere part of an immense process. It is impossible to recognise the full implications of this notion. Western man has become so accustomed to the idea of his passivity and insignificance that it is difficult to imagine what sort of creature he would be if phenomenology could uncover his intentional evolutionary structure and make it a part of his consciousness. Religion redeemed man from his sense of insignificance, but at the cost of making him a mere sleeping partner in the universal scheme, an atom whose only business was obedience to God. Newton and the romantics between them destroyed forever the idea of man as a creature; but unfortunately, science could see no way of conceding man the kind of importance he had been allowed by religion. In a way, Dostoevsky's *Grand Inquisitor* might be interpreted as an attack on religion from the point of view of science, for the Grand Inquisitor argues that men do not want the heavy responsibility of fighting for their own salvation – and therefore being, in a sense, co-partners in the universal scheme – and that the Church will keep man in his old position as the 'obedient atom', the sleeping partner. And as an existentialist (which he is generally conceded to be) Dostoevsky argues in favour of responsibility for individuals, and the rejection of the Grand Inquisitor's offer. One problem worried Dostoevsky, and apparently struck him as insoluble. The Grand Inquisitor is quite obviously right; the majority of people do not want the responsibility of their own salvation. Where, then, is the place for them in a religion that declares 'Truth is subjectivity'? Is not one forced to agree with the Grand Inquisitor that men must not be robbed of the religious illusion – and perhaps even with Peter Verkhovenskt in *The Devils* that the only really satisfactory society would be a society of mediocrities, in which men of genius were destroyed as soon as they showed the first sign of individuality?

But Dostoevsky was arguing on a naïve all-or-nothing basis, unaware that the theory of the dominant minority is sound biology, and not a disguised form of fascism. The proportion of the human race capable of grasping the principle of 'individual salvation' could hardly be more than five per cent. Whitehead writes: 'Religion is what a man does with his solitude.' In that sense of the word, the human race has never possessed more than five per cent of religious – or potentially religious – individuals.

What seems probable is that if the human race ever develops its five per cent of human beings who are capable of an intuitive grasp of evolutionary intentionality, and a certain control of the 'St Neot margin' by means of phenomenological disciplines, these beings will not experience the need for 'subjective religion' in Kierkegaard's sense, since the need will already have been fulfilled on another level. Many of the personal aspects of religion – prayer to a 'personal God' ritual, collective worship – are a means of combating the 'St Neot margin', restoring the equilibrium of a being that has been attacked by the sense of insignificance (although this is not to argue that this is their only value). Phenomenology is the systematic study of the 'St Neot margin', so that this particular need of religion will be fulfilled in another way.

Let me try to be explicit about the basis of this 'new existentialism'. Sartre summarised the objection to religious values in one word: contingency, and embodied his objection in a book *Nausea*. H. G. Wells expressed it in *Mind at the End of Its Tether* as follows: 'He (the writer) has come to believe that the congruence with mind, which man has attributed to the secular process, is not there at all. The secular process (i.e., the workings of nature) ... is entirely at one with such non-mental rhythms as ... the flight of a shower of meteors. The two processes (mind and nature) have run parallel for what we call Eternity, and now abruptly they swing off at a tangent from one another ... Man's mind accepted the secular process as rational ... (only) because he was involved as part and parcel of it.' This problem forms the basis of the 'nihilism' investigated in *The Outsider* and subsequent books. Now what is proposed is that mind and nature are not as separate as Wells assumed. Man is not as 'contingent' and accidental as he looks. He has arrived at this conclusion because of an evolutionary peculiarity of western man: the prominence of his faculty of 'immediacy-perception', and the consequent weakening of his faculty of meaning-perception. This lop-sidedness of western man has made him, up till now, a highly successful evolutionary experiment; but a time has come when it must be consciously recognised and compensated. Otherwise there can be no 'next step' in evolution.

Biology and zoology have now recognised that evolution is not a mechanical process, like the running down of a clock, but seems to contradict the physical law of running-down. It was Husserl who, without fully intending it, gave this force a philosophical status by recognising that philosophy is mistaken to think of man in terms of a contingent consciousness, and by demonstrating that man's 'intentional consciousness' can be a subject of scientific investigation. Man believes he is separate; but he is connected with the 'organism' in ways that are hidden from the observation of the natural standpoint. Wells was mistaken; the two processes are not alien to one another; their fundamental law is the same: complexification. Writing of mescalin, Huxley said: 'Like the earth of a hundred years ago, our mind still has its darkest Africas, its unmapped Borneos and Amazonian basins. In relation to the fauna of those regions, we are not yet zoologists, we are mere naturalists and collectors of specimens'. (Thereby denying, of course, Sartre's notion that consciousness=intentionality=man). Phenomenology is an attempt to raise man's status from that of the collector to that of the zoologist and cartographer of the 'mind's antipodes'. If, as seems probable, the structure of intentionality proves to be evolutionary (i.e., the 'intention' is complexification, not, as Sartre seems to assume, the static preservation of illusions that make life bearable), then it can be stated flatly that contingency is an illusion. The old objection to evolutionism – in its Shavian or Bergsonian form – was that compared to religion it is an abstraction. A convinced reader might lay down *Evolution Créatrice* or *Man and Superman,* and sigh: 'But what am I supposed *to do*?' An existentialism based upon Whitehead and Husserl is able to answer this question. The basis of the phenomenological method has been laid down by Husserl, whose role in this respect might be compared to that of Newton in science. The line of development is clear. Phenomenology – the descriptive analysis of intentional structures – must proceed until it becomes the descriptive analysis of evolutionary intentionality. This would be a fundamental step in the process that Nietzsche called 'the revaluation of values' – the changing of the direction of our pessimistically-oriented culture by reversing its fundamental premises. This is basically what is hinted at in the opening pages of Wells' *Experiment in Autobiography*. So far, human beings, like animals, have relied on the challenge of circumstances to maintain their vital intensity. And, as Toynbee points out, when the challenge vanishes the civilisation declines; human beings are incapable of maintaining their intensity without external challenges. And yet it is these challenges that prevent 'the outsider' from being able to concentrate on inner-development; this is Wells' complaint. What Wells is saying is that, whether we like it or not, we are producing a new type of human being who finds himself stifled by the irrelevancy of everyday necessities – and yet who is not strong enough to do without their stimulus. (*The Outsider* and *Religion and the Rebel* attempted to point out that such a being is by no means a new evolutionary type; nevertheless, it does seem to be true that our civilisation is producing them in larger quantities than ever before.) Hence 'the outsider' finds himself in a curiously painful position, with which his basic human instincts are unable to cope. He is self-divided because a part of him rejects the irrelevancy of everyday necessity, and the other half is honest enough to recognise that 'the world of the mind' is not a real alternative, since it requires a self-discipline beyond anything that human beings at the moment possess. What is needed, then, is that human beings should turn their power of analysis squarely upon this problem of the 'St Neot margin', and recognise that it is as urgent as the problem of the hydrogen bomb. (They are fundamentally identical; the problem of war *is* the problem of the St Neot margin.) Man's tendency to boredom is a part of the 'natural standpoint', that is to say, it is taken for granted because it has become a habit. But it is not necessary that the 'pressure in the mind' should be dependent on outward circumstances ('When his café empties, his head empties too'). This is an unnecessary habit, like a tail or an appendix. What is more, it is a dangerous habit. Whether we like it or not, the next stage of evolution has been entered upon; Newton launched it, and the romantics gave it reality. The romantics found the challenge too much; but it remains, all the same. A new kind of mental strength is required, and a new sense of purpose.

The next question, then, is that of the means to this end. A number of solutions have been offered during the past forty years. Shaw was one of the first to state clearly that civilisation cannot exist without a religion, and he went on to suggest that the main features of the world's 'greatest religions' should be combined – particularly their mythologies. In the final volume of *The Study of History,* Arnold Toynbee offered a similar suggestion. But it requires very little consideration to recognise that a consciously constructed 'ersatz' religion would not answer the need, even if individual religions could be persuaded to 'amalgamate'. Religions are formed from within by a vital impulse, not constructed. Aldous Huxley is closer to the reality of the situation in suggesting that mescalin should be made as generally available as alcohol or tobacco – at least he recognises that the problem is to produce a change in western man's mode of consciousness, to develop the perception of causal efficacy. Huxley admitted there were objections: mescalin takes longer to act than alcohol, and the effects last longer. The effects are also unpredictable: it may produce mystical ecstasy or paranoia. But he apparently overlooked the real objection: the mescalin taker remains 'passive'; it teaches him nothing – certainly not how to reproduce the experience at will. The real problem, the 'St Neot margin', remains untouched.

Ultimately, it must be recognised that if the problem is of a change in the mode of consciousness, then it can only be approached through the analytical study of consciousness, that is to say, through phenomenology, the descriptive analysis of subjective states.

In the preface to the present volume, I stated that the impetus behind the six books of the 'outsider cycle' was a feeling of frustration: that what was needed was *foundation work*. These six books constitute a re-examination of the foundations of modern philosophy, and an attempt to provide a basis for future development. With the present volume, the 'foundation work' is complete; the direction for development is clear.

It will also be seen why I have chosen to speak of these books as the 'outsider cycle', although the word was used extensively only in the first two volumes. After the publication of *The Outsider*, critics objected that the term was too loose, that almost anyone can be described as an outsider; in short, that it is a matter of degree, not of kind. To some extent, this is true. The kind of distinction between 'outsider' and 'insider' that I had in mind is illustrated by an anecdote of Tolstoy, who saw a brother officer striking a soldier, and asked him indignantly if he had never read the Gospels. The officer retorted: 'Haven't you read the army regulations?' Here the difference is clear: there are two sets of standards due to two ways of seeing the world. But the weakness of this kind of ostensive definition is that people are not usually as sharply defined as this; most of them can sympathise with both points of view.

From the present volume, it will be seen that the 'outsider' remains a fundamental concept, in spite of this objection. As a social type, the 'outsider' may be vague; as a description of a state of consciousness definable by phenomenology, it is precise.

It is described by Wells in the opening pages of his autobiography, and it is, in the sense already explained, a new evolutionary type, confronted by a new problem. This problem defeated most of the 'outsiders' of the nineteenth century, and, if we are to judge by *Nausea* and *Mind at the End of Its Tether*, is still unsolved. I have suggested that this defeat has two causes: first, that most of the nineteenth-century 'outsiders' were unable to bring the problem fully to consciousness; second, that existentialism, that has explored the problem more analytically, has been bogged down in its own false premises. The books of the 'outsider cycle' have been an attempt to examine these premises, and to suggest how they might be revised so that existentialism will no longer be involved in a self-contradictory nihilism.

What has been suggested is that the answer is to be sought in the idea of evolution, as described by Shaw, Wells or Sir Julian Huxley. The objection is that evolution is too impersonal to replace religion, that it can never satisfy the personal need in the same way as Christianity, for example. But is this entirely true? What man has lost in religion is something that, by the nature of his evolution, he was bound to lose anyway, the sense of being a mere creature whose only business is passive obedience to a master. If this was the price that man paid for his sense of 'belonging' in the world, then it was too high. With the collapse of the old religious dogmas, man has gained a kind of freedom; he has become more adult than his forefathers. It is objected that he has lost the feeling of individual purpose, of being part of a meaningful scheme – in short, the feeling of having a kind of direct telephone line to God in prayer and worship. This, say the objectors, is the thing that science can never replace.

Yet what if science *could* replace that sense of individual meaning, the feeling of having a direct telephone line to the universal purpose? For this is precisely the aim of evolutionary phenomenology: to change man's conception of himself and of the *interior forces* he has at his command, and ultimately to establish the new evolutionary type, foreshadowed by the 'outsiders'. The new element to which these 'amphibians' must learn to adapt themselves is the world of the mind and of ideas – what Teilhard de Chardin calls the 'noösphere'. This can only be achieved by means of the techniques of phenomenology. Kierkegaard recognised the basic direction of this evolution when he wrote 'Truth is subjectivity', but the full meaning of this statement only appears when it is viewed in the light of phenomenology. For the romantics, it only meant that truth is relative – is in the 'eye of the beholder'. For the phenomenologist, it means that truth is, in a paradoxical sense, both subjective and objective. It is 'within', and yet it is not relative; it must be sought by means of science like any law of nature. The law of man's evolutionary being must be uncovered and brought to consciousness by the same methods that uncovered the laws of the planets. What distinguishes religion from speculative thought is that it is 'lived by'; when the laws of evolutionary intentionality have been uncovered and brought to consciousness, they will also be 'lived by', continually present to introspection. Descartes was wrong in believing that man's only certain knowledge is: 'I think, therefore I am.' All feeling, as Whitehead pointed out, is absolute knowledge. Husserl's method of exploring 'subjective processes' is therefore the only philosophical method that can claim certainty, the only possible direction of development for a philosophy that can claim to be scientific. If we can also feel the same certainty about evolution – as a process of complexification – then post-Sartre existentialism has an unshakeable foundation.

Howard Fast has an interesting story called *The First Men*, in which he points out that, in the few known cases where a human child has been stolen by apes or wolves and brought up among them, the intelligence of the child has been permanently impaired.* The conclusion he draws is of peculiar interest: if, among human beings, there were a small number who carried the evolutionary germ of a higher type of man, we might also expect this germ to be stifled within the child's first ten years of life. In Mr Fast's story, a number of investigators select a dozen or so of these potential 'men-plus' (by investigating the intelligence quotients of very young children) and bring them up in isolation; the result, as they expect, is the production of a higher evolutionary type.

I mention Mr Fast's story because he summarises an idea that has been 'floating free' in the cultural atmosphere for a long time. (For example, Wells deals with it in a novel called *Star Begotten*. It was also the basis of my own *Outsider*.) It is impossible to doubt that man stands at the beginning of a new phase in his development,

* Mr Fast tells me that his story was based upon actual cases.

and that the germs of this development have been present for at least a hundred and fifty years. But the title of Mr Fast's story shows that he has grasped the most important implication of this idea. When one considers man as he has existed for the past five thousand years – that is, from the dawn of his cultural history – it seems clear that we cannot say that he has yet completed the transformation from animal to 'spiritual' being. Admittedly, when we consider what man has achieved through language, imagination and his social sense, the difference between man and ape is seen to be equivalent to the distance between man and god. The life of an animal is purposeless, tied to physical needs; in comparison, man is part of a great organism of purpose. And yet real purpose is precisely what man lacks. There is a sense of 'something missing'. The Christian religion has always ascribed this imperfection to original sin. But when we consider what is meant by 'original sin', we see that it is nothing else than the problem of the 'St Neot margin'. Man dreams of autonomy, of free will; yet his internal resources are too feeble. We have to describe this curious imperfection in similes. The story of the old woman in the vinegar bottle makes us think of the human situation in terms of a man climbing a glacier, who keeps slipping back to his starting point. This means that, in spite of all he has achieved by way of civilisation, man still lacks a certain fundamental quality that would distinguish him clearly from the ape. In *Heart of Darkness*, Conrad shows how the lack of this quality can lead to a reversion to the animal level.

Professor Erwin Schrödinger, in an essay called *What is Life?*, has pointed out that the workings of living matter cannot be reduced to the ordinary laws of physics; there is, as it were, a radical break between a machine and a living organism. The living organism possesses various qualities that can be summarised in the word 'autonomy'. There is no gradual shading of machine into animal; there is an absolute break. And yet in another sense, the animal is still largely a machine; its purposes can all be defined in terms of simple physical needs. Between the ape and man, there would seem to be another 'absolute break', although, again, ape and man have much in common. Yet in man, the word 'autonomy' has quite a different sense. The machine is dependent entirely on its operator; the animal is dependent on the stimuli of its environment; man inhabits yet another world, the noösphere, the world of mind.

When we have said this, we realise that, in terms of these 'absolute breaks', the transition from ape to man is still incomplete. Man cannot yet be said to 'inhabit the world of mind'. He has learned to swim in the new element, but he is not yet at home in it. (This, or course, is to reverse Wells's simile of the amphibian.) He objects to his old element, and yet has not the strength to make a complete transfer to the new one. He is not yet a 'spiritual being', for spiritual, in its ultimate sense, means capable of exercising freedom, and freedom is meaningless without ultimate purpose. For thousands of years, religion has supplied this spiritual need for purpose; yet this was not true purpose, for it depended on illusions – upon man's picture of himself as a passive creature. Religious man was also incomplete; he was walking on crutches. The crutches have now been taken away. It is impossible to evade the implication. The one thing that is required to complete the transition from ape to man is the birth of a new kind of purpose *inside* man. Sir Julian Huxley is right in calling this sense of evolutionary purpose a 'new religion'. He writes: 'Finally, the evolutionary vision is enabling us to discern, however incompletely, the lineaments of the new religion that we can be sure will arise to serve the needs of the coming era. Just as stomachs are bodily organs concerned with digestion, and involving the biochemical activity of special juices, so are religions psychosocial organs concerned with the problems of human destiny, and involving the emotion of sacredness and the sense of right and wrong.'*

All this can be summarised in a single statement: there is no point in talking about the superman, because *man does not yet exist*. Sir Julian Huxley has declared that he considers that animal evolution and human evolution are separated by a 'critical point', after which the nature of the material undergoes radical changes (presumably in the way that the nature of the 'biological material' differs from inorganic matter). The next important

* Man Without God; *The Observer Weekend Review*, September 3, 1961.

recognition is that even beyond this critical point, the change is not yet complete. One might say loosely that biological matter differs from inorganic matter in that it has a dimension of freedom – that is to say, as a plane differs from a straight line. We should be able to say that the human material differs from biological material as a cube differs from a plane – in having yet another dimension of freedom. And yet we cannot yet say this, for much of the human material still belongs to the animal sphere of Sartre's café proprietor. There *does* exist human material in which the change has started to take place; but it is not yet completed. Fast calls such material 'man-plus' (or perhaps 'potential man-plus'); in *Star Begotten*, Wells speaks of 'Martians'; in the first two volumes of the present cycle, I preferred the term 'outsider'.

Let us cast a summarising glance back over the whole problem, and try to reduce it to its simplest terms.

Idealism – belief in man's future – is fundamentally a belief that thought can make man the master of life. But the romantics soon became disenchanted with this idea when they discovered that a clever man is not necessarily a free man – that man seems to be held by invisible nets. Hence the despair of Faust, Schiller's Karl Moor, etc.

Now for modern man, the deepest of his psychological problems is his feeling of unimportance, of being accidental – contingent. Western man suffers particularly from this sense of contingency because of the strength of his faculty of 'immediacy-perception', which keeps him firmly jammed in the present, and will allow him very little access to his own past, or to the sense of meaning. (This applies far less to Eastern races, and – apparently – to Celts.)

Science, which owes its development to this peculiarity of the western mind, is an attempt to see the world in terms of immediacy, *and to reduce meaning to immediacy*. (If the mind can grasp meanings intuitively, it can see no need for science.)

Science is, so to speak, a blind man's method of describing the world. Compared to the east, western man is blind-blinkered by immediacy-perception. And yet this blindness has given the west a certain superiority over the east, for it has led western man to develop a system of labelling his ideas and perceptions (which might be compared to a kind of Braille).

In the days when Christianity was the universal religion in the west, this lack of meaning-perception did not matter greatly; Christianity offered meaning. But when science undermined Christianity, western man found himself in his present uncomfortable position – without a religion, and without an intuitive sense of meaning. His temperament now confirmed the conclusions reached by his science: that man is an accident in a purposeless universe.

There are various ways in which a man can intensify his sense of meaning – of causal efficacy. The simplest is through work, since work involves a practical succession of cause and effect. The same is true of games. Listening to (or reading) stories is almost as universal, since a story compresses many events into a brief space of time, and again produces a sense of meaningful cause and effect. Other arts seem to evoke meaning in a more sophisticated way – music for example – but the basic principle is the same. Then there are more direct physical means – alcohol and drugs. These have the effect of temporarily intensifying the vitality, fortifying consciousness against the pressure of the world. The same is true of sexual excitement. For Proust, a piece of cake dipped in tea made him cease to feel 'mediocre, accidental and mortal'. Finally, there are the so-called 'mystical experiences', which may be due to many causes, but which seem invariably to produce this sense of universal meaning. I say 'so-called mystical experiences' because they are not really of a different order from the experiences mentioned above. The main difference is that they are usually more intense, and so their meaning is more difficult to describe. But William James agreed that alcohol produces the mystical experience to some extent; drugs like mescalin certainly do.

In all these 'meaning experiences', meaning is experienced as being *out there*, in the world; nausea, the sense of futility is recognised to be an illusion, or rather an error due to our 'worm's-eye' perspective on the universe. Western man's problem is that his meaning experiences are too brief and too difficult to hold on to.

For western man, then, the central problem is not any abstract question of the scope and limits of philosophy or the decay of religion: it is the problem of contingency. What he lacks is certainty, confidence, sense of purpose. But even if he has no intuition of meaning – because of his overdeveloped faculty of immediacy-perception – he has the power to grasp meanings intellectually – which is eventually preferable to the purely intuitive approach, since meanings grasped by intuition are too easily lost. If he had more access to his own past, to memory, his sense of purpose would be immensely augmented. Hesse's Steppenwolf expressed this sense of meaning due to re-possession of the past:

> For moments together my heart stood still between delight and sorrow to find how rich was the gallery of my life, and how thronged the soul of the wretched Steppenwolf with high eternal stars and constellations ... The kernel of this life of mine was noble. It came of high descent and turned, not on trifles, but on the stars ...

Proust's *Recherche* is also a determined attempt to gain access to the past. We may feel that Proust's past was hardly worth all that trouble, and that his self-pity invalidated most of what he had to say; but the book remains a monument of evolutionary humanism because Proust clearly recognised that man *must* have such access to his past if he is to become truly human. If Proust's attempt had been successful, and he had demonstrated that man can regain his past by a long intellectual discipline, the major problem of modern man would be solved. He would have achieved sense of purpose without sacrificing the increased immediacy-perception that is western man's chief distinction.

It has been argued that Proust's aim could have been more effectively achieved by drugs (LSD or lysergic acid, for example) but this point has already been dealt with; drugs operate at the expense of immediacy-perception. Nevertheless, the use of drugs in controlled experiments could furnish valuable data; after Aldous Huxley's *Doors of Perception*, this is impossible to doubt. This road is by no means a blind alley.

Now it must be admitted that evolutionary humanism cannot provide the sense of contingency, of purpose, that was once provided by Christianity, since it will not allow man the comfort of thinking of himself as a creature who can be justified through faith. It demands a sense of autonomy and purpose, which can only be achieved through certain disciplines. But here the chief barrier is of language. Science is nothing less than this ability to fix meanings in words and symbols, so that the symbols can be made to do the work. Unfortunately, we have only the most rudimentary symbols for describing our psychological states, so that the efforts of a Proust or a Steppenwolf are doomed in advance. Language can only be developed through the expansion of a fixed co-ordinate system of general ideas. (I shall speak further of this in the final chapter.) In the meantime, evolutionary humanism provides the basic outline of a creed whose evolution (and complexification) is bound up with the use of the phenomenological method.

What is most important for man in the twentieth century is that his creed should recognise the possibility of evolution. So far, phenomenology has been made the instrument of the anti-evolutionary philosophy of Sartre and Heidegger. In such works as *The Undying Fire, The Croquet Player* and *Experiment in Autobiography*, Wells revealed that he was as profoundly concerned with an *existenz-philosophie* as Sartre, but compared to the author of *L'Imaginaire* and *L'Etre ét le Néant*, he seemed hopelessly unmethodical. It has been my purpose to show that, unmethodical or not, Wells's fundamental intuitions were sounder than Sartre's, and that they provide a basis for an existentialism that can transcend self-contradictions. Such an existentialism could fulfil Husserl's prediction that phenomenology would become the basis of a universal science.

A NOTE ON THE PROBLEM OF HUMAN SEXUALITY

The evolutionist picture of the universe of Huxley and Teilhard de Chardin has some interesting implications for sexual psychology. The animal has no power to transcend its environment and view it objectively; the human level is clearly distinguished from the animal level by its use of language and of imagination.

One of the most difficult problems for all writers on the psychology of sex has been how to define 'normality'. All sexual 'perversion' seems to be the result of the misuse of imagination, the clash between imagination and reality. No such problem arises where animals are concerned, since the female goes periodically on heat, and the male's desire is stimulated by the smell of oestrum.* With human beings, sex is largely 'mental'. Tolstoy tried to solve the difficulty by suggesting that all sex which is not directed at propagation of the species should be regarded as perversion. Gide went to the opposite extreme and suggested that there is no such thing as perversion.

But the truly human is distinguished from the animal by its use of imagination. Now the 'truly human' at present barely exists; man is still an amphibian, half-human, half-animal. He is not yet equipped for long excursions into the noösphere; fairly short journeys into the realm of intellect or imagination exhaust him, and make him glad to get back to the 'reality' of the biological sphere. Predictably enough, the level on which human imagination feels most at home is the sexual. It takes a man of the genius of Shelley or Blake to imagine social or human ideals with such intensity that his whole being hungers for their fulfilment; but a man of far less vitality can project sexual ideals with an intensity that sharpens his appetites. So we discover that an enormous number of sexual criminals are badly adjusted but intelligent neurotics.

What must be recognised is that imagination is man's organ of self-change. It is therefore a mistake for the writer on sexual psychology to keep at the back of his mind some animal ideal of normality – the notion of sex tied to propagation. The animal is oriented to present biological needs; man is somehow oriented to the future. The animal's fulfilment can be defined in terms of the relation between its 'present being' and the objects required to satisfy its needs; man's fulfilment has to be defined not only

* This, of course, is a convenient oversimplification. Many animals masturbate; and, according to Sir Julian Huxley, even elephants may make 'improper advances' to other males.

in terms of satisfaction of needs, but of a future being. The attainment of this future being is also one of man's present needs, so that the problem of fulfilment becomes, so to speak, a problem in two variables. Sexual normality in man must be involved with his future being, and therefore with his imagination. The psychology of sex *must* therefore be discussed in evolutionary terms.

Chapter 7

NEW DIRECTIONS

The existentialism of Sartre, Camus and Heidegger found itself unable to proceed further because of the nature of its premises. The stoical pessimism of *Sein und Zeit, Altona* or *La Chute* seems to indicate a limit, a closing period. In the present book, I have attempted to establish a new set of foundations for existentialism In this aim I have, I believe, been successful. What Husserl called the 'transcendental ego' is the drive to complexification. Evolution is the 'hidden achievement of the transcendental ego'. But the problem of proceeding beyond this point still remains – even though this problem is, by nature, completely different from the one we have been considering. In this final chapter I shall attempt to offer some indications – necessarily perfunctory – of the way in which a strictly phenomenological existentialism might develop.

I have already said that the fundamental objection to 'evolutionism' as a religion is that it is incapable of 'speaking to the condition' of the ordinary human being. A man who contemplated suicide would hardly be dissuaded by Teilhard's *Phenomenon of Man* or Huxley's *New Bottles for New Wine*. The idea of evolution is too impersonal; it lacks the power of any of the great religions to 'speak directly'.

It might seem that religion and evolution are opposed in a way so fundamental that it is impossible that they should be reconciled. Religion is based upon what Ardrey calls 'the fallacy of central position', the idea of the individual that he is somehow the centre of the universe, an immortal soul whose salvation or damnation are of importance to God himself. Evolution demolished this notion: man was not specially created; he is fundamentally an animal like other animals, even if of a higher type. This change of emphasis, it seems, constitutes the basic difference between religion and science.

And yet this is not entirely accurate. It is true that the primitive religions regarded man purely as a creature; yet the higher religions – like Hinduism and Christianity – already hold it as a basic tenet that 'the kingdom of God is within you'. This is immediately a shift of emphasis from 'God outside' to 'God inside'. Many nineteenth century scientists and thinkers held a view that might be called 'primitive evolutionism', in which man was a mere creature of evolution, a twig carried along in the great stream. The new evolutionism – as held by Shaw, Huxley, and Teilhard – recognises evolution as an *internal principle,* not a by-product of the running-down of nature. Now it might be said that all the disciplines prescribed by the saints and fathers of the church – mystical and otherwise – were means of bringing the 'God within' nearer to the surface, uncovering the 'atman', as it were, by a species of excavation. In fact, one has to read very little of Boehme, Eckhart, De Sales, Scupoli, to recognise that what these men are practising, within a framework of Christian dogmas, is a primitive phenomenology. This is particularly apparent in Boehme, where the outlandish terminology, much of it borrowed from alchemy, is obviously an attempt to create a language capable of dealing with the inner realities of which Boehme was constantly aware.* But in the poetry of T. S. Eliot we may find a recent example that is much more convincing. Eliot shows a constant awareness of the problem of the 'St Neot margin', particularly in the *Four Quartets* – the problem of the incompleteness of mind, the inadequacy of man's internal resources, unsupported by the comfort of everyday preoccupations. ('The Word in the desert / Is most attacked by voices of temptation.') The whole of phenomenology is expressed in the line 'And partial observation of one's own automatism' (*Family Reunion*, scene 1). (*Faber & Faber.*) Eliot's work provides an

* In *Religion and the Rebel*, p. 165, I offer an attempt to translate some of Boehme's theological language into the language of phenomenological psychology.

interesting proof of the fundamental similarity of aim of phenomenology and religious introspection.

By considering the writings of Boehme – or Eliot – it can be seen that to speak of phenomenology is to speak of the limitation of language in describing man's inner processes. Aldous Huxley underlines the nature of the problem in using a geographical metaphor to describe the mind; we have no adequate maps to describe this territory. Brentano observed: 'It is a sign of the immature state in which psychology finds itself that one can scarcely utter a single sentence about mental phenomena which would not be disputed by many.' This was written of pre-Freudian psychology; and yet, in many ways, Freud made the situation worse by shifting the emphasis from phenomenology to practical results, and allowing some of his personal prejudices to masquerade as theory. Psychology is still in an immature state, and the first necessity is the systematic creation of new concepts and language from descriptive analysis.

Consider the following questions:

(1) Define the difference between the taste of an orange and that of a tangerine.

(2) Define the degree of existence of (a) a gas mantle, (b) a limited company, (c) the address on an envelope, (d) Mahomet, (e) yourself, (f) Beethoven's Ninth Symphony.

(3) Explain precisely what happens when you prevent yourself from feeling sick by saying 'I do not feel sick'. How does it differ from the occasions when the formula fails to work?

These questions make us aware of the limitations of our language to explain (a) objective experience, (b) abstract notions, (c) subjective experience.

A positive existentialism should begin from an awareness of the limitations of our language. We are accustomed to think of ourselves as knowing too much, of having developed technical and scientific resources that are far in excess of our every day needs. It would be healthier to recognise that, as far as communication goes, we are as primitive as aborigines. Our language at present is little better than a primitive sign language.

A farmer could describe precisely how he would set about

developing a tract of rough land. Can the phenomenoloist describe how he proposes to develop language?

In the *Philosophical Investigations* (Part 1, para. 12) Wittgenstein makes a good beginning. If we look into the cabin of a locomotive, we see all kinds of handles; but they serve quite different functions, and operate in different ways. One is intended to be pulled, others to be pressed down, another to be wound in circles, another to be pumped back and forth. Wittgenstein goes on to say that when we say 'Every word in language signifies some thing', we have said *nothing whatever*. Words are of as many different types as the handles in the cabin of the locomotive; at present, we have no system of classifying them as a lepidopterist classifies butterflies.

Consider the first example I have given above. How would you describe the difference between the taste of an orange and that of a tangerine? One's first reaction is: 'Impossible.' But is it any more impossible than describing the difference between a Chinese and a Hottentot to a class of school children? It is necessary to rely on a certain *common ground* between the teacher and the children. No language is 'absolute'; it always depends on comparing something to something else.

The development of language parallels exactly the development of counting by ordinal numbers. Each unit is given a name; the seventh unit is called seven. To certain primitives, this system would seem as remote from everyday life as opening a bank account or taking out a life insurance policy. They feel that it involves as much unnecessary labour as a farmer who builds a series of vast barns in anticipation of a harvest that may never come.

And yet all thought has developed by this 'anticipatory labour' – analogous to taking out an insurance policy *to cover a thousand eventualities that may never occur*. If, for example, we wish to use language to describe the difference between an orange and a tangerine, it would be necessary for some scientist to work on a catalogue of smells, including every known smell and combination of smells, to understand the relations between smells in the way that we understand the relation between the colours of the spectrum and the vibration that produces them, and to give all these smells names, numbers or descriptions. (If it ever became necessary to the progress of science, such a 'system' could be developed in a year or less.) It would eventually become necessary for every schoolchild to learn this catalogue and associate each name with its smell in the way that he learns French or algebra. This would be 'extension of language'.

Wittgenstein draws attention to another of the inadequacies of language when he asks 'What is a game?' Wittgenstein answered that there is no simple definition of a game, for poker, football, patience, cowboys and Indians and the game a cat plays with a mouse have no common element; instead, Wittgenstein says, there is a 'network of relationships'. And yet it might be objected that this is one of the cases (there are many in *Philosophical Investigations*) where Wittgenstein's lack of phenomenological training produces difficulties that do not really exist. All games have one thing in common: their relationship to reality, which might be called a 'rehearsal relation'. But even this hint of a definition reveals the limitations of language. The reason that the word 'game' is so difficult to define is because it has no stable underpinning of accepted ideas. We can see that the Olympic Games of 1936 had a certain 'rehearsal' relation to the Nazi attempt at world domination, but what is meant here by the difference between 'sport' and 'reality'? Is it what is meant by the difference between dream and reality? Or phenomenon and reality (noumenon)? Plainly not; in each case, the word 'reality' has a different meaning.

Most of Wittgenstein's work after the *Tractatus Logico-Philosophicus* is concerned to make his readers aware of the nature of language, to destroy the 'natural standpoint' in which language is accepted as a comprehensive descriptive system of reality. Language is not one thing; it could better be described as a network of language games, having as little in common as the games mentioned above, but connected by a network of relationships.

It will at once be seen that Wittgenstein's aim and Husserl's were identical, although their methods of approach were different. Wittgenstein felt that most post-Cartesian philosophy is a muddle of misunderstandings due to inadequate definitions; his aim, he said, was to train his readers to see disguised nonsense as patent nonsense. Husserl's approach was constructive; Wittgenstein's tended to be destructive; nevertheless, both were concerned with foundation work, with the prolegomena to philosophy.

The method of extension suggested above might be called 'the frame method'. Imagine a large square frame, subdivided into hundreds of smaller squares. The scientist who was trying to expand our language of smells would take a frame, and set out all the known smells in each of the squares, giving each a name. As he discovered the secret of the inter-relationship between the smells – analogous to that between colours and atomic vibrations – the order of the smells within the frame would be altered. It would also become possible to postulate new smells, and to name them in advance, rather as the atomic chart enabled scientists to postulate elements and describe their properties before they were isolated in nature.* It is remotely possible, for example, that some such organisation of smell-words, colour words, etc., might one day reveal an interesting parallel between orange and tangerine, and the difference between, say, sea-green and grass-green.

The frame method, then, could be used for the extension of various departments of language; to begin with, the 'smell frame' would be mostly empty squares; the aim would be to fill it up, but the existence of the empty squares would be like an insurance policy, a calculation involving the future.

The third question – the description of subjective states – is a matter for phenomenological analysis. The data are 'internal'; therefore a 'frame' is of no immediate value; the relationship between the data will be dynamic rather than static, and determine its own frame. The problem here is analogous to the engineer's problem of resolving a complex force into its constituents – a kind of psychological vector analysis. We know, for example, that the kind of will that enables us to move the fingers if quite

* An interesting example of what I mean can be found in Thomas Mann's *novella, The Black Swan*. Out for an afternoon walk, two women smell an odour of musk. They discover that this comes from a small dead creature covered with blow-flies, mixed with rotting vegetation and excreta; the mixture of smells produces the smell of musk. James Joyce observes in *Ulysses* the urine smell of fried kidneys and the 'feety smell' of gorgonzola cheese; and yet no one doubts that we would be revolted by a piece of cheese that tasted of urine or a kidney that tasted of unwashed feet. What relationship of smells is implied here?

different from the kind that enables us to perform the operation of defecating, and that both these types of will are different from the kind that controls digestion. The will that enables us to make simple bodily movements could be called 'direct'; it is as simple in its action as turning a handle to open a door. The other kinds are more complex, involving relaxation as well as the act of volition. Sometimes, these more complex form of will seem to operate by the law of reversed effort; a man using all his will-power to stop himself stammering or blushing may find himself blushing harder than ever. A man trying to force himself to keep awake to read a dull book finds that it is a certain method of inducing sleep – although an interesting book will 'charm' him into wakefulness with only a fraction of the effort of will. It *is* possible to prevent oneself from being sick by an act of will; but it is a complex act, and so far we have no means of describing its constituents. There are even more complex reaches of the will mechanism; hysteria can produce curious psychosomatic effects; many people who are not necessarily saints can produce stigmata effects like those of St Francis; fakirs can drive nails through their hands without bleeding, and temporarily stop the movement of the heart. Even the simple act of trying to remember a name or a tune is beyond the present scope of pheonomenology; again, it seems to work, to some extent, by the law of reversed effort.

Expressed in this manner, it might seem that the task of descriptive analysis is hopeless; but this is only an appearance. Once the main lines are laid down, the analysis becomes simpler. It is necessary, for example, to bear in mind the distinction between inorganic material, biological material and human material. The statement that these can be compared respectively to a straight line, a plane and a cube indicates that the 'vector analysis' applies here. The peculiar attribute of human material is its third dimension of freedom – even though, as already observed, this dimension is 'incomplete'. This dimension complicates the whole problem of will and the 'St Neot margin' – turns it, as it were, into a complex variable. We can see the way in which this 'third dimension' complicates the issue in the case of sex. Animal sexuality is a physical matter, dependent upon certain appetites and energies, and upon the smell of oestrum. If an animal is tired, and there is no *physical* stimulus, then sex is unthinkable. Human beings possess the extra dimension of imagination, which makes their sex lives altogether more complicated. It means that they are no longer dependent on direct natural stimuli; the imagination can also act as a 'detonator' of the sexual energies. The psychologist writing about sex finds it impossible to offer a simple definition of sexual perversion, since he is dealing with a complex variable. The complicated needs of man's mental being might intensify his sexual experience, or produce impotence – or lead to any number of complications between these two extremes. Freud's theory of the libido fails to recognise the fundamental difference between human material and biological material, attempting, as it were, to reduce man to a 'plane' object. It is not difficult for phenomenological analysis to reveal the contradictions in Freud's theories.

The necessary starting point for all phenomenological analysis is the recognition of the difference between biological material and human material – as expressed, for example, in the opening passage of Wells's autobiography. For what Wells is saying is that *although the physical world is able to cause him pain and inconvenience, it has no comparable power to make him happy, to produce a sense of fulfilment.* This produces a split in motive, and leads to the complications of the old woman in the vinegar bottle – as well as those implicit in the writings of the Marquis de Sade. (The latter attempts to reduce sex from a complex to a simple variable; but the physical plane is incapable of the developments he tries to force on to it; hence 'sadism'.) What Wells is saying is that man – or rather, men such as himself – have transferred their hopes and ambitions to a new level of their being, the level of intellectual evolution. (I here use 'intellectual' in its fullest sense to mean all the activity of the human spirit.) The position is strange and uncomfortable, for unless the mental component possesses great power – the kind of power that can be given only by deep conviction – it is no genuine counterweight to the negative stimuli of physical existence (and the positive stimuli – physical pleasures – have lost the absoluteness that they possess for animals.) In the ages of religion, this kind of deep conviction was possible; today this is no longer true (at least, not for minds such as Wells's). It would seem that man's own mind, without the support of religion, is incapable of raising its sense of purpose like a cathedral spire. The nineteenth century bears ample witness to this; a creator like Wagner, for example, attempted to create a secular counterpart of religious conviction – and almost succeeded – but ended by bartering his humanist ideal for Christian abnegation.

And yet when we consider the problem as presented by Wells, new ground for hope emerges. Wells is saying that his desire to live depends on the evolution of his intellectual consciousness. We observe that the power of this conviction is less great than the power of negative stimuli. And yet, as Wells points out, it is only in the past hundred years or so that one could say to a man 'Yes, you live and work, etc, *but what do you do*?' It is true that there have always been men who have instinctively recognised that man should have a new dimension of freedom, and who have rejected 'the world' in the name of this freedom. But in the past, the saints have been rarities; since the beginning of the nineteenth century, this tendency to 'world-rejection' has become a commonplace. As we have seen, the urge to intellectual evolution in the romantics was often frustrated by the confused nature of their reasoning and the failure of their language. Today, this is ceasing to be true. If the culture of our time can throw off its nineteenth century legacy of defeat, there is no reason why it should not cease to be true altogether. We can now see that the whole process of becoming human ('hominisation', Teilhard calls it) *is the development of a conscious dimension of evolutionary purpose.* The 'outsiders' – such men as Van Gogh and T. E. Lawrence – only seem to be paradoxical because of an element of self-destructiveness in them; in the light of evolutionary phenomenology, we can see that this destructiveness was only rejection of the 'biological man' in an attempt to intensify the dimension of freedom, of evolution. Like Wells, their condition for consenting to live at all was evolution. (This is particularly apparent in Lawrence – see his 'midnight sermon' on freedom and self-destruction: *Seven Pillars of Wisdom*, chap. 74.) But since Byron's Manfred expressed his rejection by shaking his fist at the sky, human evolution has been considerable; it would seem almost as if it operates by a law of geometrical progression. Even though Wells knows nothing of phenomenology or the existentialist approach, his grasp of the problem is incomparably more powerful than anything we can find in the previous century. Already he is attacking it directly, consciously, no longer having to rely upon vague intuitions. The nineteenth century approach is all instinct and emotion; Nietzsche expresses his rejection of the biological level in the phrase 'human all too human', and his hope for the future in the word 'superman'. The emotional nature of Nietzsche's thought rendered it suspicious, and succeeding generations rejected it as totalitarian; yet fifty years later, Teilhard 'quotes with approval Nietzsche's view that man is unfinished and must be surpassed or completed; and proceeds to deduce the steps necessary for his completion'.* Nietzsche's idealism becomes the subject of phenomenological analysis, and is placed upon firm biological foundations. The paradoxical behaviour of 'outsiders' can be seen as a consequence of an evolutionary necessity.

Our defeatism is a legacy of the nineteenth century. Mind made a sudden violent assault upon the problems of human existence, and was thrown back. It was like a drill trying to cut into a smooth, polished surface, and failing even to make a scratch. D. H. Lawrence once wrote: 'It is the way our sympathy flows and recoils that really determines our lives.' Language has not, so far, succeeded in labelling this complex 'flow and recoil' of our response to experience, and language is the drill. Husserl and Wittgenstein have suggested what was wrong; the drill was made of base metal. That is to say, language was adulterated with preconceptions and fallacies. I have tried to show that the failure of existentialism was the failure to eliminate the preconceptions and fallacies – particularly the Cartesian fallacy. Once this is clearly recognised, the sense of frustration and limitation vanishes; creative development again becomes possible.

All this is foundation work. The real work still lies ahead. *The way forward lies through the development of language.*

Gorran Haven

1960-1964

* Sir Julian Huxley; preface to *The Phenomenon of Man.*

Appendices

Appendix One

THE MESCALIN EXPERIENCE

In July 1963, at the time of revising the chapter dealing with the experiments of Huxley and Sartre with mescalin (and their relation to Whitehead's views on the modes of perception), I decided that I would try taking mescalin. It has often been noted that no two people seem to experience exactly the same effects from the drug. So on the 18th of July, at half past ten in the morning, I took about a quarter of a gram of mescalin sulphate dissolved in water. (It tasted rather like Epsom salts.) Aldous Huxley mentioned that he had taken four-tenths of a gram – just under a half – but I wanted to be on the safe side, in case the effects were unpleasant. (I had been told, however, that it was safe to take up to a gram.)

Huxley mentions that within half an hour, he became aware of 'a slow dance of golden lights' then swelling red surfaces – then saw 'reality' far more vividly. I read quietly, determined not to anticipate the effects by excitement; but an hour later, there were still no effects of any kind. I had had a very light breakfast, and suspected that perhaps the mescalin was taking longer to work for this reason. I therefore decided to take another quarter gram. I took this at about midday. Half an hour later, there were still no distinct effects, although by now I was beginning to feel very slightly unwell – feverish, as if I had a bad head cold. Finding the house intolerably stuffy, I decided to walk down to the beach. On the way, I noticed that the 'head-cold' effect had intensified; 'reality' was further away, as when one has a slight fever. I was also reminded of my first experiences of drinking spirits. Twenty minutes later, on my way back home, I realised I was feeling distinctly ill, and found myself wishing that I had not walked so far. An acquaintance stopped me to talk, and I found that I could barely finish the conversation. On my way back along the lane that leads to our house, I had the impression that my sense of smell was far keener. The scent of various flowers in the hedgerow seemed stiflingly strong. My sense of smell has always been strong – a certain smell will bring back a scene from the past with which it is associated far more vividly than a sound or sight. But in this case, it may have been only that the feeling of physical illness made me more sensitive to smells. When I came into the kitchen and found my wife making coffee, I had to hurry into another room of the house.

I decided to make myself sick. This was not difficult. A small quantity of the mescalin came up – I could tell it by its taste. But I was aware that the rest of the mescalin was already working in my system. I felt as if I was trembling slightly – although I was not – and had a feeling of something working in my blood – the feeling that alcohol produces, but less pleasant. I felt as if I had been poisoned.

I decided to lie down on the bed and try to sleep it off. This was difficult, since I felt so sick. I can remember thinking repeatedly 'Oh God, I'll never touch this filthy stuff again', and feeling relieved that I had not been tempted to take the whole gram. For about an hour it was a question of trying to lessen the sickness by a form of mental persuasion, as one tries to prevent oneself from being physically sick. I also tried making myself sick several times more, but with little effect. My wife brought me a cup of glucose dissolved in water, since Huxley had mentioned that the effect of mescalin is due to sugar starvation of the brain. I did not expect this to work, and I am sure it didn't.

Finally, I managed to fall into a light doze for a few minutes – this would probably be towards half past one or two. When I woke up, I found that the sickness was subsiding, leaving me feeling extremely weak. I got up and walked about. There were still no visual effects of any kind – certainly none of the kind described by Huxley – although it seemed to me that there was a strangely prismatic play of colours on a varnished door. However, I later discovered that this is so even when one has not taken mescalin.

I now realised that the mescalin was finally having a positive effect – well over four hours after taking the first dose. My body was feeling the gratitude that it normally experiences after having been physically sick – the feeling of recuperating. I noticed that this feeling of pleasure was stronger than the usual relief after vomiting. As I concentrated on it, it became a well defined rhythm, a kind of wave motion, that seemed to start at my brain and travel all the way down my body, as a hand might stroke a cat, or as a raft might be gently rocked up and down on the sea. I am not sure whether becoming aware of it intensified it, or whether perhaps a negative attitude on my part had prevented me from feeling it much earlier – a resistance to it. My sleep seemed to have placed me in a receptive frame of mind, as unresisting as a baby; consequently the effects became stronger.

I soon realised that I felt as if *something outside* was trying to communicate with me. This was not an unpleasant sensation, but not pleasant either. I recalled Robert Hichens' story *How Love Came to Professor Guildea,* about a kind of idiot ghost, a mindless elemental, that falls in love with a professor and plagues him with constant attention. I felt rather like the professor in the story.

This part of the experience is difficult to describe without conveying the wrong impression. There was no sense of something *outside my body* trying to communicate. This was entirely a 'feeling'. Moreover, it manifested itself as a warmth and benevolence, a sense of *innocence* and trust. Huxley speaks about Adam on the dawn of creation; certainly this feeling was like the trust that one experiences as a baby, a sense of mother-love, a completely uncomplex innocence. When I consciously turned my thoughts towards innocence – for example, my eye fell on a volume about Marilyn Monroe on my bookshelf – I had a sudden feeling of recognition: 'Yes, *that's* it.' It seemed that the innocence of which I was so intensely aware was the innocence that I had so often instinctively recognised in people – in Miss Monroe (whom I had met on a couple of occasions), in my three-year-old daughter, in perhaps a dozen people in all (most of them women or girls).

In speaking of the 'mystical experience', Huxley has laid a great deal of emphasis on the idea of the 'not-self' as opposed to the 'self', of the freedom from the prison of personality, of the way that 'personality' usually embodies the evil and selfishness in people, the petty 'selfhood'. Now I felt most strongly that he was wrong, that there is an element of Manicheeism in Huxley, a tendency to reject the world as evil (which once led me to borrow one of Huxley's characters – Mr Propter – and transfer him to a novel of my own, merely to contradict this idea). This has led him to an equally simple equation of selfhood with evil. Now I was intensely certain that he was wrong. Although this sense of love and innocence was delightful, it was *too* innocent. I found myself fighting against it – not as Huxley says, because the Old Adam was putting up a hard fight against grace – but because selfhood is a precise instrument for a certain purpose, and this feeling was blunting the instrument. I found myself thinking about Peter Kürten the Düsseldorf sadist, or of Straffen, the child-murderer, and recognising that adult minds are intended to be the policemen of the universe. My daughter came into the bedroom and confirmed this feeling; her affection expressed precisely the same kind of thing that I was feeling inwardly; yet lying there, feeling physically enfeebled, overwhelmed by this sense of universal love and trust, I recognised that I was in the wrong position in relation to my daughter – that the job of the adult is protection and care. And the job of all responsible human beings is the same protection and care towards the universe. For this, one needs, as a preliminary step, to insulate oneself against this universal love. Having taken this step of insulation – the first step towards adulthood – all crime becomes possible, if one does not operate upon a kind of ingrained confidence that the universe means well by one. Even lapped in this sense of universal love and innocence, I could not find it in myself to condemn a Kürten completely, aware as I was that, having taken the first step towards 'adulthood', he had had no reason to feel that 'the universe meant well by him'. (Kürten's upbringing was extremely brutal and miserable.)

I should note that there was a slight erotic component in this sense of innocence, but nothing strong enough to be called sexual excitement. In any case, the sense of physical enfeeblement was so strong that sexual excitement would have been impossible.

By this time, I was feeling well enough to sit up and drink a cup of coffee; I also felt hungry and suggested something to eat. But when my wife brought me a lamb chop, I found it impossible to eat more than a mouthful. It would have been as difficult as to eat human flesh. Again, I felt overwhelmed by the cruelty of human beings. I am not a vegetarian, although I am inclined to feel that I should be. But if I took mescalin regularly, I am sure that I would have no alternative. I could no more eat a lamb chop than I could have strangled the lamb with my bare hands and eaten it raw.

A friend who took mescalin told me that she had a sensation of descending 'into the cellars of her mind' and becoming aware of all kinds of depths and of mental processes and feelings of which she was normally unaware. My own experience could be described in the same way. I felt like a radio without a VHF attachment, so that all kinds of stations were interfering at the same time. The capacity to will, which depends on clarity of purpose, was strongly diminished.

I believe this explains my body's strong resistance to mescalin, and the reason that I felt ill for so long. My own mind has a strong 'VHF attachment', a mechanism for allowing me to focus all my attention on what absorbs me at the moment, and exclude all other ideas and feelings; this has been developed by a long process of mainly unconscious discipline. Mescalin temporarily put this attachment out of action, and I realised instinctively that this was something I did not want. (On re-reading Huxley's *Doors of Perception* on the evening before taking mescalin, I remember feeling strongly: 'I don't need to take the stuff', and also experiencing a premonition that it would not give me any glimpse of 'the morning of creation'.)

I am also inclined to believe that mescalin made me 'psychic' to some extent, it certainly seemed that many of the feelings and 'messages' I was receiving were floating loose in the atmosphere, like radio waves. But it may have been an illusion due to some stimulation of imagination. For example, when I thought of the area in which I live (in south Cornwall), my mind immediately received a strong impression of *witchcraft*. My wife, who takes some interest in Cornish history and antiquities, tells me that, as far as she knows, this area was never connected with witchcraft.

I not only disliked the sense of being overwhelmed by 'feelings';

I was certain that these feelings somehow lie in the opposite direction from my moments of real insight. Huxley seems to equate the feeling of loss of selfhood, of universal love, with mystical experience. I can only say that this has never held true for me. I should say first of all that I do not believe that mystical experiences are confined to mystics and saints. Professor A. H. Maslow of Brandeis University, USA has turned his attention to the subject of *extremely healthy* human beings, and has concluded that most healthy people experience what he calls 'peak moments', mystical insights, moments of life-affirmation that seem to be based on the sense of universal love. I am certain that a 'mystical insight' depends partly on a certain kind of mental health, partly upon a mental discipline, and partly merely in 'looking in the right place'. I am inclined to suspect the kind that come through ill-health or physical privation – like Pascal's vision. My own moments of intense insight have always been accompanied by a sense of health and control. They take the form of an intensification of reality, but not in the visual sense of which Huxley speaks; they are the opposite of what Heidegger means by 'forgetfulness of existence'. We live in a world of petty preoccupations and illusions, and there is a strong element of the spoilt child in all of us – that is, we are inclined to behave as if some trivial worry or inconvenience were the most important thing in the universe. Sometimes, some outward event is kind enough to bring us back to earth – as if a man about to shoot himself because his wife has left him should hear of the outbreak of war, and recognise that his own catastrophe is unimportant in comparison. But mostly we are confined to a claustrophobic world of personal little values. We can do something to combat these by some mental discipline, by refusing to be carried away by trivialities, by refusing to make mountains out of personal molehills, by trying forcibly to 'un-spoil' oneself. (On the basis of a slight acquaintance with him, I believe that the late Aldous Huxley did this highly successfully.) But it is also possible sometimes to 'shatter' one's narrow personal values by forcing the imagination to contemplate some great challenge, or perhaps the idea of death. A poem like Wilfred Owen's 'Exposure' can have this effect of bringing reality closer; so can a passage like 'El Sordo on the Hilltop' from Hemingway's

For Whom the Bell Tolls. It might be said, of course, that in the simplest sense, these experiences of 'reality' are simply part of the process of growing up. But it should also be recognised that most people never do grow up; they remain fixed in this childish stage of self-contemplation, believing that their emotions are the most important thing in the universe.

It will now be seen why I found myself fighting so hard against the sense of love and trust brought on by the mescalin; it was the reverse of the process of becoming adult; it was sliding back to the beginning again, seeing the universe through great mists of one's own feelings – even though these feelings had no element of cruelty or selfishness. One was further away than ever from Being in Heidegger's sense. The great objection to this 'personal' world is that it blocks one's vision, exactly as if someone emptied a bucket of glue over the windscreen while one was driving. Therefore, instead of one's inner being responding healthily to challenges, it is bewildered by conflicting voices, like a host of children clamouring for attention.

I could understand perfectly why Sartre and Huxley had experienced opposite reactions, and why my reaction was different from either. When Huxley was interviewed, the interviewer asked him if he could understand in what direction madness lies, and Huxley replied emphatically '*Yes*'. 'If you started the wrong way, everything that happened would be a proof of a conspiracy against you ... If one began with fear and hate as the major premiss, one would have to go on to the conclusion.' Huxley saw the world 'quivering with meaning', somehow projecting the inner intensity outward on to things. If one started with the wrong premise – that the universe was actively against one – this 'meaning' would seem to be its malevolence seen face to face. Most children and adolescents have a certain feeling of mistrust about the universe – it is one of the first consequences of losing the innocence of babyhood (and no doubt the reason that so many young children develop self-pity, and use their pains and illnesses as a weapon for extorting affection). Ridding oneself of this feeling that the universe has a personal grudge against one is the first and most difficult task in growing to adulthood. A simple, but dangerous means of bringing it under control is to select some particular object as the target for one's sense of universal unfairness – perhaps the Jews, or the communists, or the capitalist conspiracy. One justifies the mistrust by *reason* – or something that has a specious appearance of reason.

Now Sartre has certainly used reason to justify his pessimistic view of the world; consequently it is to be expected that mescalin should introduce him to 'hell' rather than heaven. On the other hand, it is clear that Huxley has spent a lifetime in trying to free himself from 'selfhood', to 'unspoil' himself. This process involves rough treatment of one's tendency to self-pity. But the consequence is that there is no suppressed feeling of universal unfairness, no 'basic horror of existence', for the mescalin to release. Huxley's problem – as he explains – is rather that he is too intellectual, too much given to making the world bloodless by conceptualising it, and therefore too confined to this airless, sterilised world of concepts. Mescalin had the exhilarating effect of putting his reason out of action. In *Ash Wednesday*, Eliot had prayed that he might forget 'these matters that with myself I too much discuss, too much explain'. T. E. Lawrence made the same observation: the intellectual sometimes finds his reasoning mind clacking on like a typewriter until he begins to feel that his nature has been permanently dehydrated. Intellectuals are always finding themselves in this difficult position, victims of their own tendency to analyse. There are various ways of counteracting this effect: alcohol (within reason), social intercourse, listening to music, playing games, etc. Mescalin is undoubtedly more effective than any of these; the Frankenstein reason is chained; the world of feelings and objects rushes in to replace the world of concepts, and suddenly, with delight, one realises that the world is *real*, when one had begun to suspect that it is an abstraction. This accounts, I think, for Huxley's sense of release and his delight in the 'is-ness' of things.

As to myself, although I suppose I also qualify as an 'intellectual', I dislike being confined in a world of concepts, so I am inclined to keep my thinking 'existential'. I think with my instincts as far as possible, and use reason as a kind of midwife, brought in to help and clarify. I am bad at languages and at mathematics because I object to abstract thinking, to ideas or concepts (or words) for their own sake. Eliot was right when he objected to the practice of speaking about 'vague emotion' and 'clear thought', since thought is more often vague and emotion precise. I find that my own thought is clearest when connected to a strong impulse or insight; the stronger the feeling, the clearer the idea.

I am also fundamentally optimistic. When I read *Doors of Perception* and thought 'I don't need to take mescalin', it was the recognition that I experience a weaker degree of the mescalin sensation fairly frequently, and that it forms the underpinning of my everyday thinking. On the whole, I take it for granted that the universe means well by me, and always have, ever since my childhood. Throughout my childhood and teens I can remember experiencing sudden moments of certainty that 'everything is well', that the world is unbelievably beautiful, and that only our human limitations prevent us from seeing it. It always seemed therefore that the only problem is somehow to get past the limitedness of human vision, our 'worm's eye view' of the universe, and it would instantly be seen that the universe is mostly composed of good, with very little evil. I recognise that in order to achieve this distant objective, it is necessary to limit my consciousness, just as a watchmaker needs to narrow his attention to repair a watch. The universe itself may possess infinite power, and yet such power is as useless for the small and precise tasks of evolution as the power of the Niagara Falls would be for repairing a watch. In order to get this precision, we need to install a valve for cutting down this great flow of power to a trickle. We install the mental 'cut out', the VHF attachment, and it immediately becomes possible to focus the mind on its problems with a new accuracy. The only thing to watch out for is the cut out getting jammed.

I am inclined to believe, therefore, that my own cut out can be disengaged slightly more easily than Huxley's, so that there were no dehydrated tracts of my mind to be irrigated by the action of the mescalin. The mescalin experience was in no way fundamentally strange to me; but it was too strong. Instead of refreshing like an April shower, it swamped me like a monsoon.

After the attempt to eat the lamb chop, there is nothing of great interest to report. My wife said she was going to the local church fête, and I decided to get up and go too. I felt tired, but no longer ill. The wave-sensation was still going on like faint regular shocks of electricity – but less strongly. At the fête I realised with relief that the feeling was wearing off. I felt the same kind of pleasure that an athlete must feel on recovering from a sick-bed. My feelings were again controllable; I no longer felt like a female pig feeding a dozen young ones. Later in the day – particularly around supper time – I experienced twinges of the mescalin effect, a surge of feeling that had to be controlled. (There is a distinct sense of being able to give these feelings a positive or a negative interpretation, somewhat similar to persuading oneself not to be sick; the feelings seem to be like a powerful animal that is safe so long as one's control over it is absolute.) A few of these twinges recurred the following day; but they had all ceased within forty-eight hours. Thinking about this later, I was glad that I had never been tempted to try mescalin in my teens, when I might have found the forces released by it uncontrollable.

The other half gram of mescalin was taken a month later by a Soho friend; the results were not spectacular. For several hours he seemed to be intensely happy, and kept repeating: 'I feel wonderful.' (He compared the effect to marijuana.) When listening to *Tristan and Isolde* a few hours later, he burst into tears. The mescal seemed to have an un-inhibiting effect on him, similar to that of alcohol.

Another friend who took mescalin – a young novelist – has supplied me with her notes on the experience, which largely confirm the theories I have developed above, particularly that mescalin plunges the taker into a kind of dream world, a world of inaction, where one has no defence against one's latent fears and fantasies. She describes herself as inclined to catatonia – a state of mental automatism in which the will ceases to function, and the limbs remain fixed in any position in which they are placed. Her account brings to mind Greene's description of his state of mind in his teens: 'For years ... I could take no aesthetic interest in anything visual at all: staring at a sight that others assured me was beautiful, I would feel nothing. I was fixed in my boredom.'

The first effect of mescalin upon this subject was to make her creep into a corner and assume what she calls an 'Egyptian pose', and to contort her limbs in various other ways. '... the compulsion was a sort of inner necessity, similar to, but more elaborate than, the need to turn off a dripping tap or to touch every third railing. I should mention that I am normally an obsessive compulsive type, and the mescalin tightened it.'

Walking in the street, 'I felt weightless and glided along'. This was late at night, and the lights produced a sensation of pleasure; an office block, for example, looked liked 'a bunch of flowers against the sky'. She writes: 'There is a point where the verb "to see" is raised to "to experience". Under mescalin, visions have an objective, unquestionable quality; they seem to be a change in the world, rather than in you.'

'Further colour experiences occurred in the bathroom. The walls had originally been green, then whitewashed and repainted pale blue. The work had been badly done, and resulted in watery patches of discoloration. Now the walls looked like a submarine scene, with aquatic diffusions of blues and turquoises, and a submerged mountain range. The window ledge had a sort of eroded crust, formed by years of blistering paint and spattered toothpaste. I thought the spots and spores looked mildewed like the rind of a gorgonzola cheese.' Discussing these phenomena with C (her landlord), we used the word 'bathroom' so often that C made a slip of the tongue and said 'bloodbath' (from a recent newspaper headline). I told him that when advertising rooms to let, he should print on the card 'Come and see the submerged gorgonzola in our bloodbath', as he would thus attract the right sort of tenants.

'I tried closing my eyes, and saw parallel rows of tiny identical figures, made of brightly coloured tin like the scraps inside a kaleidoscope.' Huxley, also, mentions a similar experience. I myself found that closing my eyes made no difference – in fact, my eyes were closed much of the time.

After eating, they sat in opposite chairs. 'I turned the armchair into a flight of front steps, on which C ... had established his court for the night ... I further supplied a Greek pillar and some empty milk bottles. From this time on, I gave him the personality of the zany professor. My own personality was the Egyptian, whom I entitled the Egyptian Catatonic. This business of personae needs elucidating; neither C nor I were *like* something; we *were* something. Similes became metaphors. It was rather like an agreement between actors; one of them finds a policeman's helmet in the property trunk, and by putting it on becomes, for present purposes, The Policeman.'

'I was not The Egyptian all the time. Walking home, I had been for a while a face, half of which was a skull ... Later, I became a horrible Thing. A thing was a face, like the flat head of a snake, with slit, idiot's eyes. It was soft and disgusting, slug-like, and had no lower jaw, but ended in the curve of the cheeks and upper lip. I had a concept of the Thing, and knew it was me. The experience was horrible while it lasted.'

Here the experience begins to sound like Sartre's. Again, it can be seen that the usual mental filter, that one establishes by long discipline, vanishes, and the world becomes a place of fears, as in a nightmare.

'... my mescalin world mostly resembled a black and white film ... Especially it resembled the surrealist films of Cocteau; his ruinscapes in which an attic lumber room leads away down an endless corridor; than a corner is turned and we are in a desert with a group of pillars as the sole landmark.'

'I felt I had magical powers; I could see how a group of drug takers would be in the right mood to invoke the devil or practise necromancy. The feeling of possessing magical powers was, however, only subjective; the drug did not make me *think* that magic was possible, and in fact left my usual, rather objective manner of thinking unimpaired.' Again, one is reminded of Sartre's account.

'I used my feeling of magical powers to practise self-analysis; various intuitions emerged with the certainty of revelations. Later, cold consideration of these 'revelations' tended to confirm them. They were all rather depressing ... '

At this point, her account becomes more than ever reminiscent of Sartre. 'My experiences were almost all unpleasant. I was eating a pear, and suddenly noticed that its flesh was composed of granules. Where I had bitten, the granules were writhing like bisected maggots and bleeding pus. The whole thing was organic; it revolted me. I turned the pear and regarded it from an oblique angle; now it heaved and writhed like larva. I could not stop looking at it; I was hypnotised by disgust.'

This seems to confirm the suggestion I have made that the experiences described in *Nausea* were those of Sartre's mescalin experience, or its after effects. There were also visual illusions that sound similar to Sartre's 'lobster':

'Out of the tail of my eye, I saw beetles crawling over the fireplace. The grate was ferny with cobwebs and centipedes. Greenfly climbed the plastic flex of the bedside lamp. Like a shower, beetles threatened to invade my own skin. When I looked straight at them, the insects stopped moving and proved to be marks on the paint, or specks of dust.' At this point, the experience begins to sound similar to that described by American 'hopheads', and perhaps explains some of the peculiarities of 'Beat' poetry:

'I did some writing, but this was of no literary value because it was distorted by compulsions. I felt compelled to print this word in block capitals, or put that one in brackets, or to distort my handwriting ... These distortions served as a devious way to present the truth; whereas writing should be a direct statement of it.

'I could not read because the lights and sparks emitted by the page, like interference on a radio, bombarded the meaning of the words.'

'About 4 a.m. my sight started to run down, like a camera shutter that clicks rapidly between each image, and produces the jerky effect of old films. I went to bed but could not sleep until 7 a.m., when my ceiling looked as beautiful as if a pallet knife had spread it with different thicknesses of white paste.'

She adds, ' I consider that the experience had a long term effect on me' in terms of general depression and abnormal behaviour. She concludes: 'I did not like writing this account ... I do not like thinking of those years at all; the ice is so thin; it is easy to fall again into that terrible depression.'

In this account, it is clear that mescalin had two effects. The first hardly differs from the effect of alcohol – she felt a warmth towards the world and particular objects – desire to dance with a post-office van, etc. The second effect may also be associated with alcohol – the slowing down of sensation, so that objects are seen more clearly – or rather, obtrude into consciousness by their stillness. One may even experience an analogous sensation through indigestion – the feeling that the limbs are made of stone or wood, and are swelling. (This usually occurs when lying down with the eyes closed.)

At any moment, human beings are more or less aware of the 'pro and contra' of existence. But the mind's 'cut out valve' seems to work more strongly with the 'pro' than the 'contra'. It is easy to see the world as a place of misery and insecurity and cruelty. The 'pro' is a more difficult matter; it seems to have two possible forms: natural goodness and evolutionary consciousness. By 'natural goodness' I mean not only ordinary moments of pleasure – aesthetic and physical – but also the state that Boehme called 'the sabbath of the soul', which seems to be analogous to Aldous Huxley's sensation under mescalin. By evolutionary consciousness, I mean *all* pleasure associated with the intellect or intellectual sensibility (which includes music, painting – even wine tasting.) Natural goodness causes a sense of passivity, receptivity. Keats's 'negative capability'; evolutionary consciousness is an intensity in which consciousness is aware of itself *as activity*. This is the purpose of education, as described by Wells on p. 33. It is a sense of power, of control, and is different in kind from any physical pleasures. (Wells catches it admirably in the *Autobiography*, describing the exhilaration of his first explorations into science.) It involves a sense of responsibility (as distinguished from passive enjoyment), and in *Man and Superman* Shaw speaks of 'the birth of the moral passion' to describe the awakening of this sense of *active* participation in the business of evolution. (I here use evolution in its simplest sense, meaning any kind of complexification; the notion of biological evolution need not be present.)

Mescalin seems to inhibit evolutionary consciousness. Whether its effect is pleasurable or not therefore depends, to begin with, on how far one needs a rest from evolutionary consciousness. A thinker who finds himself thinking too much comes into this category. But it is clear that Huxley was generalising his own experience too much when he assumed that most people would enjoy a 'mescalin holiday'. From Huxley's early work – stories like *The Bookshop* and *Richard Greenow* or a novel like *Crome Yellow* – it seems apparent that Huxley's boyhood and youth were not haunted by a sense of insecurity; there is a freshness, a feeling of the gentle enjoyment of existence, about them. Moreover, Huxley was in his sixties when he took mescalin, and had therefore had time to develop a perception of meaning, a rejection of the idea of existence as horror and nausea. All this explains why he found the mescalin experience so pleasurable. A younger person of comparable sensitivity will almost inevitably be more aware of the 'contra' side of existence. (Dostoevsky himself was more aware of the 'contra' than the 'pro', as is apparent from *The Brothers Karamazov.*) Unless such a person possesses a strong enthusiasm for ideas, of the order expressed by Wells in *The Undying Fire*, the effect of mescalin will be to emphasise these fears, produce a feeling of 'skating on thin ice'. It may even produce a sense of total horror, nausea, as described by William James in *The Varieties of Religious Experience*. It is interesting to note that James's account of his own attack of 'horror' has much in common with the above account of mescalin-induced 'catatonia'. It came when he was in a state of ill health and nervous depression, and was accompanied by an image of a catatonic patient whom James had seen in an asylum, who sat unmoving all day looking like 'a sculptured Egyptian cat or Peruvian mummy ... looking absolutely non-human'. James adds: 'I awoke morning after morning with a horrible dread in the pit of my stomach, and with a sense of the insecurity of life that I never knew before.' This 'dread in the pit of the stomach' is the most familiar of everyday sensations to many people whose lives seem to be a constant battle against various forms of insecurity and unpleasantness. It can be seen, then, why Huxley's recommendation of mescalin for general use should not be taken too seriously. It is noteworthy that James says that his attack took place when he was in a state of 'general depression of spirits about my prospects' – a state that is familiar to most people. But James's account also confirms the thesis that I have advanced in the first chapter of this book – that the most powerful optimists are those who have swallowed a strong dose of pessimism early, or have had difficult beginnings that make them less inclined to self-pity.

Huxley's comment that schizophrenia can produce some of the effects of mescalin is confirmed by an example related to me by Margaret Lane. In 1945, immediately after the birth of her second child, she found herself in a condition of emotional oversensitivity, when any thought of pain or misfortune would bring her close to tears. It was at this time that the famous 'Hiroshima' copy of *The New Yorker* arrived, devoted entirely to John Hersey's account of the dropping of the atomic bomb and its after effects. In a state when even the mention of somebody's cat being lost could seem intolerable, Hersey's narrative was a shattering experience that had the effect of 'burning out her emotional fuses' (in her own words). She became completely incapable of any kind of feeling, as though all the 'feeling nerves' had been cauterised. Even when she had recovered physically, the capacity to feel did not return, although she 'went through the motions' of social and family life. One of the symptoms of this state of 'inner deadness' was that grass took on an artificial appearance, while the leaves on trees seemed to be cut out of green tin. Living became a kind of ritual, without any spontaneous feelings of love or hatred, pleasure or distaste. A year later, she and her husband were thinking of buying a cottage in Hampshire, and went to view it. Miss Lane went out alone into the field behind the cottage. The grass, as usual, looked a clever imitation, and the leaves like tin. She noticed some unfamiliar blue flowers in the grass; their blue was so intense that she stopped to stare. Suddenly, the blueness seemed to break through the glass wall between herself and reality, and a sense of tremendous emotional relief followed so that she burst into tears. She knew this was the beginning of recovery. During the next few days, the frozen feelings semed to thaw and break up, until the capacity to feel had returned completely.

As she described these experiences to me, I immediately recognised the state of oversensitivity following pregnancy as being identical with my own experience under mescalin, when it became impossible to eat a lamb chop. In such a state, with an almost nonexistent pain-threshold, such a revelation of pain and cruelty as Hersey's book could easily produce total and permanent insanity. Some interior safety-mechanism obviously came into operation, preventing such a collapse, completely suspending all feeling, 'blowing the fuses'. But what is significant is that grass and leaves were seen as *lifeless*. In fact, it would hardly be untrue to say that grass and leaves *really* look rather like green raffia and tin; we supply their 'life' in looking at them. The burning out of internal fuses meant that this energy was no longer available to the subconscious intentionality, so that nature was seen as dead. It is interesting to speculate what would have been the effect if, in the state following childbirth, Margaret Lane had had an experience that produced the opposite effect – a sense of universal love and trust; would this have consolidated itself later as a kind of *positive* mescalin vision?

The real significance of all this emerges if one thinks for a moment in terms of phenomenological analysis. Miss Lane described her state of 'inner deadness' as a kind of schizophrenia, and in a technical sense, no doubt she is right. But in that case, schizophrenia is not illness, like mumps, divided from normality by a definite break, but a mere point on a line, on which another arbitrarily selected point is labelled 'normality' and yet another 'mystical vision', while further in the opposite direction is suicide-mania and catatonia. And since not even a Watsonian mechanist would deny that progression from schizophrenia to 'abnormality' is an evolution, and that this evolution might be brought about, or at least facilitated, by phenomenological analysis, it follows that man's natural evolution lies in the 'visionary' direction, and that this is also partly a matter of phenomenological analysis.

Let me try to summarise one of the central ideas of this book, in the light of what has been said above.

One of the most fundamental problems of the human condition is that man assumes his reality to be identical with his present states, physical and mental. Since he is necessarily aware of himself as a 'social animal', a human personality that knows itself essentially through its interaction with other human personalities, it is inevitable that his human personality – tied to the static present – will act as a filter through which the outside world has to pass. 'Reality' is seen stained by the mediocrity of everyday existence. Man lives at the bottom of a kind of fish-tank whose glass is greasy, dusty and inclined to distort. Certain experiences can endow him with a mental energy that momentarily rockets him clear of the top of the fish tank, and he sees 'reality' as infinitely alien, infinitely strange. What is more, it is curiously *meaningful*; if a direct relation could be established with it, life would be seen in the light of purpose. (It is impossible to think of meaning dissociated from purpose.)

It should be made clear that the glass of the fish tank is not the senses – as Descartes and subsequent philosophers have assumed; it is the human *personality*, which knows itself as an active participant in the world, in relations with other people. *This fine network of relations is the distorting medium, not the senses.*

Man is mistaken, of course, in assuming himself to be a static being. Even if he fails to mature in any mental sense, he grows older physically. If he could somehow develop a faculty of seeing himself as a dynamic rather than as a static being, the problem would be solved. Unfortunately, the mind of western man has developed the faculty of presentational immediacy at the cost of that of causal efficacy. A man deeply involved in some active work that gives him a sense of development can escape the 'fish tank' to some extent; but this is no answer unless the gains can somehow be consolidated.

The mystics were all aware of this in some degree; it is the subject of all Blake's work, for example. The romantics, and later the existentialists, were also aware of it. But to be aware of a problem is not to solve it.

Husserl began to lay the foundations of a method for attacking the problem. The problem is the distorting medium, which Husserl labelled intentionality. The greatest achievement of existentialism has been to recognise that it is active human intentionality, not the 'senses', that is the distorting medium; this, so far, has been its major contribution to philosophy. The first problem is to become aware that 'the world' we naïvely take for granted is being seen through a distorting medium. Husserl's life-work was mainly concerned with developing a scientific method for getting beyond this point.

Heidegger and Sartre both believed that they were concerned with the next stage of the problem – how to clear away the distorting medium. Heidegger's chief contribution was to analyse the exact part played by human relations and by time in the distorting medium. By laying the emphasis on time, he emphasised that the problem is not a static business, as earlier philosophers had assumed; it is inextricably tangled with *action* and human personality. It must be approached kinetically.

Sartre approached the problem from a slightly different viewpoint. As I have already said, he was inclined to emphasise the need for action, rather in the manner of Fichte. This was largely because his metaphysicial foundations – his theory of consciousness and intentionality – were so shaky. For Sartre, purposive action will get man out of the fish tank. The central emphasis of his positive philosophy lay on the notion that man is not a static being, that he is wrong to accept his present 'reality' as his permanent reality, that he must learn to recognise his freedom to become something other than the self that is determined by his being-in-the-world. Sartre had stated, in less abstract terms, what Husserl had already stated: that the first step in freedom lies in recognising the natural standpoint for what it is, a temporary convenience.

Aldous Huxley brought the whole problem one step nearer the practical daylight by expressing it in terms of something that people might *do*: i.e., take mescalin.

It can clearly be seen what now remains to be done. The present book has attempted to outline the problem, to take it a step further and to show the way to future development, to 'show the fly the way out of the fly bottle', as Wittgenstein expressed it – or to show man the way out of the fish tank. Mescalin, I believe, could be used to produce the 'shocks' necessary to make the existentialist thinkers aware of the problem; but its usefulness is limited. What is now needed is a new existentialism based upon the method of Husserl, and applying this method to the material supplied by Heidegger – the network of relations that is intentionality. What is happening is that the problem expressed by the mystics – and by Blake in particular – has been first of all expressed in terms that would have been acceptable to Descartes, and second, expressed in terms of science, of phenomenological psychology, so that it can be attacked like any other scientific problem. First of all, the destruction of the natural standpoint effected by Husserl and Heidegger must be incorporated into everyday consciousness.

This is not difficult – no more difficult, say, than learning a language. The phenomenological method must then be directed upon the problem of the renewal of man's two worlds, the language world and the perceived world – both of which are composed mainly of worn out parts. Phenomenological existentialism is the systematic replacement of the worn out parts.

Appendix Two

THE ROPE TRICK – BILL HOPKINS

The Divine and the Decay

I know of only one modern novel that seems to move naturally in the direction of a positive existentialism – *The Divine and the Decay* by Bill Hopkins. This was published in England in 1957. While it is not a wholly successful novel, it seems to me in many ways one of the most important to have appeared since the war.

In *The Angry Decade,* Kenneth Allsop remarked on the violence of the attacks on the book, unlike the usual sympathetic reception given to first novels. Hopkins' AYM affiliations were not entirely responsible for these. *The Divine and the Decay* is an uncompromising book, a curiously fanatical book, showing no visible influences, making no concessions to what the reader expects of modern fiction, preoccupied only with working out its problem of 'how a man can be a giant in a world of pygmies'. It is also the work of a poet and a dramatist rather than of a born novelist; it has an assertiveness that has been missing from English fiction since D. H. Lawrence. All these led certain critics to jeer about the 'search for a Superman', and to smell out 'crypto-fascism' in the book's theme. Other critics supposed that the book is a savage satire on its fascist-type hero. Neither view is correct.

The novel concerns Peter Plowart, the young leader of a neo-fascist movement in London's East End. Plowart goes to Vachau – a Channel Island obviously based on Sark – ostensibly for a holiday before a political campaign, but in reality to have an alibi when his co-partner in the movement is murdered in London.

Plowart is in some ways a typical 'hero of our time'. In spite of his instinctive contempt for other men, he lacks real self-belief. He is the true dictator type – a romantic and dreamer who can never be contented with introspection, who needs to see his effect on men. But although he lives and works in 'society', he is no realist; he is hardly aware of anything but his own inner compulsions. This strange 'lack of contact' with the real world is demonstrated in the opening scene of the novel, where he is on the boat crossing to Guernsey, and falls into conversation with a middle-aged man; almost immediately, Plowart plunges into self-revelation. He is not aware of the unsuitability of his audience, only of his own need to speak. He tells the man: 'The outstanding trait of my personality was a strong aversion to other human beings; I saw in them all, a shabby travesty of myself and of everything that constitutes human greatness.' He goes on to tell how he deliberately went to parties, to convince himself that he could 'meet the world on its own level', squirming among the 'self-betrayers who shouted out their emotions and private lives like costermongers ... Theirs was a game of persistent self-belittlement and ultimately the disparagement of all humanity'. He drinks until he feels sick, vomits in the lavatory, then deliberately returns to the party for more drink. This is pure 'outsiderism'. In *Heartbreak House,* Shotover tells Ellie: 'At your age, I looked for hardship, danger, horror and death, that I might feel the life in me more intensely.' This is what Plowart needs; hence these exercises in self-flagellation.

Later, Plowart became a political leader, and became aware of his power over audiences. But this is precisely his problem. He is aware of his own power in contact with other human beings. But left to himself, he feels nothing. Lawrence of Arabia had the same characteristic; all who worked with him spoke of an extraordinary inner force that made him a natural leader; and yet the *Seven Pillars of Wisdom* is full of self-doubt, the fallacy of insignificance. Like Plowart, Lawrence was gripped with this ideal of being 'greater than mankind'. And a comment on Lawrence, quoted by Kennington, applies equally to Plowart: 'He is never alive in what he does ... He is only a pipe through which life flows ... '

This 'hollow men' aspect of Plowart is revealed after his conversation on the boat. He falls asleep, and has again one of the appalling nightmares that have always haunted him; it leaves him feeling exhausted and empty.

In a café on Guernsey, some Vachau fishermen accidentally smash his portable radio; Plowart had been relying on it to bring him the news of the murder; he flies into an insane rage and threatens to stab the fisherman. This episode has later repercussions in the book.

On Vachau at last, he finally takes lodging with a repulsive, self-pitying cripple named Lumas. The story of his encounter with the fishermen has preceded him, and he is generally avoided. Only one man – a drunken old villain named Buffonet – offers to carry his bags, and offers him a certain grudging regard. He is later beaten up by the other fishermen for ignoring the boycott.

Lumas, Plowart's landlord, is everything for which he feels contempt. He is intelligent, but nihilistic. For several years, his wife has been having a love affair with a tomato grower from Guernsey named Lachanell. Lumas stews in his self-pity, and drinks heavily.

Very soon, Plowart meets the other major character in the book, the young Dame on the island, Claremont.

Now, for some reason that Hopkins does not make quite clear, Plowart becomes fascinated by her. It is not a sexual attraction. For some strange reason, Plowart senses that she possesses knowledge and 'power'; not his kind of power over other people, but subjective power. He seems to feel almost that she is a supernatural being. This is undoubtedly a weak link in the book; for although Claremont comes over as an intelligent and self-possessed young lady, the reader finds it hard to imagine why she should impress Plowart more than all the other similar young ladies he must have met at London parties.

Claremont does not return Plowart's admiration. He speaks to her with his usual frankness about his ambitions, his contempt for human beings; she is secretly horrified, but takes care not to show it. She proposes a 'test' for him, which she claims is a tradition among the young men of the island. It involves crawling down a spur of rock that juts out from the cliff over the sea; this, she says, will prove whether he is merely a braggart and a coward. Plowart accepts, and edges his way along the spur; it breaks away from the cliff, and he falls a hundred feet into the sea. Badly shaken, but unhurt, he drags himself back to his room. Claremont apparently assumes that he is dead; the reader is left to suppose that this was her aim in proposing the test.

The lover of Mrs Lumas – the tomato grower, Lachanell – wants Plowart to vacate his room; it is an attic room in which Lachanell usually stays when he is on the island; the cripple cannot reach it because the ladder is too steep. Plowart refuses. But soon the tomato grower gains the means to blackmail Plowart. He finds a compromising letter – a letter that proves Plowart's involvement in the murder. Plowart decides that the tomato grower must be eliminated, and begins to play on the self-contempt and self-pity of his host to try to make him the instrument of Lachanell's destruction.

In the meantime, he sees Claremont again, spends the night at her house, and ends by raping her. At the last minute, instead of resisting, and thus acknowledging his superior strength, she becomes calm and withdrawn, and as Plowart takes her, he feels that she has defeated him again. But in spite of her apparent indifference, she now has another reason for wanting to see Plowart destroyed.

At the end of the book, the cripple murders his wife's lover – to Plowart's astonishment. He had been convinced that Lumas would never find the courage, even with the knowledge that his wife was leaving him. Plowart is delighted. He follows the trail of blood from the house, down to the shore; there the evidence shows that the dying tomato grower was pushed out to sea in a boat by his mistress.

There now follows a curious scene, the climax of the book. Claremont tells Plowart that she can reveal the secret he has been asking about – the secret of the 'inner strength' he lacks. She points to some rocks two miles away from the island, and tells him a fantastic story; she claims that when she was fifteen she swam towards these rocks, and was caught in the treacherous cross currents. Suddenly, the rocks began moving towards her through the water, and she experienced 'revelations', a sense of inner power. She claims that she has tried the experiment several times since then, and each time, the rocks have moved, and the sense of inner-power has been intensified.

Plowart believes her. They both strip and swim out to sea. It is the most dangerous time of the day, with the tide going out and creating currents. Claremont is a stronger swimmer than Plowart; but after a short time, both are caught in the currents and pulled out to sea. When she knows there is no hope of return, she tells him that she was lying. He does not believe her; as he looks through his salt-strained eyes at the rocks, he is convinced they are moving towards him through the sea. He begins to swim like an automaton, ignoring the current; Claremont stops swimming, and is drowned. But by this time, Plowart is already halfway to the rocks, gripped by the sense of inner power he has always wanted. He gains the rocks and pulls himself on to them; there is immense power in him; he experiences the revelation that Claremont foretold.

Many hours later, fishermen come out to the rocks and pick him up. He is stiff with cold and exhaustion, but happy. But the fishermen thought that Claremont was on the rocks with him; when they realise that she is drowned, they refuse to take Plowart on board. A wave tosses the boat against the rocks; while they are striving to force it away with their oars, Plowart leaps on board. One of the men is swept overboard and vanishes out to sea. As soon as the boat is away from the rocks, the men seize Plowart and throw him overboard. Fortunately for Plowart, Buffonet is on board – the villainous fisherman that Plowart befriended. Unseen by the others, he releases the lifebelt, which drifts back towards Plowart. As the boat moves towards the shore, Plowart shakes his fist after it and roars: 'I'm indestructible, you fools!'

The Divine and the Decay is a very remarkable achievement, an obsessive book. At times, it is a bad book, but it is always bad in its own particular way. Although it has a remarkable unity and simplicity, the plot occasionally becomes too much for the author, who shows his impatience and boredom in the more pedestrian patches. He is at his best in the major scenes: Plowart's climb down the rock, the scenes with the drunken Lumas, (who is perhaps the most remarkable and memorable character in the book), and the final scene. The passages in which Plowart expresses his ideas are also of uniform excellence. From this point of view, the central passage of the book is the speech in which Plowart explains to Claremont his theory of 'ultimate compassion'. An ambulance driver on a battlefield does not stop to shudder with pity for the victims; he stifles his pity and gets them into hospital as quickly as possible. This is real compassion, ultimate compassion. It is Plowart's retort to the accusation of ruthlessness. Men are self-destructive weaklings, they have lost belief; Plowart will give them belief, in the same manner as Dostoevsky's Grand Inquisitor.

To some extent, this might be dismissed as the casuistry of a power-maniac. The argument of Hitler and Mussolini was very similar: the age is dying because of anarchy – too much freedom; very well, take away the freedom and restore 'order'. Stalin's excuse for the elimination of the moujiks in the 'thirties would have been the same: in times of emergency, stringent measures are necessary. And yet this is not entirely untrue. (In the last appendix, I shall go into this problem more fully where it concerns Soviet Russia.)

This is the problem that makes the book so difficult – and so rewarding. Hopkins cannot be accused of simplifying the issues to gain sympathy. Plowart is not a sympathetic character; it would help the reader to feel that the author disapproves of him. But Hopkins' attitude is difficult to define. It is not complete approval; but it is very far from disapproval. The author obviously feels as Plowart does; the failure of men to rise above mediocrity worries him. The reaction of T. E. Lawrence to the same feeling was withdrawal from society, a refusal to offer his intimacy. With an apparently insane idealism, Hopkins obviously feels that men can be changed, that there are ears to listen to sermons on the need of man to increase his stature. In his essay in *Declaration*, it becomes apparent that he feels basically as Plowart does. He begins with a forthright denunciation of literature since the war, declaring that it lacks purpose, direction and power, has opened no new roads of imagination and created no monumental characters. He also has the remarkable sentence: 'There are only a few who demand all the truth a writer possesses.' He speaks of the need for 'writers with phenomenal powers of dedication'. The title of the essay, significantly, is *Ways Without a Precedent*.

It is unfortunate for Hopkins that his book appeared when it did, in 1957. Seven years earlier, when the critics were gloomily prophesying that there would be no literary revival to parallel the revival of the 'twenties, his book would probably have been read with more perception. (This was the time when Mr Angus Wilson's first book of stories – hardly promising his future development – was acclaimed.) As it was, it received the worst of the backwash of the unprecedented publicity of the Angry Young Man movement. Sir Charles Snow has recently spoken of the lack of magnanimity in British life today – he suspects it may spring from Britain's sense of being a waning power in world politics. Since the mid-fifties, it has been particularly evident in literature. This has been nowhere more obvious than in the reception of *The Divine and the Decay*.

For what Hopkins is trying to do is, after all, supremely worthwhile. The literature of the twentieth century has very few memorable characters. The few remarkable 'heroes' have been self-portraits of their authors: Lawrence's Paul Morel, Joyce's Stephen, Proust's Marcel, Hemingway's Nick. Aldous Huxley had tried to create a few 'positively good' characters in his later novels, beginning with Propter in *After Many a Summer*; all are quite unmemorable.

The central problem was expressed by Sartre in his novelle, *Childhood of a Leader*. Lucien Fleurier is a handsome and intelligent young man, but far too sensitive, far too introspective. He also has no sense of 'inner-power', of being somehow 'necessary'. He is even capable of wondering whether there is any proof that he exists. But unlike Huxley's Gumbril, he does not 'glory in the name of earwig'; he finally succeeds in leaving behind his self-doubts by becoming a fanatical anti-semite and a fascist thug. The story ends with his realisation that he has 'the stuff of a leader' in him.

But Sartre's meaning is unmistakable, and his book on anti-semitism underlines it: Lucien has 'sold out' by becoming an anti-semite, plunged quite deliberately into self-delusion (*mauvaise-foi*), chosen an inauthentic means of escaping his inner chaos.

This is splendid. But what would be an *authentic* way? This is the question that Sartre never tries to answer; the hero of his major novel, *Roads to Freedom,* is another hopeless weakling. Hopkins has attempted to answer the question, thereby taking existentialism a stage beyond Sartre. And he is bold enough to recognise that the problem cannot be solved in terms of the 'ordinary man' – that is, a self-divided modern man, without self-belief or any other kind of belief. At least Plowart has a fierce belief in the possibility of human evolution.

But Hopkins's major advance beyond Sartre is in the 'rope trick' at the end of the novel. Like all modern heroes, Plowart feels 'empty inside'; he is a pipe through which life flows. It is not that he does not possess the power; he does. He is in the position of Ramakrishna's grass-eating tiger who could not believe that it was not a sheep. It is self-belief that he does not possess. (In his later years, Dickens had to read his works aloud to audiences because he had to *see* them sobbing over the death of Little Nell or fainting over Bill Sykes's murder of Nancy; it somehow convinced him that he was a great writer.)

But did the rocks move or not? Claremont was lying, and yet Plowart made the rocks move and experienced the 'revelation'. It is the 'rope trick' again. It is the act of faith, of self-belief that is the preliminary of existentialism and of phenomenology. There would be no point in seeking for an intentionality if we believed that the 'phenomenon' was the only reality.

Although it is doubtful whether he had heard of phenomenology at the time he wrote *The Divine and the Decay* and *Ways Without a Precedent*, he has many things to say that might be simply a restatement of the views I have tried to outline in the latter part of this book. For example: ' ... I predict that within the next two or three decades we will see the end of pure rationalism as the foundation of our thinking. If we are to break out of our present encirclement, we must envisage Man from now on as super-rational; that is, possessing an inner compass of certainty beyond all logic and reason ... '

It is this 'inner-compass' that has so far been lacking from existentialism. Kierkegaard's 'Truth is subjectivity' expresses it only feebly, because it seems to justify the view that there are as many 'truths' as there are individuals, and all are equally valid. It would be more accurate to say: 'Truth is evolutionary intentionality.' Our basic experience of life is of fighting; from the moment we are born, gravity pulls us to the earth, and requires a constant effort to resist it. Before we have achieved a sense of balance, we fall and learn that the force of gravity and the hardness of the ground seem to be in league against us. We never overcome gravity, and when, in old age, our legs grow weak, gravity begins to win again. (Consequently, 'freedom' is often identified with floating; drugs and alcohol have the effect of making us forget gravity, or of making the body seem lighter.) It might be said, then, that man is foredoomed to lose the battle against gravity, and that his life is a 'burden' by its very nature.

On the other hand, this is to forget that there could be no human life and no civilisation without gravity; we would float away. Gravity is the basis of most machines. If gravity were regarded as man's inevitable tragedy, we would gape with astonishment at men who are eccentric enough to go walking as a hobby, or even climbing mountains; it would be regarded as self-flagellation. But we take these things for granted, because we recognise that gravity is a necessity of life that is a nuisance only to a limited extent, but that can be used in a thousand different ways. We have only to generate enough basic energy to neutralise the pull of gravity – which has to be paid like a shareholder in a company – and the rest of the profit is our own.

Human life in general is an exact parallel to this basic physical situation. It is easy enough to prove that it is a burden, that man 'can't win', that when the 'facts are weighed in the balance of logic, it would have been better if we had never been born'. *But logic alone can lead to nothing and prove nothing.* If you are watching a game of chess, and you know the rules of the game, logic will inform you whether each move has been made according to the rules or not. But unless your mind grasps the total purpose of the game and can see all the possible moves, you cannot be said to 'understand' it. Without a grasp of the intentionality that drives all life, it is indisputable that 'man is a useless passion'.

At present, man is in the position of knowing most of the 'rules of the game'. He may even accept that the game has a purpose connected with evolution. But a good chess player needs more than a knowledge of the rules and the ultimate purpose; he also needs a firm grasp of its possibilities, a pictorial intuition. The further ahead this intuition is capable of reaching, the more likely he is to win the game.

Without such an intuition of purpose, life undeniably would be meaningless. Plowart 'feels' himself to be greater than other men; all that he means is that his intuition of purpose is deeper and drives him harder. All that is lacking is one final piece of knowledge that would complete a pattern – and yet ignorance of it is as important as ignorance of just one number to open a combination lock; it invalidates all the rest.

It is difficult to define exactly what was lacking in Plowart before his 'revelation', and it is even more difficult to guess what will happen to him next. This is partly because of the difficulty and complexity of the problem itself, and partly because of the shortcomings of Plowart's creator. If we accept Plowart as he is presented, he is a strange mixture. He is oddly childish in many ways, too vulnerable. There is a scene near the beginning of the book where he meets Claremont's two younger brothers; they annoy him and end by throwing pebbles at him; Plowart loses his temper, and begins to hurl boulders at them as they run away down the cliff – any one of which could kill them. This is the violence of a paranoiac, like the scene in which he threatens the fisherman with a knife because his radio set has been accidentally smashed. Earlier in the book, Plowart recalls an occasion when an abscess swelled under his arm; the pain almost drives him insane, but he refuses to go to a doctor because 'it had become the incarnation of everything that opposed him'. When finally he is taken to hospital, he demands to be anaesthetised before they lance it, and then at the last minute, under the mask, fights the unconsciousness because he dreads losing his mind more than he dreads the pain. This begins to sound very like a persecution mania. It is a remark made by the brothers about Claremont – repeating one of her observations about Plowart, when she sees him from a distance leaping over rocks – that convinces Plowart that she is an 'oracle'. These extremes of his character – violence and gullibility – make it difficult for the reader to take much sympathetic interest in him.

In spite of its faults, *The Divine and the Decay* is an impressive performance – the only attempt I can recall to create a sympathetic hero who is not governed by the fallacy of insignificance, a man who is in some ways 'larger than life'. T. E. Lawrence has an interesting passage in one of his letters:

> I have looked in poetry everywhere for satisfaction: and haven't found it. Instead, I have made that collection of bon bons, chocolate éclairs of the spirit, whereas I wanted a meal. Failing poetry, I chased my fancied meal through prose, and found everywhere little good stuff, and only a few men who had tried honestly to be greater than mankind: and only their strainings and wrestlings really fill my stomach.

I do not doubt that Lawrence would have found something of what he looked for in Hopkins's novel. I am equally certain that he would not have found it in any of the other 'Angry Young Men'. John Braine's Joe Lampton, in *Room at the Top*, briefly produced an impression that something healthier and breezier than 'anger' was making its appearance; but when Lampton reappears in *Life at the Top*, it is seen that his 'will to power' in the earlier novel was largely a social matter. Joe shows himself willing to settle for peace and domesticity on five thousand a year. The romantic glow has vanished; Braine reveals himself as a realist, writing superlatively well about the world we know. Hopkins is a romantic in every sense; he is not interested in pleasant brooks; he wants cataracts falling from mountain tops. He does not want to make conversation about the weather; he wants to speak of tornados and bolts of lightning. The danger is obvious; the more a book wishes to achieve romantic heights, the deeper it has to cut its foundations of realism. There seems to be no prospect of Hopkins altering his aim – even the announced titles of his 'works in progress' prove this – *Time of Totality, The Titans.* The question, then, is of how deep he is prepared to cut? It would not take a great deal of 'foundation work' to turn the immense promise of *The Divine and the Decay* into secure achievement.

But the main importance of the book lies in the power with which it 'symbolises' the rope trick. There are, in existentialist fiction, certain works that symbolise the meaning of various abstract terms so well that it is difficult to write about existentialism without referring to them. No one has ever expressed 'bad faith', self-deception, with quite the same power and finality as Sartre in *Childhood of a Leader*. No one has ever embodied the ideas of 'authentic' and 'inauthentic existence' in a story so perfectly as Hemingway in *The Short and Happy Life of Francis Macomber*. *Crime and Punishment* contains the perfect symbol for the 'definitive act'. Kierkegaard's *Diary of a Seducer* embodies the idea of arbitrary choice and freedom; Briussov's *City of the Southern Cross* is an embodiment of man's hunger for 'the irrational'. Hopkins's novel is the only expression of 'the rope trick' that I know in existentialist literature: of the paradox that the untrue can be made true by an act of belief, because *the untrue was secretly true in the first place*. Because of the power with which it captures this intuition, it should be regarded as a cornerstone of the literature of evolutionary existentialism.

BIBLIOGRAPHY

In the present bibliography, it has been necessary to be highly selective for reasons of space: for example, an adequate bibliography for Chapter Two would obviously occupy a dozen pages. I have therefore restricted myself to books actually mentioned in the text, or to the essential works on any particular subject. On gestalt psychology, for example, I have mentioned only Ellis's compilation. Existential psychology and phenomenology are listed as subjects.

ARDREY, Robert. *African Genesis*, Collins, 1961

BEAUVOIR, Simone de. *The Prime of Life*, Deutsch and Weidenfeld and Nicolson, 1962

BLANCHARD, Brand. *On Philosophical Style*, Manchester University Press, 1954

BROAD, C. D. *Philosophy of C. D. Broad*, Tudor, 1959

CAMUS, Albert. *The Myth of Sisyphus*, Hamish Hamilton, 1955

CAPETANAKIS, Dimetrios. *A Greek Poet in England*, John Lehmann, 1947

CHARDIN, Pierre Teilhard de. *The Phenomenon of Man*, Harper, 1959

DIJKSTERHUIS, E. J. *The Mechanisation of the World Picture*, Oxford, 1961

ELLIS, Willis D. *A Source Book of Gestalt Psychology*, Routledge, 1950

EXISTENTIAL PSYCHOLOGY:

BOSS, Medard. *Psychoanalysis and Daseinsanalysis*, Basic Books, New York, 1963

CANTRIL, Hadley, and William Ittelson. *Perception, a Transactional Approach,* Doubleday, 1954

CARUSO, Igor A. *Existential Psychology,* Darton, Longman and Todd, 1964

FINDLAY, J. N. Hegel. *A Re-examination,* Allen and Unwin, 1958

HAMANN, J. G. See: *Hamann,* by R. G. Smith, Collins, 1960

HEIDEGGER, Martin. *Being and Time,* SCM Press, 1962. *Existence and Being* (4 essays), Vision, 1956. *The Question of Being,* Twayne, 1958. *What is Philosophy?* Twayne, 1958. See also: *Earth and the Gods, a study of Heidegger's Philosophy,* by Vincent Vycinas, Martinus Nijhoff, The Hague, 1961

HULME, T. E. *Speculations,* Routledge, 1924. *Further Speculations,* Minnesota Press, 1955

HUSSERL, Edmund. *Ideas*, Allen and Unwin, 1958. "The Crisis of European Humanity and Philosophy" (in *The Search for Being,* Edited by J. Wilde and W. Kimmel. Noonday, New York, 1962. *Cartesian Meditations*, Martinus Nijhoff, 1960

MASLOW, A. H. *Motivation and Personality,* Harper, 1954. *Towards a Psychology of Being,* Van Nostrand, New York, 1962

MAY, Rollo (Editor). *Existence*, Basic Books New York, 1960

RUITENBEEK, Hendrik M. (Editor). *Psychoanalysis and Existential Philosophy,* Dutton, 1962

UNGERSMA, A. J. *The Search for Meaning,* Allen and Unwin, 1961

PHENOMENOLOGY:

BOCHENSKI, Anna-Teresa. *Phenomenology and Science in Contemporary European Thought,* Noonday, 1962

CHISHOLM, R. M. *Realism and the Background of Phenomenology*, Free Press of Glencoe, Illinois, 1961

HUXLEY, Aldous. *The Doors of Perception,* Penguin, 1959

HUXLEY, Julian. *New Bottles for New Wine,* Chatto, 1957. *Essays of a Humanist,* Chatto, 1964. *Heredity, East and West,* Schuman, 1949. (Editor) *The Humanist Frame,* Allen and Unwin, 1961. With H. G. Wells: *The Science of Life* (see Wells).

JAMES, William. *Varieties of Religious Experience,* Modern Library, 1958

KOESTLER, Arthur. *The Sleepwalkers,* Hutchinson, 1959. *The Act of Creation,* Hutchinson, 1964

MERLEAU-PONTY, Maurice. *The Phenomenology of Perception,* Routledge, 1962. *The Phenomenological Philosophy of Merleau-Ponty*, by Remy C. Kwant, Duquesne, 1963

MILLER, Henry. *Time of the Assassins,* New Directions, 1946. *Sunday After the War,* New Directions, 1944

NIETZSCHE, F. *Philosophy of Nietzsche*, Modern Library, 1954

PIAGET, Jean. *The Psychology of Intelligence,* Routledge, 1959

RYLE, Gilbert. *The Concept of Mind,* Hutchinson, 1949

SARTRE, Jean Paul. *Being and Nothingness,* Methuen, 1957. *Sketch for a Theory of the Emotions,* Methuen, 1962. *Transcendence of the Ego,* Noonday, 1959. *Problem of Method,* Methuen, 1963. *The Psychology of Imagination,* Rider, N. D. See also: *Reason and Violence,* by R. D. Laing and D. G. Cooper, *Sartre's Philosophy, 1950–1960*, Tavistock Press, 1964

SPIEGELBERG, Herbert. *The Phenomenological Movement,* Martinus Nijhoff, The Hague, 1960

STRAWSON, P. F. *Individuals,* Methuen, 1964

STACE, W. T. *The Philosophy of Hegel,* Dover, 1955

WELLS, H. G. *Experiment in Autobiography,* 2 vols, Gollancz, 1934. *The Science of Life,* with Julian Huxley and G. P. Wells, Cassell, 1934

WHITEHEAD, A. N. *A Whitehead Anthology,* Edited by F. S. C. Northrop and Mason W. Gross, Cambridge, 1953. (This volume contains a representative selection from Whitehead's writings, including most of *Symbolism, Its Meaning and Effect.*)

INDEX

☐ Madden, David and Bach, Peggy/REDISCOVERIES II $9.95
☐ Martin, Jay/NATHANAEL WEST: THE ART OF HIS LIFE $8.95
☐ Maurois, Andre/OLYMPIO: THE LIVE OF VICTOR HUGO $12.95
☐ Maurois, Andre/PROMETHEUS: THE LIFE OF BALZAC $11.95
☐ Maurois, Andre/PROUST: PORTRAIT OF GENIUS $10.95
☐ McCarthy, Barry and Emily/FEMALE SEXUAL AWARENESS $9.95
☐ McCarthy, Barry/MALE SEXUAL AWARENESS $9.95
☐ McCarthy, Barry & Emily/SEXUAL AWARENESS $9.95
☐ Mizener, Arthur/THE SADDEST STORY: A BIOGRAPHY OF FORD MADOX FORD $12.95
☐ Montyn, Jan & Kooiman, Dirk Ayelt/A LAMB TO SLAUGHTER $8.95
☐ Moorehead, Alan/THE RUSSIAN REVOLUTION $10.95
☐ Morris, Charles/IRON DESTINIES, LOST OPPORTUNITIES: THE POST-WAR ARMS RACE $13.95
☐ O'Casey, Sean/AUTOBIOGRAPHIES I $10.95
☐ O'Casey, Sean/AUTOBIOGRAPHIES II $10.95
☐ Poncins, Gontran de/KABLOONA $9.95
☐ Pringle, David/SCIENCE FICTION: THE 100 BEST NOVELS $7.95
☐ Proust, Marcel/ON ART AND LITERATURE $8.95
☐ Richelson, Hildy & Stan/INCOME WITHOUT TAXES $9.95
☐ Roy, Jules/THE BATTLE OF DIENBIENPHU $8.95
☐ Russell, Franklin/THE HUNTING ANIMAL $7.95
☐ Salisbury, Harrison/A JOURNEY FOR OUR TIMES $10.95
☐ Schul, Bill D./ANIMAL IMMORTALITY $9.95
☐ Scott, Evelyn/ESCAPADE $9.95
☐ Sloan, Allan/THREE PLUS ONE EQUALS BILLIONS $8.95
☐ Stanway, Andrew/THE ART OF SENSUAL LOVING $15.95
☐ Stanway, Dr. Andrew/SECRET SEX $15.95
☐ Trench, Charles/THE ROAD TO KHARTOUM $10.95
☐ Werth, Alexander/RUSSIA AT WAR: 1941-1945 $15.95
☐ White, Jon Manchip/CORTES $10.95
☐ Wilmot, Chester/STRUGGLE FOR EUROPE $14.95
☐ Wilson, Colin/BEYOND THE OCCULT $10.95

☐ Greenberg & Waugh (eds.)/THE NEW ADVENTURES OF SHERLOCK HOLMES $8.95
☐ Greene, Graham & Hugh/THE SPY'S BEDSIDE BOOK $7.95
☐ Greenfeld, Josh/THE RETURN OF MR. HOLLYWOOD $8.95
☐ Hamsun, Knut/MYSTERIES $8.95
☐ Hardinge, George (ed.)/THE MAMMOTH BOOK OF MODERN CRIME STORIES $8.95
☐ Hawkes, John/VIRGINIE: HER TWO LIVES $7.95
☐ Higgins, George/TWO COMPLETE NOVELS $9.95
☐ Hugo, Victor/NINETY-THREE $8.95
☐ Huxley, Aldous/ANTIC HAY $10.95
☐ Huxley, Aldous/CROME YELLOW $10.95
☐ Huxley, Aldous/EYELESS IN GAZA $9.95
☐ Ibañez, Vincente Blasco/THE FOUR HORSEMEN OF THE APOCALYPSE $8.95
☐ Jackson, Charles/THE LOST WEEKEND $7.95
☐ James, Henry/GREAT SHORT NOVELS $12.95
☐ Jones, Richard Glyn/THE MAMMOTH BOOK OF MURDER $8.95
☐ Just, Ward/THE CONGRESSMAN WHO LOVED FLAUBERT $8.95
☐ Lewis, Norman/DAY OF THE FOX $8.95
☐ Lowry, Malcolm/HEAR US O LORD FROM HEAVEN THY DWELLING PLACE $9.95
☐ Lowry, Malcolm/ULTRAMARINE $7.95
☐ Macaulay, Rose/CREWE TRAIN $8.95
☐ Macaulay, Rose/KEEPING UP APPEARANCES $8.95
☐ Macaulay, Rose/DANGEROUS AGES $8.95
☐ Mailer, Norman/BARBARY SHORE $9.95
☐ Maugham, W. Somerset/THE EXPLORER $10.95
☐ Mauriac, François/THE DESERT OF LOVE $6.95
☐ Mauriac, François/FLESH AND BLOOD $8.95
☐ Mauriac, François/WOMAN OF THE PHARISEES $8.95
☐ Mauriac, François/VIPER'S TANGLE $8.95
☐ McElroy, Joseph/THE LETTER LEFT TO ME $7.95
☐ McElroy, Joseph/LOOKOUT CARTRIDGE $9.95
☐ McElroy, Joseph/PLUS $8.95
☐ McElroy, Joseph/A SMUGGLER'S BIBLE $9.50
☐ Mitford, Nancy/DON'T TELL ALFRED $7.95
☐ Moorcock, Michael/THE BROTHEL IN ROSENSTRASSE $6.95
☐ Munro, H.H./THE NOVELS AND PLAYS OF SAKI $8.95
☐ Neider, Charles (ed.)/GREAT SHORT STORIES $11.95
☐ Neider, Charles (ed.)/SHORT NOVELS OF THE MASTERS $12.95
☐ O'Faolain, Julia/THE OBEDIENT WIFE $7.95
☐ O'Faolain, Julia/NO COUNTRY FOR YOUNG MEN $8.95
☐ O'Faolain, Julia/WOMEN IN THE WALL $8.95
☐ Olinto, Antonio/THE WATER HOUSE $9.95
☐ O'Mara, Lesley/GREAT CAT TALES $9.95